Smart Living

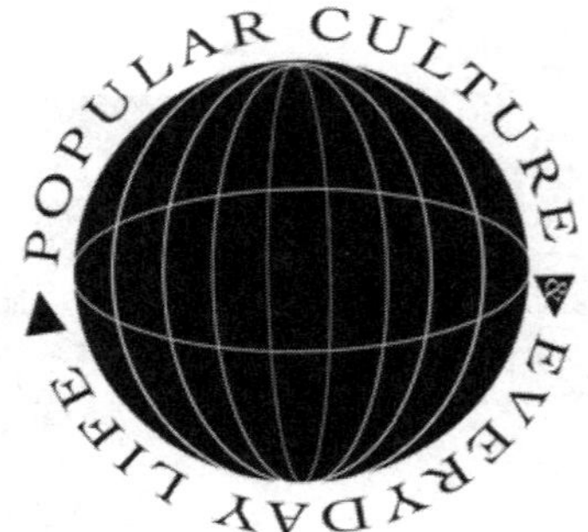

Toby Miller
General Editor

Vol. 15

PETER LANG
New York • Washington, D.C./Baltimore • Bern
Frankfurt am Main • Berlin • Brussels • Vienna • Oxford

Tania Lewis

Smart Living

Lifestyle Media and Popular Expertise

PETER LANG
New York • Washington, D.C./Baltimore • Bern
Frankfurt am Main • Berlin • Brussels • Vienna • Oxford

Library of Congress Cataloging-in-Publication Data

Lewis, Tania.
Smart living: lifestyle media and popular expertise / Tania Lewis.
p. cm. — (Popular culture and everyday life; v. 15)
Includes bibliographical references and index.
1. Lifestyles—United States. 2. Popular culture—United States.
3. Makeover television programs—United States.
4. Television—Social aspects—United States. I. Title.
HQ2044.U6L49   646.7009182'1—dc22   2007027971
ISBN 978-0-8204-8678-9 (hardcover)
ISBN 978-0-8204-8677-2 (paperback)
ISSN 1529-2428

Bibliographic information published by **Die Deutsche Bibliothek**.
Die Deutsche Bibliothek lists this publication in the "Deutsche
Nationalbibliografie"; detailed bibliographic data is available
on the Internet at http://dnb.ddb.de/.

Front cover image courtesy of NBC Universal Photo Bank
Cover design by Clear Point Designs

The paper in this book meets the guidelines for permanence and durability
of the Committee on Production Guidelines for Book Longevity
of the Council of Library Resources.

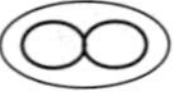

© 2008 Peter Lang Publishing, Inc., New York
29 Broadway, 18th floor, New York, NY 10006
www.peterlang.com

Printed in the United States of America

Contents

Acknowledgments

This book is not just the result of an individual author's isolated labours — it owes much to a number of other individual's valued contributions. Firstly, I owe a major debt of gratitude to Brian Morris without whose emotional and intellectual support I would never have got to this point. He read and commented on the book at various points in its development and put up with my at times unhealthy obsession with all things lifestyle related! Toby Miller also played an important role in getting this book in print and I'd like to thank him for his ongoing encouragement and support. Thanks also to Chris Healy for feedback and encouragement in the early days of the book's inception. I'd also like to acknowledge John Frow, Jane Landman, and Graeme Turner's inspiring critical responses to specific chapters in the book and Fran Martin, Anna Clark, and Ken Gelder for their useful suggestions.

The arguments in the book also benefited from feedback and conversations I had with colleagues at various conferences including the Fifth International Crossroads in Cultural Studies Conference, University of Illinois, Urbana-Champaign (2004) and the Internationalising Media Studies Conference, University of Westminster, London (2006). A particular highlight was the ESRC Centre for Research on Socio-Cultural Change's Media Change and Social Theory conference (2006) organized by David Hesmondhalgh and Jason Toynbee, where I met a fantastic group of scholars working on lifestyle media including Bev Skeggs, Helen Wood, Guy Redden, Katherine Sender, Peter Lunt, Alison Hearn, and Ruth Holliday.

The book greatly benefited from the institutional support of the Faculty of Education at Monash University, which provided me with a Research Fellowship and several generous grants along the way to support the completion of the project. I thank my colleagues at Monash for their encouragement; in particular, Jane Kenway for her professional mentorship and Ilana Snyder for her long-term support.

Two chapters in this book are based on empirical 'field research'. The chapter on *Honey We're Killing the Kids* comes out of interviews with staff from Freehand, the independent company that produced the show, and the Ten Network that commissioned and screened it. I am greatly indebted to Peter Abbott at Freehand for his enthusiasm and generosity towards my research and to the members of his production team who gave their precious time to be interviewed for this chapter. This part of the book also benefited from the input of Tim Clucas and Cathy Scott at Network Ten. Thanks also to Jane Roscoe for her role as 'medium' in recommending me to key television industry figures.

The chapter on health and lifestyle draws upon interviews I conducted in 2003/2004. My sincere thanks to the young people at the University of Melbourne and the staff and clients at the Melbourne Citymission who participated in that study.

Thanks to Zo Gay at Damage Design for the wonderful job she did formatting the book and to Mary Savigar and Bernadette Shade at Peter Lang for their professionalism. Thanks also to Christy Havranek at NBCU Photo Bank and Nikki Hartley at Jamie Durie Publishing for their assistance.

Finally, love and thanks to Ngaire Bissett, Bethan Lewis, and Malcolm Lewis.

Earlier versions of parts of this book have been published as: 'He needs to face his fears with these five queers!': *Queer Eye for the Straight Guy*, makeover TV and the lifestyle expert', *Television and New Media* 2007, 8(4): 285–311; 'Seeking health information on the internet: lifestyle choice or a bad attack of cyberchondria?' *Media, Culture & Society* 2006, 28(5): 521–539; and 'DIY selves?: Reflexivity and habitus in young people's use of the internet for health information', *European Journal of Cultural Studies* 2006, 9(4): 461–479.

Introducing the lifestyle expert
Zen and the art of spot removal

Recently I was asked by a feature writer for a broadsheet newspaper to comment, as an 'expert' on lifestyle media, on the surprise best-selling Australian book Spotless *(Lush and Fleming 2005), which had at that time sold 300,000 copies, a huge number by local publishing standards. Why, I was asked, had a guide to removing household stains triggered such huge interest in the Australian public? As* The Age *journalist Paul Heinrichs pondered in the subsequent article (2006: 15), '[I]s this book doing more for its readers than simply helping to remove last night's curry from the carpet?'*

The book was written by Shannon Lush,[1] a previously unknown great-grandmother and fine art restorer, who after ringing in to a public radio show several times to provide information on house cleaning and stain removal was given her own regular radio spot and now presents highly popular segments on thirteen radio shows around the country. In discussing Lush's overnight transformation from radio listener to expert presenter and best-selling author, Heinrichs noted her 'ability to fuse traditional household wisdom—from sources going back to the 19th century—with modern chemistry, to produce sure-fire results' (15). As Lush's book publisher puts it, 'She's tapping into some lost knowledge … Half the stuff she's talking about are things that your great-aunt or great-grandmother probably did a lot of, but it's been lost as women entered the workforce and so on' (15).

Shannon Lush's rise to fame as the Australian 'Queen of Clean'—she has since put out another guide, *Speed Cleaning* (Lush and Fleming 2006), for time-poor Aussies—presents a useful example through which some of the concerns and interests of this book might be introduced. The surprising success of *Spotless* is not an isolated incident but part of a broader trend in contemporary media. While this book primarily focuses on US, UK, and Australian examples of lifestyle media, I argue that popular media around the world today are increasingly concerned with teaching audiences, both men and women, how to manage their everyday lives through a seamless focus on food, home decoration, health, style, and grooming. This focus on 'educating' audiences has been accompanied by the rise of a 'new and emergent class' of experts concerned with lifestyle and the presentation of self (Palmer 2004): the 'ordinary' lifestyle experts who are the central focus of this book.

Defining popular expertise

In the past the term 'expert', at least in the West, has tended to have a fairly narrow range of associations. Experts were remote figures associated with a distant realm of rational objective inquiry, such as scientists, or individuals possessing specialized professional modes of knowledge, such as doctors and lawyers; figures, in other words, whose credentialed knowledge was seen as far removed from that of the realm of ordinary, 'lay' knowledge. In contrast, the popular media's understanding of what constitutes expertise has historically been relatively more catholic—gardening specialists, self-help gurus, and chefs have all at different times shared the label 'expert' with more traditional 'talking heads'. However, these different modes of expertise have tended to be marked by a clear hierarchy; on television, for instance, this has been reflected in the traditional divide between 'serious' educational television of the current affairs/documentary variety and entertainment-oriented programming. In other forms of media, too, there has tended to be a clear distinction made between credentialed experts and more popular figures associated with the world of domestic and personal advice.

In this book I analyse the relatively recent proliferation of experts associated with the 'soft', entertainment-oriented end of the media spectrum, figures whose expertise is intimately connected to the 'ordinary' (Lewis 2004). In particular, I am interested in the ways in which skills and knowledges associated with everyday life and with 'ordinary people' such as Shannon Lush are becoming valued as forms of expertise in their own right. Such a shift can be seen as part of a growing 'informationalization' of everyday life, a process that has seen advice and expertise become relatively democratized and presented in increasingly accessible forms. This has been accompanied by a growing commoditization of information and advice whereby everyday life skills and expertise have become professionalized and incorporated into the market. Hence in contemporary popular media—particularly those forms oriented towards lifestyle advice, such as makeover television and lifestyle supplements in newspapers—'domestic goddesses' and 'style gurus' (figures associated with these more 'ordinary' modes of knowledge and skills) increasingly find themselves placed in the same discursive category as other 'experts', such as doctors, psychologists, and dieticians.

While the notion of 'ordinariness' underpins many scholarly discussions of lifestyle media, it is a somewhat slippery term (Bell and Hollows 2005: 15). At one and the same time it can be seen to refer to the way in which contemporary media increasingly addresses its audience in a familiar, colloquial manner; the way in which experts themselves are repositioned in such media as friendly guides rather than authorities; the growing role of 'ordinary people' in lifestyle media as both 'participants' and themselves sources of advice and expertise; and the blurring of the boundaries between media celebrity and ordinariness (with Shannon Lush again being a good example of this) (15). What is also 'ordinary' about the experts featured in lifestyle media and beyond is the specific focus of their 'specialist' know-how. While the group of people I am examining together in this book under the rubric of 'ordinary expertise' comprises a wide range of seemingly different figures—from food coaches and celebrity chefs to child behaviour gurus and style mavens—what they have in common is a focus on skills and knowledges associated with the domestic and the everyday.

While some of these skills have previously figured as forms of expertise in the media, they have tended to be cordoned off and associated with more conventional modes of instructional television such as cooking shows, hobby-oriented DIY shows, or gardening programmes, or, in the print media, with women's 'service' magazines. That is, they have appealed to feminine or specialist audiences. As Moseley argues in relation to television (2000), the 'primetime-isation' of previously feminized forms such as the makeover, alongside an unprecedented focus on ordinary people and ordinary lives more broadly, has seen a mainstreaming of domestic and ordinary modes of knowledge. While daytime TV and women's magazines continue to offer advice around personal self-care, family health, and all things domestic, similar modes of advice reframed as 'lifestyle' expertise are targeting a broader range of media audiences, including men and youth.

This mainstreaming of, and obsession with, forms of expert guidance has been played out across media, a good example being the relatively recent emergence of glossy lifestyle supplements in broadsheet newspapers carrying (often heavily consumption-oriented) modes of advice on everything from personal finances to grooming and etiquette. The explosion of expertise has been particularly prominent on television, however, which has over the past few years produced apparently limitless types of lifestyle programmes oriented towards instructing us in every aspect of our daily lives.

While lifestyle television has been particularly popular in the United States and the United Kingdom, lifestyle programming has also been on the rise in a range of TV markets around the world from Spain and China to Australia and New Zealand. On an average week on Australian primetime television, for instance, audiences are offered a range of advice-based programming from more traditional locally made magazine-style shows such as *Better Homes and Gardens* (featuring a variety of home renovation, cooking, and gardening experts) and *What's Good for You?* (a health-oriented magazine show that aims somewhat confusingly to 'debunk the myths of life's little mysteries') to a range of 'sexed up' cooking shows, often featuring 'food personalities' or international celebrity chefs such as Jamie Oliver. Recently this more traditional fare has been boosted by a growing number of reality-based makeover shows from the 'transform-your-pet, transform-your-life' variety such as the UK show *It's Me or the Dog* to lifestyle programmes that aim a little higher by offering to fix unruly children (*Supernanny*) or, on a less everyday level, that teach 'ordinary' Australian girls the style and manners they need to pass as members of the British aristocracy (*Australian Princess*). Among the more popular lifestyle makeover shows to air in recent times in Australia has been a locally made version of the US show *The Biggest Loser*, a show that has also sold franchises to the Netherlands and Israel.

As I discuss in this book, while these new makeover programmes (particularly competitive reality game show formats such as *The Biggest Loser*) appear on the surface to be less concerned with instructing audiences and more focused on entertainment than earlier modes of DIY TV, these hybridized popular–factual formats in many ways offer more potent models of pedagogy, teaching audiences about social norms and values through processes of identification and (self-)surveillance. And while the flavour and feel of localized versions of lifestyle shows often vary quite considerably in different national contexts, central to all these shows is the figure of the ordinary expert—from 'diet doctors' and on-call nannies to etiquette coaches and style gurus—hell bent on passing on his or her lifestyle skills and advice to the hapless makeover-ees and in turn to the audience.

The rise of lifestyle culture and expertise

As I have noted, many of the skills taught on these shows have been traditionally relegated to the realm of 'women's issues' (or, in the case of topics such as pet handling, arts and crafts, or DIY, associated with 'special interest' audiences or targeted at forms of domestic masculinity). Today many of these modes of ordinary advice, however, have been repackaged for a broader audience via glossy newspaper supplements and, in particular, the reality makeover format. This broadening out of the scope of popular advice has seen a shift in the kind of terminology used in association with advice-based media forms and in particular a growing use of the term lifestyle. Used today as a descriptor for everything from New Age religious choices to sports drinks, lifestyle is a term that has become so ubiquitous in contemporary consumer culture it is increasingly hard to pin down. At the same time, its very ubiquity attests to the way it has now become a form of everyday 'common sense'. Representing far more than just a convenient new way for the industry to re-label popular advice media, lifestyle has become one of the dominant frameworks through which we understand and organize contemporary everyday life.

As Bell and Hollows note (2005: 2), the term lifestyle, on the surface at least, has rather different meanings in different contexts. Marketers, for example, often categorize consumers into different lifestyle groups or personalities. In medicine and public health, on the other hand, 'healthy' or 'at-risk' lifestyles tend to be associated with certain kinds of behavioural choices (2). They also note that these seemingly disparate uses of the term can all be seen as variants of a choice-based or voluntarist notion of social identity. In general, the concept of lifestyle is underpinned by an individualistic, consumption-oriented conception of the relation between selfhood and the social, where rather than being constrained by traditional forms of identity such as class, race, or gender, the individual is seen as a site of endless choice and potential transformation. Similar to the premise of the makeover show itself, lifestyle media and culture addresses an essentially DIY self.

The question of why this lifestyle-based conception of the self has become dominant at this particular moment, along with the associated rise of forms of lifestyle media and expertise, is a multifaceted one. While shifts in the gendered content and mode of address of media, alongside a growing focus on 'the ordinary', have played an important role in the 'lifestyling' of popular advice, the rise and popularity of forms of expertise that speak to lifestyle issues needs to be more broadly understood as emerging out of a complex conjuncture of historical, social, and cultural developments.

In the next section, I want to introduce the reader to a range of critical accounts and approaches, drawn variously from media studies, cultural studies, and sociology, as a way of both situating the rise of the lifestyle expert and signalling some of the recurring themes and concerns of this book. While lifestyle advice and expertise is a feature of popular media around the world, the book is primarily concerned with shifts occurring within Anglo-American popular media and culture and as such draws upon Western scholarship and theoretical concerns. Some of the critical approaches used here (from class-based analyses to critiques of consumerism) have, of course, considerably broader international relevance given the increasingly globalized nature of media culture and of consumer capitalism more broadly. At the same time, it is also important to recognize significant regional and national variations in the role and meaning of lifestyle media and culture given the often very different socio-cultural and political contexts framing media production and reception in such sites.

The 'ungendering' of expertise?

From my perspective, one critical approach crucial to understanding contemporary shifts in the role and status of popular expertise in the West is a gender-based analysis. While contemporary media has sought to repackage the kinds of knowledge associated with personal care and domesticity as forms of lifestyle expertise, these skills have often been traditionally marked out as women's territory (although, as I discuss in more detail in Chapter 1, DIY, home improvement, and other types of 'productive leisure' connected with the home have also been associated with masculine forms of domesticity). In broad terms, however, issues related to the home and to personal style continue to carry feminine connotations and there are still strong tendencies within contemporary media to divide off certain types of life skills and know-how along gendered lines (within the lifestyle genre, male experts tend to focus on more masculine or relatively 'neutral' arenas such as physical fitness, professional modes of cookery, gardening, and carpentry). At the same time, I think Moseley is right to suggest that we are seeing some 'more general cultural shifts around gendered expertise' (2000: 309), even if these shifts have not yet marked an 'ungendering' of TV programming and its modes of expertise.

One of the contexts for these shifts has been an economic one. The relabelling of personal and domestic skills as expertise marks a growing trend in late modernity towards outsourcing domestic work, reflecting shifts in the gendering of the labour force, and in particular, the growing numbers of 'time-poor' professional working women (McRobbie 2004b). While the focus of this book is on media-based forms of popular expertise, the rise of popular advice has occurred in a context marked by a broader commodification of areas of life once relatively marginal to the market and the world of work (Schiller 2007), a context that has witnessed a proliferation of commercial modes of advice from life planners and personal coaches. These experts-for-hire offer services oriented towards organizing and streamlining people's domestic arrangements, from de-cluttering houses to advising on family dynamics.

Tasks that have tended to be associated with the hitherto unpaid and often hidden labour of housework (and with the personal presentation and life management skills associated with femininity more broadly) have, for the middle classes at least, been marked by a growing professionalization and commercialization. A recent series on one of Australia's public TV channels (SBS),

The Lifestyle Experts, focused on precisely these issues documenting how middle class families (and in particular the working women in these households) were paying lifestyle experts to help manage their home life and achieve a 'life–work balance'. As one of the women on the show put it when asked to justify her use of a 'life assistant', while women have been 'traditionally tied to the home … outsourcing is definitely the way ahead'.

While *The Lifestyle Experts* focused largely on the perspective of the women in the households concerned, these shifts in the economics of domesticity and the breaking down of distinctions between the public world of work and the home have also affected men. Alongside the 'outsourcing' of domestic labour, the so-called feminization of work more broadly over the past few decades has been marked not only by a growing number of women in the workplace but also by the emergence of more service-oriented work cultures. Just as the home has become a space of expertise, so too this shift in the gendering of the realm of work has seen a revaluing and professionalization within the public sphere of competencies previously coded as feminine and, to some extent, queer forms of expertise (Miller 2005), such as personal presentation and people skills. At the same time, the 'identity politics' associated with the rise of the new social movements in the 1970s, such as feminism and the gay rights movement, alongside developments in consumer culture and a more recent focus on physical appearance and fitness in the workplace (Miller 2005) have seen masculinity come under intense scrutiny. The lifestyle makeover show *Queer Eye for the Straight Guy*, discussed in Chapter 3, can be seen as exemplary of these shifts over the past four decades, with its emphasis on the need for men to 'get ahead' both economically and socially through acquiring the valuable cultural competencies or 'cultural capital' traditionally associated with feminine/queer skills of self-fashioning (Lury 1996: 154; Miller 2005).

In *Queer Eye for the Straight Guy*, the spaces of domesticity and style are, to a certain extent, reworked as masculine sites of (productive) play and expertise, extending upon masculine modes of domesticity oriented around DIY, for example. Ehrenreich and English (2005), however, highlight the ongoing complexity of the cultural politics surrounding this focus on and apparent revaluing of the feminine expertise around domesticity. They note that the popular cultural turn to domesticity and in particular the 'domestic nostalgia' associated with figures such as Martha Stewart (who is discussed in some detail in the final chapter of the book) dovetails with calls by US cultural conservatives for a return to family values (357), a trend also apparent in Australia, where the prime minister John Howard has publicly encouraged working women to be 'stay-at-home' mothers (Summers 2003). Such trends suggest, then, that while marked by some shifts in the gendering of expertise, lifestyle media offers a plethora of market-driven and often contradictory images of home and personal life, where the complexity of shifting gendered social roles tends to be reduced to a focus on lifestyle 'choice' and privatized decision making.

Gurus of 'good taste'

While lifestyle experts tend to place an emphasis on domestic style and the acquisition of consumer choice-making skills, their concern with instructing audiences as to what constitutes the bounds of 'good taste' is underpinned by a strongly class-based set of assumptions (Palmer 2004; McRobbie 2004b). The particular kinds of feminine skills and knowledges increasingly valued within a consumer-oriented neoliberal setting tend to be those tied to middle class competencies and values (McRobbie 2004b). Featherstone (1991: 86) argues in his classic essay on lifestyle and consumer culture that the growing 'stylization of life' marks an apparent displacement of traditional class cultures by cultures of consumption. While the notion of lifestyle was once associated with the 'ways of life' or traditions of particular communities (Chaney 2001), within contemporary culture the term is increasingly associated with the notion that individuals are 'free' to choose the style and type of life they want to live, a concept that strongly dovetails with the choice-based ideological 'logic' of lifestyle consumption.

While this emphasis on freedom and individuality within lifestyle culture assumes a shift to a post-class social milieu, a central and recurrent theme in this book is the ongoing but often masked class-based interests of lifestyle media. Such structures are particularly evident on 'educational' lifestyle shows such as *It's Me or the Dog* and *Honey We're Killing the Kids*, where the unruly behaviours of the dogs and children to be 'made over' by the middle class expert are implicitly framed as indicators of the deficient life competencies of the overwhelmingly working class and lower middle class owners and parents on 'display'. While class is not necessarily 'named' in these highly moralizing shows (although on one episode of *It's Me or the Dog* they do quip that 'even high class dogs can have low class problems'), working class life and ordinary people are overwhelmingly positioned as markers of social aberrance, whereas middle class taste, morality, and values are upheld as 'neutral' skills and norms to which we all should aspire.[2] So while the claims to ordinariness of lifestyle TV can be seen to represent a relative democratization of its mode of address and concerns, and a seeming embrace of diversity—as witnessed by the number of working class accents and faces now seen on our screens (Taylor 2002: 486; Redden 2007: 155–156)[3]—it can also be seen to be underpinned by a process whereby the difference and diversity that marks everyday life is being reframed and reconfigured according to a set of universalizing, middle class norms and values.

As numerous commentators on lifestyle media have noted, lifestyle experts can be characterized as crucial 'cultural intermediaries' in this process, a term drawn from French sociologist Pierre Bourdieu's famous account in *Distinction* ([1979] 1984) of the relations between social distinction, taste, and class. Based on a survey of more than 1,200 people in France in the 1960s, *Distinction* mapped, among other historical developments, the rise of a professional class of symbolic workers or 'cultural intermediaries' who acted as mediators between bourgeois culture and a growing petit-bourgeoisie. In an analysis that remains surprisingly relevant to contemporary lifestyle culture, Bourdieu described the emergence around this class of a strongly individualized, aspirational culture of self-expression and continual self-improvement (367). Along with a concern with self-shaping, he noted the rise of a 'domestic ethics' (369), marked by a preoccupation with the body as a sign for communicating the self and with a systematic, rule-driven approach to daily living. Central to this emphasis on a set of essential competencies for living was the rise of a new group of cultural professionals 'offering (or selling) [their] own art of living as an example to others' (370). As Bourdieu commented, while these 'ethical prophets' offered fantasies of social mobility and liberation, presenting themselves as somehow free of class distinctions, the life competencies or forms of 'cultural capital' they promoted all 'speak of classification' (370).

In many ways today's lifestyle experts are the direct descendants of Bourdieu's new class of cultural workers, although they arguably function in a world where class boundaries are less clear and where the democratization of the symbolic practices associated with consumption is now much more widespread. It is precisely because of the increasing fluidity around class categories (at least at the level of conspicuous consumption), however, that the new lifestyle experts have taken on such a prominent role today. As Gareth Palmer notes in his analysis of television shows such as *What Not to Wear* (2004), class and social distinction is a particularly pervasive feature of lifestyle makeover television and its brand of popular expertise. Like Bourdieu's earlier cultural guides, figures such as Martha Stewart, Nigella Lawson, and the Fab Five from *Queer Eye for the Straight Guy* function as the highly prominent, celebrity arbiters of good taste and style at a time of uncertainty around shared social norms and values.

Alongside their celebrity and televisual 'presence', social distinction is central to the authority held by these figures, who legitimate themselves by passing on symbolic capital to others at the same time as they continue to mark out their own distinction from them. With their transformative power, makeover experts work to make good taste and discrimination seem effortless and therefore easily acquired. This is particularly foregrounded by more ordinary figures of expertise such as Jamie Oliver whose 'mockney' accent works to signify a kind of 'anti-posh'. Such figures distance them-selves from class distinction, re-badging their middle class expertise along leisure-based lines, or as essential life skills, while reinforcing an aspirational culture of consumer-based class mobility.

However, in the case of the pre-eminently posh queens of style, Trinny and Susannah from *What Not to Wear*, part of their fascination for (particularly UK) viewers stems from the obvious class gap between these experts, who literally embody class distinction, and the hapless makeover-ees who often 'don't get' their critical assessments (and who very occasionally even have the audacity to refuse to submit to the middle class taste culture promoted by the show). Overwhelmingly though, lifestyle makeover shows attempt to resolve such dilemmas through reasserting the good taste and values of the expert in contrast to the bad taste of the ordinary person. The potentially disruptive issue of class difference is managed by reducing such difference to questions of style and taste—that is, a matter of 'choice' around home décor and personal style—again reinforcing a fantasy of class mobility through consumption.

Lifestyle and consumption

Lifestyle makeover shows, like lifestyle media more broadly, offer modes of advice that while often distinctly middle class in terms of taste and values (as well as being often associated with traditionally feminine, domestic life skills), work continually to disavow these origins, to universalize lifestyle advice as a marker of a broader post-gender, post-class society. The emphasis on an individualized, malleable self, alongside a broader focus on aesthetics and the art of living, also involves naturalizing consumption, with the lifestyle expert working 'to alert viewers to the existence of more products and services for their utility in the endless project of the self' (Bonner 2003: 104).

What lifestyle programming 'sells' to the audience here, however, are not just products but ways of living and being. In *Consumer Culture and Postmodernism* (1991), Featherstone argued that in the West, the growing conflation of lifestyle (and with it lifestyle advice)—once a term associated with traditional identities and ways of life—with consumption practices was linked to various shifts associated with the emergence of postmodernism. Crucial to the shift to a postmodern mode of consumption was 'the triumph of signifying culture' (83), where consumption was no longer just about purchasing goods or making 'rational' consumer choices but was marked by a broader stylized *culture* through which one experienced and performed identity.

Underpinned by a shift to a post-Fordist mode of production oriented towards 'variety and differentiation' (87), the rise of postmodernism saw lifestyle increasingly refigured as an individualized set of consumer-based stylistic choices. As Featherstone (1991) put it:

> The modern individual within consumer culture is made conscious that he speaks not only with his clothes, but with his home, furnishings, decoration, car and other activities which are to be read and classified in terms of the presence and absence of taste. The preoccupation with customizing a lifestyle and a stylistic self-consciousness are not just to be found among the young and the affluent, consumer culture publicity suggests that we all have room for self-improvement and self-expression whatever our age or class origins. (86)

More than a decade on from Featherstone's influential account, lifestyle culture and advice is concerned not only with questions of individual style and self-presentation but also increasingly with how lifestyle choices are linked to broader concerns around selfhood and citizenship. Discussing the rise and role of what he terms 'cultural citizenship', Miller (2007) argues that there has been a growing convergence between civic culture and consumerism. Within media culture this is evidenced by a privileging of discourses of individualized consumption, and in particular a lifestyle-oriented commercial culture focused on bettering the self through 'ethico-aesthetic exercises' (11). Marking a broader shift away from traditional modes of organized civic culture and the rise of a personalized 'lifestyle politics' (Bennett 1998: 745), the ethics and practices of selfhood and citizenship have become reduced to a series of commodified cultural practices and lifestyle choices; as Miller puts it (2007: 11), '"Good taste" becomes a sign of, and a means toward, better citizenship.'

In not only promoting certain kinds of aesthetic norms but also more broadly addressing the realm of ethical conduct, many of today's lifestyle experts, from super-nannies to life planners and organizers, appear not to be overtly concerned with selling products; rather, they can be seen as producing the responsible, rational 'subjects' of consumer capitalism. Targeting health, behavioural, and relationship issues, as well as increasingly emphasizing 'good' modes of consumption from healthy eating to consuming less energy in the home, the field of lifestyle media and expertise has expanded to embrace broader civic and community concerns, with domestic space and everyday life increasingly colonized by discourses that assume a merger between consumer choice and behaviour and the duties and responsibilities of citizenship. Celebrity lifestyle experts such as Jamie Oliver can be seen both to legitimate and to embody these broader models of lifestyle consumption, naturalizing consumption-based models of civic agency through presenting lifestyle consumer advice as 'information' and 'essential life skills' while performing certain lifestyle ideals and norms in their own highly mediated everyday lives.

Meanwhile 'living brands' (Lury 1996: 93) such as Martha Stewart offer particularly rich insights into the growing commodification of lifestyle advice. Schiller argues that the through-going marketization of culture, aesthetics, and everyday life that characterizes contemporary experience marks a broader 'transition into informationalized capitalism' (2007: xiv), in which previously marginal cultural practices and skills have now been turned into commodities. As I argue in Chapter 6, Stewart's career as a celebrity expert represents an exemplary case of the branding and commoditization of an advice culture tied to everyday life, with her sought-after domestic know-how and aesthetic judgment now underpinning a huge multimedia empire.

This 'informationalization' of domestic space via the figure of the lifestyle expert not only reflects the growing ubiquity of a market logic but also can be seen to offer security and guidance to an increasingly anxious consumer–citizen. Via extensions of her Omnimedia corporation, such as the lifestyle advice magazine *Blueprint* and Martha Stewart–designed housing communities, Stewart offers the 'choiceoisie' (Probyn 1997: 130) a kind of pre-packaged lifestyle imaginary— highly systematized and rationalized ways of living seamlessly tied to the everyday consumption of style. Consumer-based lifestyle expertise, then, has become increasingly tied to a broader search for new rules and traditions for living, for both a rationalization and a re-enchantment of everyday life.

The new 'traditions' of lifestyle expertise: Post-traditionalism, risk, and reflexivity

The growing role of lifestyle experts in providing guidelines for living marks the way in which individual choice has become central to the management of everyday life. The rise of lifestyle consumption can be linked to a broader shift to what Giddens (1991) has termed a 'post-traditional society' and Beck (1994) has referred to as 'reflexive modernization'. Both terms mark a shift away from the predictability and the structural certainties of 'traditional', class-bound societies, with post-traditional life characterized by a growing sense of pervasive doubt and anxiety, what both Beck (1992) and Giddens (1991) have famously talked about in terms of a 'risk culture' or 'risk society'.

The surge in popularity of lifestyle experts over the past decade or so, then, can be seen in terms of their role as an antidote to this sense of risk and doubt and as a source of new codes for living. As Giddens argues (1991: 5), as '[r]eflexively organised life-planning … becomes a central feature of the structuring of self-identity', people are increasingly turning to abstract, rationalized systems of expertise for guidance, much of which is provided today through the consumer marketplace (Lury 1996; Rose 1996; Petersen 1997). In this broader context, the lifestyle expert—a familiar and seemingly reliable figure who meditates, translates, and popularizes a range of expert (and consumer) discourses—offers easy how-to guides to choosing between and managing optimal lifestyles in a context of growing complexity and information overload.

In contrast to other rational and expert systems, the tremendous appeal of lifestyle experts and lifestyle media is tied to the familiar everyday-ness of the knowledge and skills on display. Lifestyle experts are comforting, neighbourly figures whom we often feel we 'know' on a first-name basis—Jamie and Martha being classic exemplars of this—familiar faces who regularly pop up on our screens or in magazines giving us various 'how-to' tips for our everyday lives, people who, in their emphasis on their own role as homemakers, wives, husbands, and parents 'like us', feature almost as an extension of our friendship network.

As Taylor argues in her discussion of the huge popularity of gardening and other lifestyle TV shows in the UK (2002: 480), lifestyle culture and expertise has been effective in filling the gap left by the shift away from traditional forms of communal culture because it 'hooks into the ordinary rhythms, practices and sites of everyday life'. The power of lifestyle programming and expertise, then, is that while it celebrates a post-traditional ethos of consumer choice, it also offers to fill the void left by the death of traditional culture with new 'traditions' and rules for living, which are in turn inextricably bound to popular rituals of consumption. In a culture of risk and uncertainty, the focus on lifestyle is a particularly effective 'stabilizer' as it taps into 'the habits of dailiness' of domestic life (Taylor 2002: 486), while also figuring domesticity as a refuge from the external pressures of late modernity. From TV programmes such as *How Clean Is Your House?* to family makeover shows such as *Honey We're Killing the Kids*, domestic space is presented as a site that can be rationalized, managed, and controlled.

Governing the citizen–consumer

In providing new rules for living, lifestyle experts can be seen to play an important role not only in teaching the public personal life skills but also, through their focus on 'lifestyle issues', in promoting and validating certain models of the 'good citizen'. On food TV, for instance, '[t]he dominant interpellation is about learning to govern the self through orderly preparation, style and pleasure' (Miller 2007: 143). The rituals and new traditionalism of lifestyle programming can thus be seen to mark a convergence between questions of lifestyle choice and a broader model of selfhood, an ethical or moral model emphasizing the role of personal and domestic lifestyle management as a site of pleasure *and* responsibility. This conflation of lifestyle choice with responsibility sees a growing connection between the self, the home, and the everyday, on the one hand, and more public, community-based concerns, on the other, with the personal aspirations of the self-improving lifestyle consumer being refigured as those of the citizen.

An important critical approach that has sought to contextualize the rise of the 'lifestyled' consumer–citizen can be found in Nikolas Rose's work on the central role of therapeutic culture and psychological modes of expertise in shaping contemporary modes of selfhood and citizenship (1989, 1996).[4] Influenced by Foucault's conception of modern power and governance as being played out through the 'freedoms' associated with liberal selfhood, Rose argues that the rise of neoliberal governments in many nations in the 1980s, alongside the emergence of a wider 'enterprise culture', has seen a shift in the dominant paradigms through which we conceptualize modern citizenship. In particular, the figure of the self-governing citizen, an individual who is constructed as 'enterprising' and self-directed, has become a cultural dominant. This has occurred in the context of the state increasingly seeking to devolve questions of social and political responsibility to the level of the individual consumer–citizen, a situation shored up by a 'therapeutic culture' that pairs freedom and moral development with self-mastery and self-development.

While Rose's argument focuses primarily on the role of experts of 'interiority' such as psychologists, the privatized 'therapeutic culture' that he sees as central to the contemporary focus on self-governance dovetails with the individualistic concerns of lifestyle culture and expertise. A crucial aspect of the ethos of self-governance is the increasing rationalization of subjectivity via the figure of the expert, whereby

> … the conduct of everyday existence is recast as a series of manageable problems to be understood and resolved by technical adjustment in relation to the norm of the autonomous self aspiring to self-possession and happiness. (Rose 1996: 158)

Such processes of rationalization go hand in hand with an increasing focus in society on self-surveillance and confession (Andrejevic 2004), where the 'gaze' of the expert is turned inwards upon the self. Confessional modes of neoliberal self-surveillance are particularly central to reality-based lifestyle formats, whose narrative development is often strongly reliant on self-disclosure, often straight to camera, inviting the audience to both identify with and judge the self-surveillant subject. These shows are also heavily reliant on the use of more literal 'technologies' of surveillance, such as hidden cameras aimed at capturing anything from fashion bungles to moments of 'anti-social' behaviour. Technologies that again can be seen as an extension and normalization of therapeutic conceptions of selfhood as a site 'opened up for expert judgment, and normative evaluation, for classification and correction' (Rose 1989: 244).

In TV shows such as *The Biggest Loser*, lifestyle media and expertise can be seen to promote self-governance in highly moralized and overt ways through the 'scopic regimes' of reality-style fly-on-the-wall formats, through the use of strongly didactic modes of expertise, and through techniques of shaming and humiliation. For the most part, however, lifestyle experts encourage 'softer' forms of governmentality, with their focus on the banal, everyday aspects of the privatized self promoting a more subtle and insidious 'ethicalization of existence' (Rose 1989: 263–264). Contemporary popular advice culture, then, can be seen to emerge out of a context in which social structural issues, such as the issue of obesity in the West, are increasingly privatized and psychologized, and where 'the well-being of all', to quote Rose again (1989: 264), 'has increasingly come to be seen as a consequence of the responsible self-government of each'. In targeting individuals as sites of relentless self-improvement, the lifestyle expert can be seen to play a crucial role in both legitimating and providing the tools and techniques for the governmental self.

Overall, the lifestyle expert can be seen to emerge out of a complex conjuncture of social, cultural, and economic factors. Linked to the growing push towards modes of reflexive, consumer-based individualism, lifestyle expertise and lifestyle media are also seen to be increasingly articulated to a neoliberal culture of self-governance and self-surveillance. Despite claims that the self-governing consumer–citizen now exists in a post-traditional realm marked by the growing irrelevance of social categories such as class, the individualistic ideals and norms held up by lifestyle experts are often underpinned by class-based (particularly middle class and lower-middle class or 'aspirational') models of taste and lifestyle. Lifestyle expertise also continues to be strongly inflected by gender; with the enterprise self borrowing from a masculine culture of rational self-interested individualism and calculated consumption and from a culture of femininity concerned both with the symbolic work associated with the performance of identity and with the labour that goes with the management of the home and familial relations.

While lifestyle expertise tends to target individuals, the 'women's culture' that lifestyle media taps into is also one strongly tied to familial and community networks, with reality makeover formats in particular being seen to draw upon the talk-based culture of chat shows and magazines. In discussing the normative, governmental dimensions of lifestyle media and expertise, it is important also to recognize the complex pleasures that accompany people's actual everyday engagement with lifestyle discourse. Speaking directly to ordinary issues through powerful personalized narratives of transformation, lifestyle-related advice addresses audiences not only as individual consumers but also as members of an emotional or affective community. Rather than late modernity being conceptualized purely in terms of 'the evolution of individualism', social existence can also be seen to be marked by 'networks of solidarity' forged around sensual and emotional ties (Maffesoli 1996: 72). The shame and humiliation, surveillance, and self-monitoring associated with the lifestyle makeover, then, is also accompanied by the pleasures of identification, of sharing personal experiences with the relative diversity of individuals who populate lifestyle media and with an imagined community of viewers/readers. There are also obviously significant textual pleasures associated with the makeover, with its focus on transformation through acquiring expertise in the management of daily life, and its often emotionally satisfying narrative resolutions. This is not to suggest that the immense popularity of lifestyle media can be reduced to questions of fandom and pleasure but to argue for the complex and negotiated relationship audiences have to such media (see Hill 2005; Sender 2006; Wood et al., 2008). It is also to recognize, after Foucault, the way in which processes of governmentality work not in a punitive fashion but through discourses of liberation, marked by productive and positive (albeit normative) constructions of the self and of social relations.

Specifying lifestyle media

While this book examines the lifestyle expert as a broad socio-cultural phenomenon, I am also interested in contextualizing this figure's role in relation to media. One of the concerns of this book, then, is with mapping the way in which the rise of lifestyle expertise and lifestyle culture has been played out across various media sites. Deciding which media forms to include in a discussion of the lifestyle advice industry is no easy task. The term 'lifestyle media' encompasses a huge range of types of media and related practices, from advertising and 'spin-off' videos and books to the celebrity culture of personal appearances and promotional practices (Bell and Hollows 2005: 9). The very fact of lifestyle as a ubiquitous cultural phenomenon presents a difficulty in 'claiming exhaustivity' or indeed in drawing clear boundaries between forms and genres of lifestyle media (Bell and Hollows 2005: 9).

While 'branded' lifestyle experts such as Martha Stewart function across a highly converged media environment with a presence in television, radio, and print media and on the internet (and in other 'non-media' commercial environments), in this book I am interested in addressing issues of both media convergence *and* specificity. Questions of genre, aesthetics, audience address, and industry economics are all important in understanding the way in which popular advice has been shaped in very distinct ways by distinct media. Acknowledging the breadth of the field and the problem of singling out media forms, I focus primarily on three specific and pre-eminent media sites of lifestyle expertise—magazines, the internet, and television—although I necessarily touch upon other media sites, forms, and practices along the way. Here, by way of gesturing to some of these concerns about media specificity and convergence, I briefly discuss the role of these media in terms of lifestyle advice.

Television has certainly been the most central and visible player in the emergence of the lifestyle expert as a contemporary cultural icon and has also been the focus of the bulk of critical scholarly interest in lifestyle media. Its central role in lifestyle culture is also reflected in the interests of this book, with two of the chapters specifically discussing modes of expertise on makeover TV. At the same time, the book also examines lifestyle expertise as it moves across and between different media forms, and it pays attention to the historical role of the magazine in the development of lifestyle advice as well as the emerging role of the internet as a site of lifestyle expertise and consumption.

While media scholarship tends to separate out media industries and forms into separate analytic categories, in practice the culture of media is one in which TV programmes, websites, and magazine features are often linked through commercial ties and shared audiences. This is particularly the case with lifestyle media and lifestyle experts, where a range of media products from TV programmes to magazines and books are all offered together as one 'branded' package. While magazines, for instance, have not featured as prominently as television in recent discussions of lifestyle media, they play a crucial and ongoing role in the lifestyle advice industry, both as important sources of information and expertise on domestic, family, and personal matters in their own right and in their links to other media forms such as television (Bonner 2002). Lifestyle experts and personalities on television will thus often feature cross-promotionally in magazines in adverts, gossip columns, and so on, and also in syndicated expert advice columns or feature articles, or in magazines co-produced alongside a lifestyle show such as *Better Homes and Gardens*.

The internet, in contrast, is seldom analysed as a form of lifestyle media and is often discussed as though it existed outside the realm of popular media culture, as a privatized technology somehow distinct from the realm of 'old' broadcast and print modes. Nevertheless, its relationship to these other media is also rather more converged, complementary, and co-dependent than such accounts would suggest. Many lifestyle-oriented websites, for instance, are extensions of other lifestyle media such as magazines or lifestyle programmes, often offering extensive forms of (at times personally tailored) advice and services. Lifestyle experts who have risen to fame on television often have personalized websites (such as www.jamieoliver.com, which features a blog and a downloadable podcast), with the website functioning as a further media extension of the expert's brand and celebrity persona and enabling a degree of audience interactivity with the expert 'in person'.

While these media all complement and reinforce one another, they are clearly marked by certain differences in regards to media form and aesthetics (as well as, in the case of TV and magazines, different industrial contexts and histories), all of which uniquely frame the way in which lifestyle advice is presented in these media. Women's 'service' magazines, such as *Woman's Day* (which continues to have a large readership in the United States and in Australia), have been providing expertise on food, nutrition, fitness, beauty, and fashion since the 1930s, training readers as consumers of lifestyle advice and representing an important site for the development of increasingly sophisticated approaches to the merger of 'service-based' informational and consumer concerns. For instance, magazines in many ways have led the way in terms of the 'ordinari-zation' of lifestyle advice, with these specific women's magazines offering a friendly, familiar, and everyday mode of address, supported by the inclusion of readers' letters and feature articles on ordinary people. The use of helpful 'informational' features such as weekly menu planners enables magazines to offer 'neighbourly' modes of advice that fit into the rhythms of people's lives, while also naturalizing the role of consumption in everyday life. Further, in contrast to TV, the print format enables the provision of considerable in-depth information on lifestyle and health topics that can be reflected upon and revisited at the reader's convenience—hence, the ongoing role of co-productions between lifestyle TV and magazines as well as other information-oriented spin-offs from lifestyle TV (such as how-to guides based on makeover shows).

Similarly, the internet offers a strongly informational aesthetic and is increasingly used as an adjunct to lifestyle TV. In contrast to the more generic quality of the information provided in magazines or on television, the internet promises personalized, just-in-time access to a range of in-depth expertise (Lewis 2006a). At the same time, it offers the potential for distinct experiences of communality and interactivity. Visitors to www.jamieoliver.com, for instance, are invited by Oliver himself to engage with a broader fan community by joining 'my online gang to swap recipes or get help and advice'. These (increasingly dominant) popular commercial forms of lifestyle advice compete in this medium with numerous not-for-profit websites and web-based communities where ordinary people share advice and offer support.

In relation to form and aesthetics, lifestyle television, particularly in its earlier forms, also shares some of its conventions with advice magazines. Early forms of lifestyle television, for instance, borrowed strongly from the segmented format of magazines—hence the term 'magazine show'—while the 'before and after' imagery central to today's makeover TV formats can be linked back to home renovation magazines such as *Better Homes and Gardens* in the 1930s (Goldstein 1998: 19). Lifestyle television can also be seen to extend into the familiar, neighbourly mode of address of service magazines, with its focus on ordinary, everyday life.

Today's reality-based lifestyle shows point, however, to some of the unique aesthetic qualities and modes of address associated with television, such as its ability to create a sense of 'liveness', enabling viewers to participate in a shared national/communal space while being profoundly linked to the daily temporalities of privatized domesticity. These shows exploit television's claim to represent 'the social' through its focus on ordinary people and their lives (Couldry 2002), erasing the distinctions between public and private space and marking it as a medium particularly suited to educating self-governing citizens (via the figure of the lifestyle expert). While laying claim to 'the real', lifestyle makeover TV also has links to melodrama (Brunsdon et al. 2001: 55), pointing to the importance of an 'emotional' aesthetic in today's lifestyle formats. In putting ordinary people and their lives on show, the educational aspects of makeover TV are increasingly tied to the emotional journey undertaken by both makeover-ees and the audience, which involves an often complex mixture of identification, critique, and self-surveillance.

Having pointed to some of the similarities, differences, and intersections between various lifestyle media in terms of what might be seen as their 'informational aesthetics', I turn in the the following section to another important context for understanding the rise and popularity of lifestyle expertise, namely, questions of cultural context, focusing in particular on the example of the flow lifestyle TV formats across (trans)national and industrial spaces.

Television on the move: Global and local lifestyles

In his book, *Big Brother* (2005: 40), Bignell discusses the way in which the transnational mobility of reality TV—with formats increasingly being sold into markets such as India and South America—might be seen as evidencing the universalization of a Western preoccupation with 'personal confession, modification, testing and the perfectibility of the self'. While I have talked about lifestyle media and culture in rather generic terms thus far, this last section raises questions about the relationship between the contemporary rise of lifestyle expertise and the national and the global through focusing on the international exchange of lifestyle TV formats and modes of expertise.

One factor crucial to the global popularity of lifestyle TV has been a significant growth in the transnational exchange of format-based programming. The deregulation of the television industry around the world in the 1980s and 1990s has seen a growing global integration of the medium in terms of production and commerce (Waisbord 2004). Television, once 'an enclave service for the affluent', has now spread throughout the developing world, becoming a major presence in most national cultures (Schiller 2007: 118). Internationally, technological developments and the emergence of a multi-channel environment have produced a situation where the pressure for content has encouraged local producers to create programmes that can potentially move across a range of markets (Moran 1998; Waisbord 2004). This situation has seen a relative challenge to US hegemony in global TV traffic and trade as TV formats increasingly emerge from the United Kingdom and Western Europe as well as from smaller players such as Australia and Mexico (Magder 2004; Waisbord 2004; Moran and Keane 2006).

As Waisbord comments (2004: 359), the rise and rise of format television has resulted in a situation whereby '[a]round the world, television is filled with national variations of programs designed by companies from numerous countries'.

For instance, Endemol, a company that originated and continues to be based in Holland, first created the global reality TV phenomenon *Big Brother* for the Dutch market, going on to sell the format to numerous countries. Now owned by the Italian commercial television network Mediaset, Endemol has managed a number of internationally successful lifestyle formats, including *Changing Rooms*, *Ready Steady Cook*, and *Ground Force* (all initially made by the UK production company Bazal for the BBC), with local versions being made in New Zealand, Australia, and the United States.

The kinds of popular factual formats associated with television producers such as Endemol have had a particularly strong commercial edge within what is an increasingly fragmented and competitive market. Reality lifestyle programmes offered up as format 'shells' have been shown to have considerable transnational mobility and saleability, as they are amenable to being readily indigenized, even in the case of programmes emerging from non-English markets (such as the Dutch market) and are relatively risk free, having been previously tried out on an audience (Waisbord 2004). They are also a cost-effective way of filling gaps in local production schedules and—owing to growing flexibility around definitions of local content and the burgeoning role of transnational co-productions and joint ventures (Schiller 2007: 132–133)—they also often fulfil the requirements for local production quotas (Steemers 2004: 174; Waisbord 2004).[5]

Part of the reason for the global success of lifestyle formats, then, is precisely their ability to adapt to national contexts. However, while lifestyle programmes travel well as format shells, lifestyle shows featuring foreign experts and 'ordinary' people from other countries are not necessarily readily accepted by national audiences. As Bonner notes (2005), writing from an Australian perspective, while foreign cooking shows and celebrity chefs tend to translate into a range of different national markets, DIY and makeover shows and their specific brand of experts are not so easily exchangeable—a fact that she puts down to the way in which lifestyle TV and lifestyle experts are so thoroughly embedded in everyday life and articulated to national culture.

While overtly bourgeois figures such as Trinny and Susannah from *What Not to Wear* and Nigella Lawson have been very successful in the UK, where class culture is a common preoccupation within popular culture, these figures have been much less popular in Australia. Lifestyle experts (and TV personalities more broadly) in Australia are often relentlessly ordinary, tending to disavow any class credentials they might possess. Don Burke, for instance, the host of the long-running but now defunct Australian gardening-oriented lifestyle show *Burke's Backyard*[6]—while possessing considerable horticultural expertise—presents very much as an 'average Aussie' male.

In the period following Bonner's analysis, however, the situation has become a little less cut and dried as some foreign reality lifestyle programmes that feature ordinary people in their homes (such as *Queer Eye for the Straight Guy*) have gained high ratings with Australian and other international audiences.[7] Lifestyle experts also seem to be becoming more mobile, with figures such as Australian celebrity gardener Jamie Durie gaining a regular spot on *Oprah* and *Supernanny's* Jo Frost featuring in the US version of the UK format. *Queer Eye's* mobility could be put down to the way it combines the exotic spectacle of queer (and American) otherness with the now highly familiar traits of the DIY/makeover show. On the other hand, Jo Frost on *Supernanny*, while English and authoritative, is a very ordinary expert dealing with everyday issues in a familiar domestic setting, albeit it again (for international audiences) a slightly exotic version of UK or US ordinariness.

The translatability of these lifestyle experts suggests that audiences are increasingly able to negotiate, and may actively be seeking out, 'foreign' versions of everyday life. At the same time, there are often considerable differences between the way in which audiences read and respond to these shows in different cultural contexts.[8] The reception of makeover formats in the United States, Britain, and Australia, for instance, continues to be framed by differences in the cultural emphasis on and meaning of class, race, sexuality, and gender. The potential meanings of these shows are also influenced by different industrial contexts of reception, such as scheduling and programming contexts as well as televisual traditions. In the United States, for instance, 'reality' television has associations with early MTV formats such as *The Real World* and crime surveillance shows such as *COPS*, whereas in Britain popular factual formats emerge out of a tradition of social observational television and docusoaps.

Television formats, then, represent sites marked by complex negotiations between globalizing forces and domestic concerns and contexts (Moran 1998). Writing about the recent emergence of a host of consumer-oriented advice shows in China, Xu (2007) notes that a growing demand for programs has seen Chinese television adapting Western lifestyle formats to local needs, with local hosts fronting the shows and presenting lifestyle content relevant to an emergent Chinese consumer class. Shows such as the Beijing Television Station program *Jojo Good Living*, whose host has been compared by the *New York Times* to Martha Stewart, can be seen to emerge from an increasingly uniform global media culture, contributing to the shaping and formation of a growing strata of middle class consumers in China and promoting a distinctly Western lifestyle model way beyond the reach of most Chinese (Xu 2007: 372).

Other locally made shows are more attuned to the realities of China's emergent market economy, focusing on local and national concerns and emerging out of a longer public service tradition within Chinese television—for instance, China Central Television's Life Channel, which produces shows ranging from real-life stories of ordinary people to tips on household management, including programs such as *At Your Service*, which advises viewers on everything from remaking old clothes to 'alternative uses of toothpaste' (Xu 2007: 371). Another show, *Life 315*, also addresses the concerns of more ordinary Chinese viewers, offering advice on how to avoid 'traps and scams in their everyday consumption activities' (371). As *Life 315*'s mission statement puts it, emphasizing the show's function as a media watchdog: 'When counterfeit and shoddy goods emerge, when legal rights are violated, when fair trade is threatened, when individual dignities are challenged, *Life 315* will be there' (371).

The rise of lifestyle TV in China and the transnational mobility of lifestyle advice culture more broadly can be seen to reflect a globalization of the television industry, which in turn is linked to a range of developments from the growing integration of the structure and ownership of the industry to the increasing international mobility of its personnel (Waisbord 2004). It can also clearly be seen 'as an instance of new transnational … configurations of subjectivity and functions of television as a medium' (Bignell 2005: 40–41). At the same time, these global processes are articulated to and played out via specific national cultures. Xu, for instance, outlines a range of political, social, and economic factors, as well as distinctive industry traditions, that have shaped and continue to shape China's unique lifestyle television industry. While the spread of lifestyle media and expertise suggests, then, that the model of the aspirational, DIY self is being exported across a range of TV markets and cultures, such processes are clearly marked by a 'complex connectivity' with existing socio-cultural contexts 'rather than the simple distribution of a particular Western … lifestyle' (Tomlinson 2004: 26).

Book outline

This book looks at a range of popular expertise—from makeover experts on TV to the lifestyle advice available on the internet, focusing on forms of advice tied to everyday life skills and 'domestic' concerns such as food and cooking, health and diet, style and aesthetics, and care of the self and the family. I use a range of theoretical approaches to analyse the recent explosion of lifestyle advice, some of which have been previewed in this introduction. The research methods employed range from textual analysis to interviews with media producers and users. The book is organized as follows.

Chapter 1 examines the history of advice manuals and magazines from the Victorian era to the present. While the book primarily has a contemporary focus, this chapter highlights the important role played by print-based forms of popular expertise over the past two centuries. Exploring the connections between various developments in capitalist modernity and the changing role and meanings of gender, work, and leisure within domestic space, the chapter sets the scene for the subsequent analysis of the contemporary role and status of domestic and personal modes of advice and expertise.

Chapter 2 examines the role of popular expertise in food culture, focusing on a range of forms of food expertise, from TV chefs and nutritionists to food coaches and nutritional therapists. In examining the way in which food has become a contested site in late consumer capitalism, the chapter highlights a range of themes that recur throughout the book, including the growing emphasis on individual responsibility and on optimizing one's health for the 'public good', the focus on consumption as a site of informed choice and lifestyle ethics, the 'informationalization' of everyday life, and the increasing awareness of the risks and side effects associated with modern life and industrialization.

Chapter 3 turns to an analysis of expertise on television, examining the highly popular lifestyle makeover show *Queer Eye for the Straight Guy*. Mapping the shifting nature of expertise on television and the growing role of feminine and queer knowledges around individual style and identity performance, the chapter locates the emergence of new performative modes of masculinity on lifestyle TV in the context of a wider shift to consumer-based, reflexive, and enterprise modes of selfhood. Discussing the complexity of the cultural politics marking these shifts, the chapter argues that the transformational elements of makeover television can be seen as marking a potential opening up of the meanings of masculinity through a reflexive foregrounding of the constructed nature of identity at the same time as working to reinstate (heterosexual) social norms.

Chapter 4 offers an industry perspective on lifestyle programming and popular expertise. Based on observation and interviews with production staff, the chapter discusses the production of the Australian version of *Honey We're Killing the Kids*, an educational lifestyle makeover show that focuses on families and in particular children with dietary, health, and/or behavioural problems. The chapter examines the complex relationships between production processes, conceptions of audiences, national television culture, and TV's role as a social institution in promoting and shaping conceptions of 'good' citizenship and responsibility to community. In terms of this latter process, the focus is both on the educational role of the show's expert–host, in the Australian case a child development specialist, and on the role of the production team as themselves important 'cultural intermediaries'.

Chapter 5 moves from a production angle to thinking about the role and perspective of media audiences in relation to the use of online health advice. The chapter frames this discussion by noting the increasing centrality of health to lifestyle-oriented conceptions of the self and the social and the growing role of popular media in teaching citizens to manage their own health and well-being. Drawing upon research on young people and their use of the internet for health information, the chapter examines the debates around the figure of the DIY health consumer. Noting the different ways in which young people from different social backgrounds both make use of online health information and conceptualize health more broadly, the chapter notes the limits of the voluntarist, middle class 'healthy' ideal promoted by lifestyle media.

Chapter 6, the final chapter, discusses the increasingly central role played by celebrity and branding in domestic advice culture. It argues that the celebritization of expertise (via the figure of the lifestyle guru) can be seen as a marker of a growing convergence between a public sphere of commodity production and spectacle and an 'intimate' private sphere of consumption and everyday life. In focusing on the increasing role of celebrity-endorsed and -branded modes of lifestyle consumption, the chapter highlights the mutually dependent relationship between branded celebrity experts as lifestyle role models and the consumer imaginary in a context where information, entertainment, privatized lifestyle consumption, and ethical modes of citizenship have become increasingly interconnected.

Notes

1   Along with her radio producer at the Australian Broadcasting Corporation, Jennifer Fleming.

2   Writing from a somewhat tongue-in-cheek perspective, Australian TV critic Catherine Deveny's (2006) review of *It's Me or the Dog* highlights the centrality of constructions of class to lifestyle TV, lamenting as she does the way in which such programming forces viewers to watch the daily lives of 'the average Bogan family' (with the Australian term 'bogan' very roughly approximating the US term 'white trash' or 'chav' in the UK context). Decrying the average bogan lounge room as a book-free zone where 'the coffee table groans under the weight of remote controls', she smugly quips, 'It would be easy to criticize these people as ignorant, uninformed and selfish. So I think I will.'

3   Redden (2007) comments, for instance, on the 'inclusiveness' of British lifestyle TV, populated as it is by experts and participants drawn from a range of ethnic and class backgrounds and from across gender, age, and sexual divides. He notes, however, that these diverse individuals are figured as just that: individuals rather than representatives of a particular social category, thus serving 'to generalize aspirational individuality across the social field' (156).

4   Some important developments in popular expertise not covered in my book include the role of the self-help movement and of self-help gurus. For a comprehensive account of the historical development of therapeutic culture and the emergence of self-help literature see Miller and McHoul (1998).

5   Australian media content rules, for instance, require commercial and free-to-air TV stations to screen Australian programs for at least 55 percent of a station's air time between 6:00 a.m. and midnight. In meeting such quotas, locally made versions of foreign reality and lifestyle formats often represent a cheaper alternative to locally made drama.

6   Although there has been talk about resurrecting the show, which ran in Australia on the Nine Network from 1987 to 2004.

7   For instance, it is now reasonably common on Australian TV for channels to purchase the format rights along with the original version of a show and to air that original version as a way of prepping audiences for the subsequent local production, as in the case of *Queer Eye* and *What Not to Wear*.

8   For instance, while many popular factual formats travel readily across cultural borders, as Bignell notes (2005), cases like the relative disinterest in *Big Brother* in the United States and *Survivor*'s relatively poor ratings in the UK indicate that one should be cautious about overgeneralizing the universal appeal of such formats.

Chapter 1

From manners to makeovers
A history of modern lifestyle advice

Many accounts of the rise of lifestyle culture and media make the assumption that these phenomena are peculiar to the mid- to late 20th century, ignoring 'the longer historical reach' of present lifestyle concerns (Bell and Hollows 2006: 3). In their edited collection *Historicizing Lifestyle* (2006), Bell and Hollows discuss a range of earlier and potentially relevant historical analyses from Pierre Bourdieu's landmark study of taste, social distinction, and the new middle classes in France in the 1960s and Norbert Elias's sweeping historical work on taste and civility from the Middle Ages onwards to Michel Foucault's mapping of the history of self-care, which in turn looks as far back as the classical era (13).

For the purposes of this book, it is useful to provide a genealogy that situates contemporary popular expertise in relation to a number of trajectories within modernity. In particular, a range of interrelated social and cultural shifts that have occurred around domesticity, gender, class relations, and changing notions of selfhood, consumerism, and the relations between labour and leisure from the industrial revolution onwards. Mapping these shifts provides a deeper framing context through which we can see contemporary lifestyle expertise as a product of a complex range of developments in late modernity such as the growing privatization and individualization of once public and governmental concerns.

Modernity has been marked in its development by an unprecedented number of people turning to experts for advice and guidance. This crucial rise in forms of popular expertise emerged around, and as a response to, a series of dramatic social changes associated with modernity from the 19th century onwards. I discuss some of the implications of the ongoing rise and reconfiguration of popular expertise from then to now in three sections: the first maps the role of popular advice and expertise primarily in relation to the domestic sphere, focusing historically on the period from the rise of the Victorian domestic advice manual in the 1830s to the emergence of domestic masculinity and DIY culture in the first half of the twentieth century. The second section focuses on the 1950s and the mass magazine market; it examines the broadening out of domestic advice culture to incorporate a growing focus on the self and on forms of leisure and lifestyle that embrace masculine concerns while also attempting to negotiate shifting notions of femininity. The third section deals with the 1980s, which saw a marked intensification of the stylization of everyday life and a seamless merger between consumption and lifestyle advice. In discussing these selective moments of popular expertise in modern Western culture, the aim is not to see advice culture in a reductive sense—as merely a 'side effect' of particular social developments—but to situate contemporary lifestyle expertise as an active player in a complex conjuncture of both long-term and relatively recent historical, cultural, and economic developments.

In attempting to sketch crucial shifts across such a long period and over a broad sphere of cultural production, I have strategically chosen to focus primarily on popular advice literature and in particular magazines. The magazine format emerged as a pivotal mass medium in the late 19th and early 20th centuries and, despite growing competition from other media, continues to figure as an important source of popular advice today. In this overview of magazine culture and its relationship to broad shifts in modernity, the examples and secondary literature drawn upon here refer specifically to developments in the United Kingdom and the United States; to a certain degree these trends can be applied to the West more broadly, but it should also be noted that these developments in popular expertise are articulated to and have emerged out of quite distinct cultural, economic, and political contexts.

The Tastemakers:
Class, gender and the Victorian advice manual

The Victorian era was a pivotal period in terms of the emergence of popular advice literature. In the US and the UK, in the context of the dramatic social upheavals that accompanied the industrial revolution, the 19th century saw the emergence of a plethora of taste, etiquette, and domestic advice manuals, with one of the most famous and lasting examples being Isabella Beeton's *Book of Household Management*, which sold 60,000 copies in its first year (Langland 1995: 32).

As I noted in my introductory chapter, one of the central roles of lifestyle experts is their function as arbiters of good taste and distinction, a role that can be seen to have taken on particular potency within the context of modernity and its move away from traditional modes of identity and cultural value. Bourdieu's pivotal work on the emergence of the new middle classes in 1960s France highlighted the role of cultural intermediaries (at that time associated particularly with the new consumer-related professions of the media and marketing) in negotiating and legitimating new normative regimes of taste and lifestyle in the face of shifting social identities and consumer-driven class mobility. However, such struggles over taste and cultural capital are not just a product of the rise of contemporary consumer culture but can be traced back to well before the 20th century.[1] The history of class and taste is also complicated by issues that are relatively marginalized in Bourdieu's account, such as the pivotal historical role of gender in questions of taste formation and social distinction. In the 19th century especially, the home became an important site where class distinction was on display and where women in particular played a key role in performing social status through their dress and manners (Bell and Hollows 2006: 12). Etiquette manuals and management guides were important at the time in shaping a middle class set of cultural values and identity. While men were also the target of advice manuals, Victorian etiquette manuals were primarily aimed at women, 'implicitly acknowledging that the evolving signifiers of bourgeois identity properly belong to women' (Langland 1995: 25).

The broader context for the rise of the popular advice manual in Victorian England was the emergence of a large aspiring bourgeoisie who sought to emulate the taste and manners of the aristocracy (Langland 1995: 25). Growing economic wealth in the late 18th century saw a relative democratization of consumption, with increasing class mobility making the role of consumption practices as a marker of taste and status even more pivotal (Bell and Hollows 2006: 7). Likewise, in the 19th century, massive urban migration and shifting social relations, alongside the mass production of goods, saw the working classes also increasingly participating in consumption processes, and the growing role of 'positional goods' in visibly marking the social status of modern citizens (Bell and Hollows 2006: 8).

As Lynes notes in *The Tastemakers* (1954: 8–9), the invention of technologies of mass production in the United States, such as William Compton's weaving loom in 1837, and the importation from England of the first wallpaper printing machine in 1844 resulted in home goods once accessible to an elite few being available to a growing consumer market. The home décor industry rapidly expanded from the 1840s, with a concomitant explosion of designer styles. A growing preoccupation with the latest style meant that '[h]eirlooms began to find their way to the attic as the new chairs and sofas, bedecked with fruit, flowers, and beasties and standing on twisted spindles, crowded into living rooms and parlours'

(Lynes 1954: 9). While some guidance in household taste was clearly required, Lynes argues that US women's magazines were slow to pick up on this opportunity to advise consumers on the latest goods and continued to be preoccupied with European fashions 'and sentimental and moral tales' (10). He contends that '[i]t was not until the 1850s that housewives were deluged with hints about what they should do to be tasteful and genteel in the appurtenances of their homes' (11).

Leavitt's (2002) account of 19th-century domestic advisors in the US suggests that questions of domestic taste and décor did feature in the earlier domestic advice manuals that emerged in the 1830s but were inextricably linked to moral rather than consumerist concerns. In particular, the Victorian era's focus on home and family saw these manuals constructing the ideal white middle class woman as one devoted to the domestic sphere and not distracted by outside concerns such as seeking a career (Leavitt 2002: 9). Issues of moral responsibility and aesthetics were brought together through the discourse of home décor, where advisors saw the appropriate arrangement and choice of furniture as reflecting 'honesty, faith and good judgement' (Leavitt 2002: 9).

The social shifts that accompanied modernization processes in the United States and in Britain thus witnessed a growing focus on symbolic markers of social status, where questions of taste and moral standing were increasingly externalized via domestic consumer practices and the idealized figure of the homemaker. As definitions of status became increasingly tied to the intangible symbolic realm of taste and manners, 'women sought stability in detailed decorums, which were in the hands of women [who in turn] were in the hands of the etiquette books' (Langland 1995: 26). The setting for the rise and success of advice manuals and magazines, then, was one where modernization processes in the West led to a generalized sense of fluidity around social status and an increasing focus on 'the manipulation of social signs' (Langland 1995: 26), with domestic space positioned as an important site for the display of good taste.

Rationalizing domesticity: The rise of the 'domiologist'

As the Victorian era came to a close and modernism emerged as a cultural and aesthetic movement, definitions of good taste and style and the meanings of domesticity itself were challenged. While many women clung to Victorian ideals of taste, women's magazines in the early 20th century sought to teach women to appreciate the masculine style of modernism, emphasizing the benefits of stark, sleek, and efficient home interiors (Leavitt 2002: 98). For domestic advisors at the time, '"modern" was a code word for "simple" and "uncluttered", for "taste" and "good character"' (Leavitt 2002: 98), in contrast to the feminine excess associated with the Victorian aesthetic.

This attempt at bringing masculine modernist ideals into the feminized space of the domestic reflected a longer struggle over the meanings of home and the place of women in a modernizing world. Ehrenreich and English (2005: 7–18), for instance, link the rise of the 'Woman Question' and associated forms of expertise aimed at managing femininity and domesticity to the shift from agrarian societies centred around production in the home to industrial societies marked by a split between a public and a private sphere. The result was a sense of ambiguity around definitions of the status of women as industrialism on the one hand freed them from 'the endless round of household productive labour' but at same time stripped them of the skills that had underpinned their productive role in the agrarian home (17).

As a new modern order emerged, it increasingly relied on setting up an opposition between a rational, masculine economic sphere and the romantic, feminine realm of the domestic, a symbolic divide that, in reality, was characterized by considerable traffic and exchange. Many domestic advisors, for instance, sought to bring modernity, science, and rationality into the home (Leavitt 2002: 99). The introduction of efficient, rational systems of domestic management was encouraged in Victorian etiquette manuals, which attempted to 'harmonize' the labours of management with femininity more broadly (Langland 1995: 46). Men were advised not to interfere with the sphere of domestic management, including the realm of home finance, over which women were constructed as having authority (Langland 1995: 47).

These early attempts at rationalizing the household anticipated the later emergence in the early 20th century of domestic science advisors, figures who attempted to bring together feminine concerns with aesthetics and care of the self and family with the rationalized processes of modernity. The emergence of expertise around domestic science dovetailed with the rise of the housewife in the 20th century as the new feminine ideal. As Ehrenreich and English argue (2005: 156), 'The idea of housekeeping as a full-time profession was elaborated by a new set of experts who were … largely women themselves.'

The attempt to professionalize housework saw the rise of 'Home Taylorists' or 'domiologists' who sought to bring Frederick W. Taylor's rationalist principles of factory floor production into the home (Leavitt 2002: 54). The domestic advisor Christine Frederick, for instance, who was consulting household editor of the *Ladies' Home Journal*, ran a 'home experiment station', where labor-saving modes of food preparation were tested, along with a variety of different products, from household appliances to food stuffs. Frederick, the author of Taylorist-inspired books such as *The New Housekeeping: Efficiency Studies in Home Management* (1913), was also a precursor of the celebrity expert (a figure discussed in Chapter 6), offering 'scientific advice' on products such as washing machines as part of paid endorsements (Coolidge-Consumerism 2007).

Rather than resolving the 'Woman Question', however, these attempts to apply scientific and economic expertise and advice to the domestic sphere marked the ongoing ambiguity of the role and status of the home and femininity within modernity. The history of the struggles over the meaning of housework reveals the way in which the public/private split strived for in Victorian times never fitted comfortably into the either/or logic ascribed to it (Mellencamp 1992: 362–363). The domestic sphere was positioned ambiguously, then, as at once a privatized, feminized realm and a space of modernization and rationalization—and, above all, as the site of a cacophony of expert voices that sought to offer guidelines for dealing with these ambiguities.

Leisure, domestic masculinity, and the DIY movement

These attempts to rationalize domestic labour reflected a broader set of concerns addressed by home experts from the 19th century onwards around definitions of work and leisure within domestic space. Central to this process was the attempt to negotiate, on the one hand, a conception of the Victorian home as a haven where men could escape from the pressures of modern life and, on the other hand, the notion of the home as a space shaped by processes of modernization.

As the rise of industrialization saw public space emerge as the primary site of 'productive' work in the 19th century, domestic space increasingly began to be constructed as a site of leisure as well as a kind of moral sanctum. One of the new roles that emerged for women at this time, aided by taste manuals and etiquette guides, was as representatives of social status on behalf of the household. In his classic work *The Theory of the Leisure Class* (1957), Thorstein Veblen outlines the role of 'conspicuous leisure' for those 'superior pecuniary' classes who seek to emulate elite lifestyles while attempting to disavow the labour that has granted them their privileged status. At a time of considerable social mobility and fluidity, one of the roles signalled for middle class white women in 19th-century advice literature was clearly to embody this notion of conspicuous leisure as a marker of superior social status. While Veblen acknowledges the considerable effort expended by women around 'the maintenance and elaboration of the household paraphernalia' (1957: 57–58), the rise of industrialism thus saw the domestic, symbolic, and aesthetic work done by women increasingly not constructed as productive labour but instead associated with the realm of leisure and consumption—although, again, the presence at the time of other counter-discourses of domesticity such as home economics within the realm of popular advice books and women's magazines indicated that the public/private, labour/leisure split was not necessarily clear-cut.

One way in which the problem of the work/leisure distinction was managed in the 19th century—particularly in relation to male participation in the domestic sphere—was through the notion of 'productive leisure'. In contrast to the idle leisure associated with, for instance, frequenting public houses, the home was offered up as a place where Victorian men could indulge in self-improving, domestic leisure such as hobbies, privatized modes of leisure that encouraged individual expression while also functioning to bring together work and leisure within the domestic realm (Rosenberg 2005). This attempt to recuperate the home as a site of productive leisure was also linked to class-based concerns (Holliday 2006: 74). While pubs offered comfortable, companionable spaces away from the cramped living conditions of working class houses, the large number of potentially 'unmanageable' workers who gathered in these public places was a source of considerable anxiety, a situation that saw middle class reformers promoting a discourse of working class improvement through 'rational recreation' (Holliday 2006: 71–72). The emergence of leisure time more broadly was seen as 'dangerous' by employees, 'as both manager and factory hand were away from the controls imposed by a centralized workplace'(Gelber 1999: 25). Thus, the domestic advisor Catharine Beecher, while urging fathers to spend more time at the home, also emphasized the need for them to engage 'in domestic amusements which at once refresh and improve' (cited in Gelber 1999: 25).

This refiguring of the home as a site of worthy modes of recreation was also a way of integrating middle- and working class men into domestic space in ways that articulated with the era's emphasis on the role of masculine productivity and rational self-control. While thus far I have primarily focused on advice manuals targeted at women, the social upheaval of the 19th century saw the rise of popular modes of expertise aimed at men at a time of instability around male codes of behaviour (Mechling 2003: 13). The domestic sphere at this time was seen as a refuge from 'the amorality of capitalist competition' (14). But while men were encouraged 'to cultivate domestic ties', there were also concerns about the need for adolescent boys and men to manage their emotional selves and their biological urges through forms of productive activity (14). Advice manuals thus emphasized the need for 'self-control and self-discipline of the body', traits all essential to be a morally upright and economically productive citizen (13).

A pre-eminent site where the popular experts of the day sought to target the domestic male was in the area of home improvement, an arena that would later develop into the DIY movement. The emergence of popular advice around this topic is of particular interest here not just because of its role as an obvious precursor to the contemporary obsession with home makeovers but also because of the way in which it prefigures the growing role more broadly of men in lifestyle and makeover culture, marking shifts in the gendered nature and meaning of domesticity, aesthetics, and moral discourses of (self-)improvement.

In the late 19th century, Victorians became increasingly interested in acquiring manual skills as a home-based 'hobby'. Hobbies offered a way of bridging 'the worlds of work and home', enabling an escape from (and potential resistance to) the world of work at the same time as affirming 'the work ethic' of market capitalism (Gelber 1999: 2). While handicrafts had hitherto been seen as a feminine activity, the emergence of modernism in the home saw craftwork reconfigured along more masculine and less ornamental lines (193–194). Furthermore, crafts began to be conceptualized as psychologically fulfilling activities through which, in contrast to the alienated labour processes that marked industrialism, men could produce a unique and authentic artifact by hand (196).[2] Craft skills, which started to be taught in schools at the time under the banner of 'manual education', were framed as a 'socially beneficial form of leisure' that taught men and boys about aesthetics and taste, contributing to their overall personal development (201–202). While the Victorian and early 20th-century home in the United States was often seen as an emasculating environment—hence the emergence of fraternal orders and clubs such as the Boy Scouts—the rise of hobby-based activities saw a space cleared within the home for 'the masculine role of artisan, if only in a leisure-time environment' (205). A kind of 'domestic masculinity', then, emerged around the pre-industrial manual skills associated with men's craft work (204).[3]

While the term DIY was not yet commonplace in the early decades of the 20th century, magazines and advice columns at the time promoted an early DIY culture, in particular 'disseminating a visual language of "before" and "after"' that was to become a central trope in consumer advice culture more broadly (Goldstein 1998: 15). In 1932, for instance, *Better Homes and Gardens* started the trend of home remodelling competitions when it asked readers to send in before and after photos of their home renovation projects (19). Such magazines shaped tastes and stylistic values, with competitions and articles on transforming the home emphasizing the need to improve the home through modernization, replacing (feminine) Victorian features with efficient modern features (19).

Despite these early developments, DIY only really took off as a widespread consumer-based movement in the wake of the post-war economic boom that swept 1950s America. In 1952, *Business Week*, proclaiming 'the age of do-it-yourself', helped turn the term into a household word, assisted by 'do-it-yourself' expositions that were held around the United States in the same year (Gelber 1999: 271). The rise of suburbia and the focus on homeownership also provided an important context for the emergence of a domesticated DIY culture.[4] DIY dovetailed with a mode of consumption oriented towards 'a family-centred way of life' and family-based leisure and was seen as offering a personal refuge from the corporate world and mass cultural conformity (Goldstein 1998: 38–39).

The rise of post-war suburbia saw the development of a large home-based consumer market for DIY goods. While before the war manufacturers advertised primarily to professional customers, during the 1950s a whole range of new easy-to-use home materials aimed at the DIY market appeared, such as '"ready to wear" wallpaper' (Goldstein 1998: 54–57). These were accompanied by 'amateur-friendly tools' (Goldstein 1998: 48), the ultimate being the portable electric drill, which 'became the emblem of the do-it-yourself movement' (Gelber 1999: 278).

The growth of a consumer market was also marked by the rising popularity of instruction manuals and the emergence of magazines such as *Family Handyman* in 1951, publications that, compared with previous instructional literature, were more aimed at the layperson, coming complete with detailed instructions and step-by-step pictures (Goldstein 1998: 39–40). These magazines were also marked by the growing use of a combination of information and advertising—strategies now central to lifestyle media—as 1950s magazines ran feature articles on DIY while also featuring advertisements for what products to use (Gelber 1999: 276).

While the manual skills involved in home renovation in the earlier part of the century were marked out as a largely masculine domain, the rise of DIY in the 1950s saw a more complex and shifting set of gender relations emerge around the productive leisure activities performed in the home. On the one hand, the growing focus in magazine advice in the 1950s on practical home improvement tips (such as 'the creative use of masking tape') saw the rise of the new idealized role 'of the suburban husband as handy man', where the handyman role was seen as 'building family bonds' (Gelber 1999: 268). At the same time, the post-war period was characterized by growing anxiety about the place and role of men, with popular culture at the time marked by recurrent images of the emasculated male (Ehrenreich and English 2005: 264).

During the war, many women worked in factories, replacing male labour while also managing the household. In the post-war period, men found themselves returning to a domestic space marked by 'shifting expectations' regarding their role 'as both providers and nurturers' (Goldstein 1998: 67). Women's growing power in the home was contrasted to that of 'the degraded dad' facing an 'overly mechanized, rationalized and organized' world of work (Ehrenreich and English 2005: 261). Stripped of his individual identity in the bureaucratized world of work, 'the man in the gray flannel suit' turned to the home as a site of potential 'masculine redemption' (262–263).

However, while DIY was often depicted as an escape from the grey conformity of mass culture, it could also itself be seen as a site of intense regulation and discipline. In the 1950s DIY was increasingly figured as an essential part of masculinity, and popular images at the time depicted the pressure overly insistent wives put on their 'henpecked husbands' to engage in their manly duty to maintain the home (Gelber 1999: 286–287). As Gelber puts it, 'The hammer, saw, and quarter-inch electric drill became the emblems of the new masculinity, and men who refused to master them did so at some risk to their standing in the eyes of spouse and community' (294). These pressures on the 1950s male witnessed the emergence of a mode of advice literature emphasizing the limitations and strictures of men's 'breadwinner' role, with publications such as *Playboy*, launched in 1953, encouraging men instead to pursue 'self-fulfillment through leisure activities and consumption' (14).

Consuming advice:
From home improvement to self-styling

The rise of this emblematic new kind of advice literature marked a significant shift, one that saw both men and women increasingly addressed as consumers. Although popular advice culture began to be shaped by the growing intrusion of commercial pressures and a burgeoning consumer culture from as early as the 19th century, the 1950s (particularly in the context of the United States) has traditionally been seen as the birthplace of mass consumerism, marked as it was by a post-war economic boom that was accompanied by a massive growth in the advertising industry and a rapid expansion of the new lifestyle-oriented middle class. Along with this expanded class of lifestyle consumers emerged a new cadre of symbolic and cultural specialists, who in turn populated the rapidly expanding public relations and marketing industries. In the 1960s and 1970s, alongside the rise of various forms of 'identity politics' associated with new social movements such as feminism, these cultural industries started to come to the fore as Fordist approaches to mass production began to give way to more flexible, specialized modes of production oriented towards the discerning individual consumer. For theorists of postmodernism, this period begins to be distinguished from modernism by the growing role of the symbolic and cultural dimensions of consumption, a development that, as we will see, becomes a dominant feature of consumer culture and everyday life from the 1980s onwards and that heralds the increasing participation of men in processes of self-styling and lifestyle consumption. To speak of the emergence of a postmodern culture of consumption is to acknowledge the growing role of the symbolic rather than the utilitarian dimension of goods as well as the increasing circulation of cultural goods oriented towards a lifestyle culture (Featherstone 1991: 84). The growing importance of symbolic culture, however, cannot be reduced to the logic of consumer capitalism. Rather, it involves a complex interplay between consumer culture and new types of 'symbolic specialists, cultural intermediaries and audiences' attuned to the cultural shifts of postmodernism (Featherstone 1991: 64). Thus, from as early as the 1950s and 1960s consumption processes, along with the growing complexity and differentiation of products and markets, were not only articulated to economic and rational imperatives but also increasingly involved in the production of complex new lifestyle-driven forms of agency and individuality.

Targeting the female consumer
Like the advice literature of the previous century, the new modes of lifestyle media that began to emerge in the 1950s provided expert guidance on managing the self in a context of shifting social mores, from the more conventional domestic imagery found in, for instance, DIY culture to the more transgressive and individualistic

modes of leisure celebrated in glossy lifestyle magazines. Lifestyle magazines such as '*Playboy*, *Cosmopolitan* and *Ebony* became virtual instruction manuals for living' (Arvidsson 2006: 28). These magazines also saw the mainstreaming of elite and avant-garde consumer practices and tastes, catering 'to an experimenting, interactive attitude' (29). This story of growing consumer agency and the democratization of taste and consumption practices across class lines, however, was once again complicated by gender. While men were increasingly targeted by lifestyle media and advertisers, consumption practices were still closely associated with the home and with femininity. As modernity saw the family household moving away from its earlier pre-industrial role in production towards consumption, the figure of the suburban housewife emerged in many ways as the archetypal consumer. Certainly, as the main point of access to household consumption practices and the chief shopper for the family, the female consumer was a central target for marketers. From the 1950s onwards, media-based advice about home management and care of the self thus became increasingly complicated by pressures from commercial interests and a growing emphasis on consumption, with much of this consumer advice media oriented towards the female consumer.

Cynthia White's classic study of the history of women's magazines in the UK (1970: 283) maps the emerging dilemma of 'service' magazines that saw themselves as having a 'social responsibility' to work 'in the best interests of their readers' while facing growing commercial pressures. Whereas during the Second World War magazines counselled their readers to economize, the 1950s saw a shift towards a culture of consumption in which the emphasis was increasingly not so much on mending and 'making do' as on purchasing new household items (123). In the context of growing affluence and the spread of middle class taste and lifestyle orientations, female consumers turned for information and expert advice on the latest consumer goods to the new glossy magazines (whose cover price was heavily subsidized by the advertising dollar) that were starting to emerge.[5]

The growing encroachment at the time of commercial pressures on editorial freedom in these advice-oriented magazines was reflected in the increasing use of 'branded products' in advice columns and the 'next-matter positioning of advertisements' (White 1970: 282). This consumer-oriented mode of address, however, was also marked by a shift away from a more authoritarian editorial style to a relatively democratized approach, emphasizing readers' needs and encouraging a sense of dialogue and participation with the magazine (159). Improvements in the look and quality of the magazines also saw a growth in the information and advice they provided on all manner of topics (160) and an increased emphasis on raising 'the tastes of their readers' (161) by 'promoting higher standards of nutrition, childcare and general home comfort, as well as personal adjustment' (298).

Despite wider social changes, such as the growing number of working women, British magazines in the 1950s were still rather conservative in their outlook, tending to emphasize traditional female roles and values. It was not until the 1960s that a range of magazines aimed at young working women, such as *Nova* launched in 1965, began to emerge. In part, the rise of these new magazines reflected a concern on the behalf of marketers with tapping into new social movements such as feminism, attempting to link feminine consumption to the new forms of agency associated with the progressive politics of the times. By the 1960s and early 1970s, marketers and advertisers were increasingly focused on the rise of the singles lifestyle, with magazines such as the hugely popular US publication *Cosmopolitan* introducing its female readers to the joys of 'instant gratification' and spending for fun rather than for the home and family (Ehrenreich and English 2005: 317). Consumer advice at the time thus began to broaden out from a focus on the household to targeting women as individual consumers of lifestyle-related goods and services.

Emergent consumer masculinities

In the post-war period consumer culture also saw an expansion—and a crucial shift in the mode of address—of consumer advice aimed at men, marked by a growing focus on the stylized male self. Men's magazines played a central role in addressing, advising, and shaping the identity of the emergent male consumer, representing an important site for the development of a masculine culture of popular expertise organized around lifestyle consumption, discourses of individualization, and the 'style-ization' of everyday life. As I have noted, the 1950s in particular saw the emergence of a growing advice literature expressing dissatisfaction with men's traditional roles, with magazines such as *Playboy* offering men alternative consumer-based identities.

Playboy, however, was not breaking completely new ground here: a number of earlier men's magazines had to a certain extent prepared the way for the emergence of the 'swinging' bachelor–consumer. *Esquire*, the first US 'magazine for men', a consumer-oriented publication that was concerned with what it termed 'the Art of Living', was started in 1933 (Osgerby 2003: 57). As Osgerby sums up the magazine's ethos, 'Combining colour illustrations of the latest men's fashions with regular features on foreign travel, cuisine and interior décor, *Esquire* encouraged its readers to think of themselves as autonomous men of taste who expressed their identities and status through the purchase of distinctive goods and signifiers' (57). The 'modern masculinity' portrayed on the pages of *Esquire*, while aimed at a cross class audience, did not include black readers, who had to wait until the emergence of *Ebony* in 1945 to participate 'in the full range of pleasures available to the American middle class' (Pendergast 2000: 209).

These early attempts to address and advise white male readers in primarily consumer-based terms were marked by an ongoing struggle to negotiate and reframe the feminine connotations of consumption practices. Much of men's advice literature in the early 20th century continued to emphasize Victorian masculine ideals of a strong work ethic and moral prohibition around 'indulgent leisure' (Osgerby 2003: 64). By contrast, *Esquire* unreservedly embraced the joys of consumption, focusing on leisure and shopping as well as venturing into the thoroughly feminized realms of fashion and cooking. However, in heading into this potentially dangerous territory, the magazine at the same time sought to reassure male readers of the thoroughly manly nature of its concerns, balancing style-oriented advice with stories on adventure and sport as well as fiction by 'literary tough-guy' Ernest Hemingway (Osgerby 2003: 69-71).[6]

The 1950s then were characterized by a growing acceptance of 'models of masculinity rooted in personal consumption', a process highlighted by the 'phenomenal success' of magazines such as *Playboy* (Osgerby 2003: 75–76). Men's advice culture was still marked, however, by ongoing anxieties around masculine consumption, reflected in particular by concerns about the associations between a focus on individual style and connotations of sexual 'deviance'. Similar to later developments in male consumer culture such as the emergence of the figure of the 'New Lad', *Playboy*'s popularity can be linked to the way it effectively detached itself from such associations by pairing its lifestyle and consumer advice to aggressively (hetero) sexual imagery. Through its groundbreaking mainstreaming of pornography in particular, *Playboy* distanced itself from '[a]ny suggestion of effeminacy … [offering] its readers "safe" passage into the realm of narcissistic and self-conscious consumption' (Osgerby 2003: 77).

The 1980s and beyond:
New Men, New Women, and the lifestyle consumer

I want to turn now to focus on more recent developments in popular magazines in the 1980s and 1990s. This crucial period witnessed an explosion of advice literature oriented towards men, marked by the rise of numerous men's magazines, as well as a number of significant changes in the women's magazine market. This final section of the chapter outlines these shifts, emphasizing in particular the growing trend from text-based advice to visual modes of communication, the foregrounding of a highly aestheticized construction of lifestyle consumption and selfhood (played out in particular in men's consumer culture) and the increasingly integrated nature of advice and consumer discourse and imagery.

The 1980s has often been proclaimed as the era that ushered in a fully fledged postmodern consumer culture. Mort (1996), in his classic account of the UK men's magazine industry in the 1980s, however, has warned against making easy generalizations about the decade. As the previous discussion suggests, such developments need to be understood in the context of longer-term trends from the 1950s onwards (while also recognizing distinct variations in different national contexts). We can nevertheless see the 1980s as witnessing a number of significant shifts in the arena of consumer and advice culture, particularly in relation to questions of gender and lifestyle consumption. In particular, this period can be seen as heralding the normalization of consumption 'as a whole way of life' when consumption practices started to thicken into a 'culture of consumption' (Mort 1996: 2). Central to this integration of consumption into everyday life was the growing role of men in consumer processes, illustrated by the following discussion of the emergence of a series of new men's magazines concerned with style and aesthetics.

Style magazines, the New Man, and the New Lad

While the rise of magazines such as *Playboy* suggested a growing interest in addressing and advising the male consumer, in the 1960s and 1970s the magazine market was still primarily attuned to a female readership. Women's magazines continued to dominate the market in the 1980s, but the decade also saw the emergence of numerous glossy lifestyle magazines aimed at men. These magazines saw young men move from the margins to the centre of consumer culture, with the innovative techniques developed to speak to the male consumer impacting across the media and consumer market.

The growing focus on men's consumption practices at this time can be understood in terms of a range of wider cultural pressures. In the wake of social movements such as feminism and the gay movement, roles, rules, and norms around gender and sexuality were marked by a degree of uncertainty and instability (Winship 1987; Mort 1996; Stevenson et al. 2003). Commercial culture's preoccupation with the figure of the 'New Man' can also be linked to the rise of popular psychology as well as the emergence of the men's health movement and concerns around 'toxic' forms of masculinity (Gill 2003: 43).

The rise of the New Man also took place at a time of significant economic change, with a shift towards more flexible, post-Fordist modes of production and a growing interest in and targeting of individual niche-oriented modes of consumption. These economic changes were accompanied, at least in the United Kingdom and the United States, by shifts in the political sphere and in particular the emergence of free-market-oriented governments. Critical of centrist models of government control and welfarism, the ethos underpinning 1980s-style neoliberal politics was one of privatization and entrepreneurialism (Gough-Yates 2003: 31–32). Alongside the increased visibility of masculinity as a form of social identity and the search for new markets within the magazine industry, the rise of this neoliberal culture of competitive individualism set the stage for the emergence of 'a new category' of men's magazines (Winship 1987: 150).

The possibility of producing a lifestyle magazine that would, similar to women's magazines, speak to a general audience of men had for some time been the holy grail of commercial publishing (Mort 1996: 18). The failure of well-backed ventures in the 1980s such as *The Hit*, however, contributed to an ongoing sense that a magazine that foregrounded the maleness of its audience was 'a risky business, because it raised the troubled question of identity as gendered' (21). The publication that broke this impasse in the UK context was *The Face*, a style magazine emerging out of a post-punk 'independent' youth and music culture (23). Although it did not sell to huge numbers of readers, *The Face* was seen as highly influential in creating a space for a sophisticated mode of postmodern journalism in which the foregrounding of style rather than fashion per se saw avant-garde aesthetics brought together with (elite) consumer culture (23–26). In terms of its influence on mainstream magazine practices, design and visual experimentation was central to the magazine, which became known for its groundbreaking photographic images and its creative and playful representations of men's bodies that borrowed in part from gay iconography. The visual focus that marked the creative, stylized consumption promoted by *The Face* also saw a shift in emphasis from largely text-based consumer advice to complex forms of symbolic communication, a shift that contributed to a wider stylization of magazine advice culture.

While *The Face* promoted itself as a style rather than a men's magazine (although its readership was largely male and its production team overwhelmingly so), it paved the way for the subsequent emergence in the UK of publications specifically targeting men, including *Arena*, which was launched by the editor of *The Face*, Nick Logan, as 'Britain's first magazine for men' in 1986 (Mort 1996: 74). A more advice-oriented magazine, *Arena* emphasized a 'superior model of consumption', with a monthly focus on goods and services called 'Arena Recommends' (75). As Mort puts it, 'The magazine functioned explicitly as a consumer manual, selecting those films, books and other items which were the current emblems of fashionability' (75). *Arena* paved the way for the subsequent 'spectacular' rise and mainstreaming of the men's magazine market in Britain, which saw the emergence of a range of publications from the late 1980s onwards not only aimed at 'upmarket' readers (such as *GQ* and *Esquire*) but also attempting to cover a range of social categories and interest groups as well as a more 'mass-market' circulation (Stevenson et al. 2003: 117–118).

While Mort highlights the dissent in the industry over the male consumer in relation to defining appropriate target audiences, he argues that some sense of a coherent mode of address did emerge at the time from these various men's magazines. Promoting the notion that selfhood and identity were intimately connected to choices made in the field of consumption, these new men's magazines were dominated by a focus on 'bodily appearance', offering advice on products for body maintenance and constructing '[p]ersonal hygiene' as a form of 'pleasurable labour' (Mort 1996: 77–78).

Similar to women's magazines, these magazines spoke to a community of men in a spirit of friendship, with advice provided by journalists who identified with the shared experiences of new masculinity rather than 'distant experts' (Mort 1996: 78). In *Arena* magazine's special issues on clothes shopping, which specialized in providing 'sought-after information' about hard-to-find products and shops, however, that shared community was seen to be a discerning, metropolitan reader (78). Letters from disgruntled readers suggested that these constructions of masculinity around a 'fantasy world of wealth' did not go uncontested (79).

The limitations of this focus on the 'New Man' as a bourgeois, London-based member of the social elite were evident in the emergence in the 1990s of another attempt to renegotiate masculinity within the UK consumer marketplace, the 'New Lad'. Interpreted largely as a reaction against feminism, like the readership of *Playboy*, this emblematic figure can be seen more broadly as reacting against the strictures of masculine roles tied to marriage and family, while also rejecting the modes of masculinity offered by the New Man, a figure perceived as 'narcissistic' and 'inauthentic' within lad culture (Gill 2003: 47–48).[7]

Magazines in the UK in the 1990s were pivotal in the construction of the New Lad, with *Arena* magazine itself publishing a 'ladifesto' in 1991 that 'sought to expose the "myth" of the sensitive, caring and non-sexist New Man, and celebrate the arrival of his hedonistic, libidinous, postfeminist alter ego' (Gill 2003: 49). With its celebration of 'working class machismo' (Edwards 2003: 144), clearly the reactionary stance of the New Lad was built strongly along class lines and could be partly seen as attempting to target a more massified consumer market. Here the New Lad was particularly associated with the more 'down-market' magazine *Loaded* launched in 1994, which stated its goal as being 'life, liberty and the pursuit of sex, drink, football and less serious matters' (cited in Gill 2003: 49).

Despite the jokey, ironic tone adopted by *Loaded* and many of the other men's magazines at the time, these publications were marked by a 'profusion of "how to" sections' and an abundance of advice on everything 'from the monitoring of sexual performance to changing a car tyre', reflecting uncertainties around masculine roles and norms (Stevenson et al. 2003: 128). In providing the male equivalent of the lifestyle advice offered in women's magazines, however, much effort was made to avoid being taken 'too seriously' or setting up a hierarchy between the magazine and the reader (120). Instead, these magazines sought to 'address the reader as a "mate", offering to become the "reader's friend" by providing handy hints, pointing out obvious pitfalls and providing useful advice' (120).

The rise of a range of men's magazines in the 1990s (accompanied by a broader men's self-help literature advising men, for instance, on how to be better husbands and fathers) reflected some opening up of debates around men's traditional roles and heterosexual norms. At the same time, the ironic tone that marked New

Lad publications and the broader cohort of men's magazines also worked to provide a buffer zone for readers from the difficulties and contradictions of the new masculinity and its relation to consumption (Stevenson et al. 2003: 122). Nevertheless, the rise of the New Man and the growing focus on masculine style from the 1980s onwards can be seen as, in part, paving the way for the recent push towards a (relatively) more mainstreamed culture of lifestyle advice and consumption.

From the New Woman to the lifestyle consumer

Alongside the success of men's magazines, the 1980s also brought about a sea change in the women's magazine industry. If the women's magazine market was defined in the 1950s, the mid-1980s might be seen as a moment when this 'heritage was finally jettisoned' (Winship 1987: 148). However, the reality, as Winship points out, was rather less dramatic and more contradictory than such a statement would suggest. In the United States in the 1980s, for instance, the 'seven sisters', the industry name for the main women's 'service' magazines in the US market (*Family Circle, Woman's Day, Good Housekeeping, Better Homes and Garden*, etc.) continued to provide large numbers of women with advice and information oriented towards domesticity and care of the self and family. Suggesting an ongoing commitment to a traditional service model of the women's magazine, in a letter from 1983, the editor of *Woman's Day* summed up her role thus:

> Our goal as journalists and editors is to help the women who are loyal readers in whatever arena they need support, from something as simple as do-ahead recipes that are as nutritionally sound as possible to something as serious as significant illness or financial need or emotional support. (cited in McCracken 1993: 9)

While magazines like *Good Housekeeping* made some attempt at updating their content by featuring, for instance, feminist articles on the value of housework, by and large the advice offered by these magazines continued to emphasize women's traditional roles (McCracken 1993: 186–187). The women's magazine market in the US and the UK was at the time under considerable economic pressure. While some of the service magazines retained their readerships, many of the traditional domestic advice publications were showing minimal growth or a decline in revenue, suggesting that these magazines were in some ways failing to meet the needs of contemporary women and also losing their appeal with advertisers (McCracken 1993: 87).

This relative downturn in the market, alongside growing unemployment and broader social trends such as claims within the media of a shift to post-feminism, saw the women's magazine industry under pressure to redefine its focus (Winship 1987: 149). Against the backdrop of the longer-term incursion of television and other media into the women's advice market, as well as the broader shifts to post-

Fordism outlined above, a mass-market-oriented approach gave way to a greater emphasis on quality and niche lifestyle markets.

This sense of transition and uncertainty in the women's market was captured by an article published in *The Times* in 1988 on the women's magazine business, complete with a mock magazine cover entitled 'The New Woman' (Gough-Yates 2003: 1). While concerns with addressing the New Woman had underpinned the emergence and revamping of magazines such as *Nova* and *Cosmopolitan* in the 1960s and 1970s, here the term marked a more widespread push within the magazine market towards addressing and targeting working women, whose numbers and wages, despite rising unemployment, were on the increase (70).

It is from this context, then, that we see the emergence of a number of new magazines in the 1980s aimed at working women, including monthly 'glossies' such as *Elle* and *Marie Claire* as well as, in the United States, updated versions of traditional service magazines such as *Working Woman*. Where the glossy magazine market expanded in Britain, US magazines such as *Working Woman*— with their focus on providing advice to the 'superwoman' juggling the double labour of home and work duties—failed to gain a substantial readership in the UK market.[8] As with the rise of British men's magazines, part of the success of the new glossy magazines was their repackaging of women's advice through a focus on aesthetics and style. In contrast to magazines such as *Working Woman*, UK glossies 'disengaged their editorial from issues relating to work, describing the mood of the "New Woman" through her attitude to "style", and her presumed interests in "personality", "individuality", "relationships", "sex", "the body", "health", "child-care" and so on' (Gough-Yates 2003: 117).

This 'lifestyling' of women's magazines saw a relative shift away from a primary preoccupation with class- and age-based demographics and an embrace of discourses of individualism, trends that dovetailed with a 'post-feminist' milieu dominated by media imagery depicting women as having made it and feminism as *passé* (Gough-Yates 2003: 34). The discourse of the New Woman 'incorporated a "feminist" language of "freedom", "independence" and "pleasure", but reduced these to matters of lifestyle and consumption' (34). This individualistic approach was also reflected in the strong emphasis placed in these magazines on the identities of their editors, who were portrayed as embodying the image of the magazine through stories on their 'working style, lifestyle and career trajectory' (118). These editor–personalities thus worked to model good taste and consumption, with a strong emphasis on individuality, for an imagined readership of lifestyle-oriented 'new middle class' women (121–124).

This shift from a more straightforward mode of consumer advice and information to a lifestyle-oriented approach also reflected wider trends in the marketing world, with advertisers realizing the 'need to suggest philosophies of living and styles of behaviour, rather than simply pushing a product' (Mort

1996: 97). A growing focus on the psychology of people's consumer choices saw a 'privileging of visual and emotional systems of communication', an approach often referred to at the time as 'lifestyle advertising' (98).

While magazine culture had been marked by a long-term tension between its service goals and the growing incursion of advertising, lifestyle advertising was marked by a subtle culture of convergence between advertising and magazine content. In both glossy and service magazines, with the extension of high-quality graphics and photography into every section of the magazine, it was becoming increasingly hard to visually distinguish between features and advertising. There was also a convergence of linguistic codes as informational articles increasingly adopted 'the language of advertising' while adverts presented themselves as informational, offering, for instance, how-to advice to readers (McCracken 1993: 50–52).

Despite these innovations, advertisers were increasingly looking to other media outlets. While the editors of women's magazines 'continued to promote themselves in industry publications as mappers of contemporary taste', the 1990s saw declines in readership numbers and a relative loss of confidence in the pulling power of magazines.

The industry tried to re-capture readers in a number of ways. Established glossy periodicals reframed their approach to lifestyle consumption through, for instance, a growing focus on celebrity culture, with specific celebrities being held up as 'indicative of the lifestyle "attitude" of the magazine itself, embodying the dispositions and aspirations of the "ideal" reader' (Gough-Yates 2003: 136). Meanwhile numerous new titles emerged that offered up images of femininity targeted, for instance, at the 'middle youth' market—child-less, professional 'thinking' women in their late twenties and thirties whom market researchers predicted to be 'a significant group of consumers for the British economy of the twenty-first century' (145).

These new publications emerged into what was by now an increasingly fragmented, diversified, and competitive lifestyle advice market that saw the addition of glossy lifestyle supplements to newspapers at the same time as supermarkets and department stores were starting to produce their own publications, such as Woolworths' magazine *Australian Good Taste* (Bonner 2002: 192). And of course television was by this time an increasingly major player in the provision of consumer and lifestyle advice, with early lifestyle programming directly imitating the look and feel of magazine culture in the form of magazine shows—some of which were joint ventures with existing service magazines such as *Women's Day USA* and *Australian Family Circle* (McCracken 1993: 293; Bonner 2002: 192).

Despite the growing diversity and competition within the field of advice culture in the 1980s and 1990s and the increasing prominence of lifestyle television, as I have suggested, magazines in this period (themselves emerging out of and influenced by earlier developments) have played a vital role in shaping today's lifestyle advice culture. A crucial development here was the articulation of the visual and symbolic language of women's advice culture with a (masculine and elite) postmodern aesthetic and with the increasingly sophisticated iconography of advertising. While the New Lad was a reaction against the style-oriented male yuppie of the 1980s, this aggressive mode of 'new' masculinity also represented an attempt at negotiating a place for a more 'ordinary' male audience within an increasingly lifestyle-oriented consumer culture—a strategy that partly explains the 'cross-over' popularity of Jamie Oliver in his more 'laddish' *Naked Chef* days. Style magazines such as *The Face*, of course, came out of a very specific moment in UK 1980s culture. Through promoting a particular mode of sophisticated, male-friendly lifestyle consumption, however, they can be seen as playing a significant role (along with other factors such as the self-help movement and the men's movement) in the subsequent 'malestreaming' of domestic and personal advice increasingly evident within other 'new' lifestyle media contexts such as television, newspapers, and the internet.[9]

Setting the scene for contemporary advice culture

In highlighting pivotal moments in the history of popular advice in print and then magazine culture, the concern here was to situate today's lifestyle experts within a broader historical context. The rise of expertise tends to be associated with times of relative uncertainty and social fluidity when people look to popular forms of advice for guidance and reassurance. While the tenor of this advice has shifted somewhat according to the concerns of specific historical conjunctures, it has been marked by certain persistent themes. Discourses of popular expertise, for instance, have often constructed the home as a space of refuge from the pressures of modernity and the world of work. Such discourses have not only targeted women as guardians of domestic morality and good taste but also—through a focus on home improvement and productive modes of leisure—sought to negotiate a role for men within domestic space.

Advice culture has also been centrally concerned with questions of personal style and self-care as important sites of consumption and moral regulation. While women have historically been positioned as central to practices of identity-related shopping and self-improvement, with the rise of consumer culture, the growing role of advertising images, and the emergence of a class of *specialists* in style and taste, popular practices of display and self-styling have become professionalized, commercialized, and mainstreamed. As both cultural intermediaries and consumers, men have increasingly played a role in the culture of style, refiguring the visual politics of feminine (and queer) identity to masculine heterosexual ends.

An important trajectory, then, in the history of popular advice around the self and the home has been the ongoing dialogue and negotiation between the boundaries and norms of masculine and feminine culture and identity, played out through shifts in the meaning and value of visual, symbolic, and lifestyle culture (as well as variously articulated to questions of cultural context, class, and race). While, in this process, men have increasingly been addressed as home-makers and self-managing subjects, as Lury (1996) reminds us they have been positioned rather differently than women in relation to consumer practices. While masculine lifestyle consumption, for instance, involves reflexively adopting the 'skills involved in the work of femininity' and then discarding them, women's practices of masquerade and self-styling have often been tied to compulsory forms of identity rather than to the voluntarist world of leisure and play (Lury 1996: 154).

As we will see in the following chapters on food expertise and TV chefs and the makeover TV show *Queer Eye for the Straight Guy*, contemporary lifestyle media continues to be characterized by ongoing uncertainty around the gendered connotations and status of the skills and expertise associated with the care of the home, family, and the self and with questions of style. The ongoing relevance and importance of gender distinctions around domestic labour and consumption practices, however, is discussed here in the context of a refiguring of such distinctions via a growing universalization and normalization of middle class values, played out as I note in the following chapter on food expertise through discourses of rationalized individualism, good taste, and ethical consumption. The flipside of contemporary advice culture's mainstreaming and democratizing of certain domestic and personal life skills and knowledge, then, is a tendency to marginalize questions of social identity and difference, with both men and women increasingly addressed by ordinary experts via a discourse of compulsory, self-managing individualism.

Notes

1   For instance, Bell and Hollows (2006: 6–7) point to the Elizabethan Royal Court in the late 16th century as a crucial site for the emergence of 'fashion' and the deployment of consumer items as markers of social status.

2   Whether these items were destined for actual use in the home seemed less important than, as one craft enthusiast put it, 'the clear joy of creation … a man experiences when he makes a shaky table' (cited in Gelber 1999: 196).

3   Gelber notes that while in popular magazines of the time women were also increasingly encouraged to join in with home improvement activities, in general manual craft work was coded as an area of 'uniquely male household competence' (1999: 217).

4   Another contributing element to the popularity of DIY was the fact that many citizens, both men and women, had acquired manual skills in the Second World War, which popular

magazines such as *Time* constructed as easily transferable to the home (Goldstein 1998: 31; Gelber 1999: 271–272).

5   By the 1960s, magazines were major players in terms of providing consumer advice, with a British survey indicating that, in an average week, 75 percent of women over the age of sixteen read one of the top five weekly magazines (White 1970: 217).

6   Another way in which new models of masculine consumption negotiated the feminine, particularly in more working class and aspirational publications, was through a focus on external transformation and 'perfectible masculinity', a discourse that Pendergast links to the recurring figure of the 'self-made man' as an individualistic ideal central to capitalist modernity (2000: 134).

7   Offering a cross-cultural analysis of commercial masculinity, Edwards (2003) contends that anxieties around the figure of the stylish male have tended to be more of a concern in the Anglo-American context than in Europe, where there has been a much longer tradition of selling style to men. He also notes that, in the United States, these tensions have been worked through via the emergence of 'various iconographies of masculinity' such as the US version of *GQ* with its 'stronger emphasis on corporate masculinity, and suited style in particular, than its UK counterpart' (143). In contrast, the later development of the New Lad in the United Kingdom addressed a concern with class and with limited economic means given the economic recession of the early 1990s, setting itself apart from the 'aspirational and individualistic' concerns of the New Man (144).

8   Winship (1987: 155–156) argues that the superwoman 'solution', which saw the concerns of 'aspirational feminism' tied to an elitist, individualist model of 'success', was a more prominent feature of US magazine culture.

9   The magazine industry continues to play an important role in providing advice and expertise to readers. However, despite the innovations outlined above, compared with contemporary lifestyle media, and in particular television, the top-selling magazine titles still tend to be divided along overtly gendered lines rather than targeting readers more broadly as lifestyle consumers (see Bonner 2002: 193).

Chapter 2

Eating expertise
From nutruitionists to TV chefs

The structural anxieties of our age are made manifest in discourses about food.

(Warde 1997: 56)

A two-page spread in the health section of a 2005 issue of the Australian version of *Vogue* (accompanied by a close-up of a gaping mouth biting into a doughnut) carried the headline 'Food for Thought' and was subtitled 'To eat it or not to eat it? We need a new set of food rules to make eating well a piece of cake' (Hawkes 2005). Addressing the issue of how to be a smart, healthy consumer in an increasingly complex food culture, the article turned to a variety of 'health experts' for advice. Quoting a range of sources including a 'leading international nutritionist', a 'food coach', a naturopath, and the *New England Journal of Medicine*, the article suggested that to attain health we need to 'learn to shop and eat like the experts do' (158).

The *Vogue* piece is a useful snapshot of contemporary food culture. Capturing the anxieties and fears that surround food and eating today—as we move from the realm of 'gastronomy' to what French sociologist Claude Fischler (cited in Warde 1997: 31) describes as 'gastroanomy'—it emphasizes the growing role played by experts and expertise where the 'rules' for eating healthily are far from clear-cut. Of course, food and eating has never been a purely 'material' matter, a question of fuel for the body and nothing more; it has always been a complex domain connected to issues of social status, ritual, and identity. Nevertheless, nowadays the tensions surrounding food culture are particularly heightened and the social meanings of food are unusually contested. I would suggest that this is because food has become emblematic of a number of broader themes within modernity under late consumer capitalism. Some of the central concerns and drivers of contemporary life—the emphasis on individual responsibility and on managing one's health for the 'public good', the focus on consumption as a site of lifestyle optimization and choice, the growing 'informationalization' of everyday life, and the increasing awareness of the risks and 'side effects' associated with modern life and industrialization—are played out in food discourse, not only in critical academic, nutritional, and health promotion debates but also in popular culture.

While contemporary culture has been marked by an explosion of lifestyle expertise focused on ordinary, everyday life, food in particular has become the target of an enormous array of advice and claims to expertise. This chapter examines some of the different types of experts—from TV chefs and nutritionists to food coaches and nutritional therapists—who have had an important influence on contemporary popular conceptions of food. The first section discusses the rise of a new type of nutritional expert, one who tends to address 'the public' in highly individualized and privatized terms, breaking with the historical role of nutritionists in promoting a more population-based model of food consumption. The second section discusses the emergence and role of a rather different figure of popular expertise in the area of food, namely, the TV chef. Here I examine the various and often contradictory discourses of pleasure, aesthetics, ethical consumption, selfhood, and community played out on food TV and embodied in complex figures such as British TV chef Jamie Oliver, discourses that also mark the terrain of lifestyle media and consumption more broadly. Through analysing the role of these contrasting figures of expertise, this chapter examines the way in which everyday encounters with food are marked by important questions around the role and politics of lifestyle consumption in an increasingly privatized civic culture.

Smart food and expert consumers

One of the central figures to have played a role historically in popular understanding of food in the West is the nutritionist, a figure who, like the 'domiologists' discussed in Chapter 1, has worked to bring 'public' masculine discourses of science and rationality into the feminine space of the home. The rise of nutritional science, particularly in the post-war period, has been accompanied not only by a growing interest at the state level in the connections between diet and population health but also by a broader spread of knowledge among laypeople of food content and nutrients (Mennell et al. 1992). Despite this democratizing process, nutritionists have tended to adhere to a paternalistic public health model, applying systematized, rationalist approaches to the daily rituals of feminine domestic food preparation and consumption. Thus, traditionally the concerns of nutritional science have dovetailed with those of the modern welfare state and its drive toward developing rational techniques for monitoring and managing populations en masse. As Warde asserts (1997: 37), 'The nutritionists' mission is to persuade everyone to consume a similar set of nutrients in order to maintain a healthy body', a process that has involved in particular targeting housewives as the primary managers of food purchasing and preparation in the home.

In recent years, however, we have seen a growing number of new forms of expertise around diet and nutrition. While many of these figures draw on nutritional science and scientific rationalism as an authorizing discourse, these new nutritional experts tend by and large to distance themselves from the one-size-fits-all model of public health associated with their predecessors, instead orienting themselves to individual consumers, both men and women. The rise of these more individualized, neo-rationalist modes of food expertise is, of course, in part tied to the broader burgeoning industry of lifestyle expertise discussed in this book. However, it also emerges out of the specific context of food production and consumption in the West, which I want to discuss briefly here before going on to focus on some specific examples of the new breed of nutritional expert.

One of the main ways in which food production, consumption, and associated forms of expertise have become reoriented toward the figure of the informed consumer is through the increasing emergence of what I term 'smart food'. This umbrella term aims to describe a set of food products and a particular approach to food, both of which privilege an essentially rationalist and calculative approach to consumption, one that is linked strongly to discourses of health and to scientific expertise (Lawrence and Germov 1999; Parker 2003). Over the past few years, in the area of food production, for instance, we have seen the rise of a growing range of products that involve the 'technologization' of food. Here I am referring not only to the more obviously 'manipulated' foods such as genetically modified (GM) and genetically engineered (GE) foods but also to what Lawrence and Germov (1999) call 'pharmafoods' or 'nutriceuticals', that is, food that is modified by adding or fortifying a specific nutrient to improve its health-giving properties, as with vitamin-enriched or 'fortified' breakfast cereal.

More insidious, however, is the related rise and acceptance of a 'commonsense' understanding of food that frames consumption in highly medicalized terms, a paradigm that builds on nutritional science's concerns with reducing food to its biochemical parts (Scrinis 2002) and directs the consumer to view foodstuffs as the source of particular health-giving, anti-aging, or disease-preventing properties—in other words, in highly functional terms. Walnuts, for instance, are seen as sources of 'good' oils (*Business Wire* 2004), cinnamon is touted as having 'potent antioxidant properties' as it contains 'heart-healthy phenols' (RealAge.com 2005), and half an ounce of chocolate taken one hour before a test is said to improve test results for school students (Zdeb 2004).

This type of scientized food discourse is now an increasingly common feature of popular culture, with terms such as 'glycemic index', 'omega-3', and 'antioxidants' seen everywhere from popular magazines to the labelling of foods in supermarkets. The widespread adoption of this kind of language involves imagining a certain kind of idealized consumer. Rather than positioning the public as undifferentiated receivers of standardized dietary advice (as per the traditional nutritionist), the emergent culture of smart food instead addresses consumers as rational and self-motivated, concerned with actively hunting out a range of products and services that serve their particular needs.

As an article in *The Times* on 'Self-Service Health' argues, the development of consumer-centred measures, such as the emergence of food labels indicating how 'healthy' foods are, marks the rise of the informed consumer as 'expert' (Crompton 2005). While this shift to the individualization of health and dietary management addresses consumers as experts on their own diet and health, the increasing amount of information available means that consumers are arguably more dependent than ever on external forms of advice.

Privatizing expertise: The new nutritionists

The role of the food expert is crucial to this mode of consumption, but increasingly this figure occupies a rather different place and status from that of the traditional nutritionist. The new food expert tends to be constructed more as a mediator and an interpreter of knowledge than an overarching authority, although some of these figures continue to make broad claims to expertise within the mediatized public sphere. Indeed, their legitimacy and status as food experts in the commercial realm is often linked to their public status, although it is the discourse of familiarity and celebrity as much as the discourse of authoritative expertise that comes into play here. The traditional figure of the nutritionist, of course, continues to play a role in contemporary culture and is often drawn upon by the media and the state to intervene in debates over national dietary health, such as in recent discussions in Australia, the United States, and the United Kingdom about the best ways to manage the rising problem of obesity. Many nutritionists, however, are 'repackaging' themselves for the commercial sphere, combining more traditional roles as commentators on public health issues with lucrative careers as health consultants, diet gurus, or nutritionists to the stars. At the same time, a growing number of new food experts combine expertise in a range of areas, from naturopathy to nutritional science, and represent themselves as private consultants on the lifestyle and well-being of individuals as well as providing expert commentary on public health issues.

'Food coaches' are a classic example of this new breed of expertise. Characterized by one 'consumer trend expert', Faith Popcorn (2002), as 'part psychologist, part sociologist, part family therapist and part nutritionist', these commercially based figures exemplify an emergent smart food culture in which food consumption is reframed around the figure of the enterprising individual. While diet and nutrition has often traditionally been badged as a solely feminine concern, with dieting being associated in particular with feminized issues of body image and lack of control around food consumption, the new crop of experts refigure food and diet in what might be seen as more masculine terms, oriented toward optimizing health and bodily functions.

In certain ways, they can also be seen to extend on the discourses of domiology and domestic science that emerged with the rise of industrial capitalism and sought to retrain housewives as scientific managers and refigure the home as a site of rationality. In a consumer-driven, 'postindustrial' era, however, food choice and diet has been refigured as a site of privatized consumption where food choices are strategic, instrumental, and focused on optimizing one's individual health. As one food coach consultancy states on its website:

> A food coach can show you how to make the best choices for you. No two people are identical, and what works for one won't necessarily be right for another. Armed with knowledge from your food coach, you can make healthy eating choices in any situation, confident you know what works best for you. (Thefoodcoach 2006)

While 'food coaching' has recently gained some public recognition in the United States and Australia, a comparable form of expertise emerged rather earlier in Britain, termed 'nutritional therapy'. The UK-based body that accredits 'nutritional therapists' describes the field as 'the application of nutrition and health science to enable individuals to maximize their health potential' (NTC 2005).

Like food coaching, this 'new' area of expertise is a hybrid of nutritional science and alternative medical and other health approaches. Patrick Holford, one of the better-known proponents of nutritional therapy, represents a particularly good case study of the new food expertise. Holford, touted on his two websites, www.patrickholford.com and www.holfordhealth.com, as a best-selling author of more than 20 books, including *Patrick Holford's New Optimal Nutrition Bible*, and founder of the Institute for Optimum Nutrition, is a complex mix of nutritional expert, international commentator, and educator on everything from nutrition to environmental and health issues. Holford's public persona involves juggling a range of (often self-styled) expert identities. While his background is primarily in psychology (in which he did some research on the impact of nutrition on mental health) and later in the field of nutritional therapy (a field he helped to create), he is often referred to in the media as a 'leading British nutritionist', and on his '100% health for life' website his publicists refer to him as 'top nutritionist Patrick Holford'.

One of the hallmarks of contemporary representations of expertise is this tendency to conflate different modes of expert advice so that 'alternative' perspectives, for example from naturopaths who comment on food and health, and more 'traditional' approaches associated, for instance, with nutritional science are often given equivalence. However, this is not to suggest that science does not still carry authority within the popular sphere. As my discussion of smart food suggests, scientific conceptions of food and nutrition have become increasingly dominant. And part of Holford's success (and partly the reason he can claim the title of nutritionist) stems from the strongly medicalized approach he takes to food. For instance, emphasizing his scientific credentials, a profile of Holford on his www. holfordhealth.com website notes that his hero is Linus Pauling, whose 'philosophy of health' was based on 'orthomolecular medicine'. As the website puts it, Pauling predicted 'that the future of medicine would be about putting the right chemicals, namely nutrients, into our bodies'. Holford, through his notion of 'optimum nutrition', takes up Pauling's medicalized approach to food, treating nutrients as not only potentially disease preventing but also health enhancing. Dovetailing with the rationalist tenets of the smart food paradigm, food is portrayed on Holford's websites in biochemical terms as a source of particular chemical nutrients that can be used to optimize one's health and well-being and minimize the effects of aging, with the goal of '100% health for life'. This approach is reflected in the glossary of nutrients provided on one of Holford websites, which informs the reader about the beneficial health effects particular substances such as retinol might have, while listing the food sources that provide optimal amounts of the nutrient in question. Likewise, another of his websites provides recommendations about nutritional supplements whereby certain nutrients extracted from food such as antioxidants are taken in tablet form. Here we see a strongly calculative approach to food, as suggested by Holford's advice on consuming fats as supplements:

> There are two ways of meeting your essential fat requirements: one is from diet, either by eating a heaped tablespoon of ground seeds every day, having a tablespoon of special cold-pressed seed oils and/or eating fish three times a week; the other is to supplement concentrated oils.

While Holford's mode of food expertise draws strongly on the tenets of more traditional versions of nutritional science and professes a concern with educating the public at large on nutritional issues, its construction of food and diet in terms of privatized questions of individual health and well-being links it more broadly to a new breed of consumer-oriented expertise centred on therapeutic discourses of self-management and self-improvement.

In this case, the authority of the new food expert is not only based on scientific credentials but is also reliant on personal charisma and life experience. Thus, on the www.holfordhealth.com website we are told that it was 'Patrick's own experience that convinced him of the role of nutrition in good health'. Once a lethargic, overweight person who suffered from skin problems and migraines, Holford, by changing his diet and taking a number of dietary supplements over a two-month period, transformed himself into a healthy, energized individual. And, as evidence of this personal transformation, the header of each website and webpage features an image of a slim, handsome, and healthy-looking Holford.

Drawing on a rhetoric of personal growth and self-actualization similar to that found on the TV makeover programme, these websites invite the reader to follow Holford's example and take control of their life biographies. Thus, on his '100% health for life' website Holford asks the reader, '[D]o you want to: increase energy … say no to cancer … improve your mood?' The implication is that the potential for 'a total health transformation' lies in the hands of the empowered and informed individual. Exhorting the consumer to 'find optimum nutrition for yourself so that you'll feel like a new person', the wellness advisor website adopts a quasi-religious tone in describing the transformational potential of Holford's philosophy on health and nutrition.

Holford's approach addresses the consumer as an expert in and driver of his or her own health while providing a systematic belief system and approach to food that gives a sense of comfort, security, and certainty to consumers faced with innumerable and confusing nutritional choices. Here optimum nutrition not only represents 'a better way' of approaching diet and food but, as the website mode of address intimates, also marks a better way of living.

From smart to slow:
'Alternative' models of food consumption and the TV chef

While at times these figures speak to broader public health issues, the new breed of experts represented by Holford and others are centrally concerned with the role of individuals rather than the state in taking control of their own health and lifestyles. The Holford worldview is one in which food is seen then as a site of potential self-improvement and investment in one's personal growth. By controlling one's diet, the implication is, one can not only optimize one's health but also gain control over one's destiny. In a rather odd blending of science, rationalism, and new-age psychology, informed dietary consumption is linked to success, happiness, and fulfilment—evidenced by Holford's own personal story of the transformative potential of 'taking control' of one's health and well-being.

In Holford's world of optimum health, it is assumed that individuals all have the time, money, motivation, and capacity to become smart, informed food consumers. Social position, however, continues to be a good indicator of one's relationship to food consumption, with members of the middle classes being much more likely to adhere to 'the scientifically defined diet prescribed by nutritionists' (Warde 1997: 184). The average consumer is unlikely to be in a position (socially or economically) to engage in the kind of high-maintenance techniques of bodily and dietary management prescribed by these kinds of life specialists. Furthermore, as Miller (2007: 116–117), discussing US dietary habits, points out, 'Despite half a century of nutritional advice as to the benefits of grains, fruits, and vegetables', government, the food industry, and the media all contribute to an environment that normalizes and legitimates 'industrialized meat manufacture and consumption'. The global rationalization of food production and consumption, or McDonaldization as Ritzer (1993) terms it, can be seen to result in a decrease rather than an increase in individual choice and personal control.

Nevertheless, as I have suggested in my discussion of smart food, the rise of this new brand of food expertise is indicative of a broader symbolic shift in popular conceptions of food and diet today. Whether people are modifying their actual food habits or not, they are now shopping and eating in an environment in which food is commonly thought of in rationalized and medicalized terms—and in which it is not uncommon to hear people, from a range of backgrounds, discussing the merits and pitfalls of various types of diets.

While I have argued thus far that the discourse of rationalism and smart food has come to play a powerful role in framing 'commonsense' understandings of food, this kind of approach has not gone uncontested. Another important source of popular conceptions of, and knowledge about, food and diet are cooking shows on TV and in particular the TV chef/cook, one of the more popular and prominent players in the shift to lifestyle entertainment on TV. In many ways, the TV chef can be seen as representing a kind of 'antidote' to the smart food approach, offering both a critique of and an apparent alternative to the world of rationalized food production and consumption. The often-seductive images of food and eating provided on cooking shows can in turn be linked to a broader discourse of escapism and indulgence in contemporary food culture. For instance, while contemporary women's magazines in recent years have become increasingly focused on the links between health and food, they have also been marked by an increase in recommendations to indulgent behaviour and to enjoying the benefits of 'comfort foods' (Warde 1997: 90).

The enormous popularity of today's TV chefs can also be linked to the rise of various other models of food consumption that offer themselves up as an apparent alternative to the massified, supermarketized world of industrial food. The slow food movement, for instance, with its focus on *cuisine de terroir*, or food that is sourced, prepared, and consumed within local communities and regions, presents itself as a form of resistance to the globalization and industrialization of food. As the www.slowfood.com website states, it is 'an international organization whose aim is to protect the pleasures of the table from the homogenization of modern fast food and life'. Likewise, the growing popularity of food markets with a focus on local produce and community can be seen as representing a conscious attempt to find lifestyle alternatives to the rationalized and massified approaches to production and consumption that have come to dominate global foodways (Yue 2003).

It is within this broader context then that I want to locate the explosion of cooking shows over the past decade, the most popular of which feature well-known and highly charismatic chefs or cooks, some of whom (such as the UK's 'domestic goddess' Nigella Lawson and her compatriot Jamie Oliver) have gone on to become international celebrities. In the next section, I discuss the way in which food TV and its cooking personalities construct food as a site of pleasure, aesthetics, and ethics, ending with a case study of Jamie Oliver as a TV chef and all-round food expert who attempts to juggle a number of, at times contradictory, public roles.

On (not) watching what you eat:
Vicarious consumption, spectacle, and aesthetics on culinary TV

For many consumers, there is no doubt a certain degree of pleasure associated with being able to control and regulate one's dietary intake. The push to smart consumption promoted by food coaches and others, however, tends to align food choice and eating not so much with enjoyment and leisure as with rationality and restraint. Indeed, the continual monitoring and self-assessment involved in dietary control can be seen as a form of labour, a mode of working on and investing in the body/self.

In contrast, many of today's lifestyle-oriented TV chefs construct food as a site of pleasure and 'productive play'. The burgeoning number of new lifestyle cooking shows can be seen to employ many different strategies to refigure eating and food preparation as a site of enjoyment and escapism. For instance, these lifestyle shows tend to distance themselves self-consciously from the more traditional instructional variety of cooking shows associated with figures such as UK TV cook Delia Smith. Like the new generation of nutritional experts, these figures reflect a shift to a focus on personality and charisma as a means of mediating expertise, while reworking food as a site of fun, spectacle, and fantasy lifestyles, distanced from the mundanity of everyday life and the labours of domesticity.

Today's food programmes thus increasingly work at the level of 'vicarious consumption', offering viewers an imagined escape from their everyday experiences of cooking and consumption (Adema 2000). For many cooking show fans such escapism is no doubt linked to being able to take pleasure in the products of someone else's (highly skilled) cooking without having to provide their own time and labour. While viewers who actually want to cook the meals prepared on cooking shows are often able to go to a show's website and get a detailed recipe, such shows are as much about emphasizing 'the symbolic power of food' as they are about the practicalities of learning about new recipes and ingredients or actually cooking (Adema 2000: 118).

Food escapism is also played out here in relation to the gendering of cooking. A number of scholars have pointed out the way in which the previously feminized realm of cooking and its associations with banality and drudgery have had a masculine makeover on many contemporary cooking shows. As on other lifestyle TV in which expertise around personal style and the home has been refigured for a mainstream audience, the 'lifestyling' of cooking programming around the world has witnessed the process of cooking being refigured as a fun leisure activity. This has seen the rise of a number of new cooking show genres whose formats can be seen to merge with other TV genres such as the game show and reality TV. The internationally popular Japanese cooking show *Iron Chef*, billed as 'Ultimate Fighting Champion meets Julia Child' (Gallagher 2004), represents cooking as a hybrid spectacle of extreme sport, extraordinary culinary skills, and camp fantasy, all shot in a massive 'kitchen stadium'. Taiwan Public Television's contribution to the hybridized cooking format, the rather literally titled *Taiwan Fun Cuisine*, describes itself as an 'edutaining food programme' that combines expert cooking advice and cooking competitions with 'amusing drag queen performances' (PTS 2007).

Another crucial way in which TV chefs distance food preparation and consumption from both the realm of mundane domestic labour and the rationalized approach associated with smart food is through 'a heightened focus on aesthetics' (Ketchum 2005: 231). A growing phenomenon within food culture over the past decade has been the enormous popularity of *images* of food and cooking (not to mention of attractive chefs and cooks), as marked by the record sales of cookbooks and food magazines. This focus on the stylistic and sensory qualities of food has also been taken up by lifestyle-oriented cooking shows, which, in contrast to the instrumentalist approach associated with nutritional expertise, are concerned with teaching viewers about how food and cooking can be seen as part of a broader 'art of everyday life' (Hollows 2003: 243).

As on makeover shows such as *Queer Eye for the Straight Guy*, the 'transformative aesthetic' central to the new crop of lifestyled cooking shows (Solier 2005: 467), despite being presented in terms of the attainable and even the ordinary, is often underpinned by bourgeois values and taste. The role of the charismatic TV chef or cook is crucial here, both in demonstrating the art of the everyday through magical food transformations and in disseminating middle class food culture and its values to a range of audiences.

This process of aestheticizing food involves reworking gender issues around food and expertise. Despite attempts to take the genre out of the kitchen, cookery TV, particularly in its more traditional instructional form, continues to be associated with the feminine domestic sphere and the everyday labours of the housewife. The TV chef, through his or her focus on aesthetics, acts as a mediator and translator for a set of 'life skills' that is associated both with the elite world of the professional chef and with the realm of 'women's work'. Through presenting food and cooking as a question of style that is linked to a broader lifestyle aesthetic, these figures give class and gender a makeover for a new demographic of emerging male lifestyle consumers and aspirational audiences more generally.

One increasingly popular way in which this mediatory process is being dealt with on today's cooking shows is through the figure of the male, working class chef made good. Figures such as the US Food Network's celebrity chef Emeril Lagasse, who is presented as rising from humble beginnings to become a well-known chef and restaurateur in New Orleans, showing that 'blue-collar masculinity can broker cordon blue' (Miller 2007: 132), or the foul-mouthed UK chef Gordon Ramsay, a 'childhood survivor of domestic violence', are not just mediators of polite middle class taste. These figures literally embody the dreams of class and lifestyle mobility promoted by lifestyle TV—while presenting processes of mobility as accessible and ordinary through the use of regional accents, colloquialisms, and, of course, a deliberate distancing from the dispassionate manner of the traditional food expert. Food preparation and consumption are thus constructed as sites of heightened symbolic and cultural value by the popular TV chef. Through fantasies of escapism, a labour-free transformational aesthetic, as well as the vicarious pleasures of class mobility offered by the figure of the celebrity chef, the imaginary world constructed by culinary TV is one in which food becomes a vehicle for an idealized fantasy lifestyle.

Ethical expertise: Authenticity, tradition, and place in food television

In contrast to the hyperrationalism of nutritional discourse, the TV chef's focus is on pleasure and excess rather than self-control, and on style and spectacle rather than calculated consumption. This focus on fantasy and escapism, however, belies a growing moral concern within certain lifestyle-oriented modes of food TV with 'educating' the public about what constitutes 'good' food. The elite, leisure-oriented lifestyles modelled by today's TV chefs are concerned not only with questions of pleasure and aesthetics but also with a personal ethics around food choice. In teaching viewers to embrace middle class taste, taste here encompasses a broader set of notions than just style, embracing bourgeois concerns about what constitutes informed and ethical consumption in today's globalized food culture.

One of the TV genres that perhaps most self-consciously concerns itself with teaching viewers about the joys of 'real' food is the genre of 'food tourism'. Bearing much in common with the slow food movement, these shows position themselves as 'other' to the world of rationalized convenience food. Food and cooking instead is framed in terms of place and locality, with a strong emphasis on tradition and authenticity. The TV chef on these shows is thus unlikely to be found in the generic 'nowhere' space of the studio kitchen but instead is shown cooking in a range of locations—strange kitchens in foreign locales as well as often makeshift outdoor kitchens in out-of-the-ordinary places where the camera is as likely to be focusing on the scenery as on the cooking (Strange 1998).

Whether travelling in exotic destinations (as per Jamie Oliver's 'adventures' in Italy in *Jamie's Great Italian Escape*) or following Rick Stein around his native UK as he investigates various local produce and cooking practices, these shows all emphasize the links between locality and food, often demonstrating a nostalgia for traditions of cooking that have become 'endangered' by the rise of industrial and globalized food practices. Central to such shows, then, is their focus on tradition as a kind of antidote to a contemporary food culture marked by a scientization and rationalization of food production and consumption, a process that for these shows is clearly associated with alienation and social anomie. Today, as food practices become increasingly individualized and socially disembedded, the appeal to tradition, no matter how 'invented', is a powerful source of security and comfort (Warde 1997).

In contrast to the abstract rationality that marks nutritional expertise, the TV chefs who feature in what Strange (1998) refers to as the 'Tour-Educative' genre of cooking shows continually emphasize the authority, authenticity, and moral superiority of local food traditions. Indeed, these shows often play with and foreground the tension between the chef's expertise and the local knowledge of the 'ordinary' cooks appearing on the show, with the 'tour-ed' chef often deferring to the 'superior' knowledge of the local cook and the quality and authenticity of local produce.

This focus on tradition and the local does not need to take place in exotic climes, however. Increasingly, both tour-ed shows and cooking shows more generally are rediscovering 'tradition' within the context of national and regional cooking, with figures such as New Orleans chef Emeril Lagasse teaching the US nation how to cook Cajun-style food and Rick Stein teaching the British about their own local food traditions. This concern with emphasizing the importance of localism and regionalism in cooking and sourcing produce is also evident in the focus of many cooking shows on rural life. Despite (or perhaps because of) the fact that the bulk of the population live in highly urbanized environments, Australian cooking shows are particularly enamoured with images of country cooking and produce. In a recent Australian TV series, *The Cook and the Chef*, for instance, a self-conscious opposition is set up between the fast-paced life of a hotel-based city chef, Simon Bryant (who is British and unknown to Australian audiences), and the bucolic existence of the country cook, here represented by Maggie Beer, already known to well-heeled Australian consumers as the name behind a range of niche-market gourmet products.

In the tradition of Jamie Oliver's classic 'lifestyled' cooking show *The Naked Chef*, the show's protagonists are shown venturing out and about to gather produce for the subsequent cook-up in which they compete with each other using the same food to create different dishes (with 'the chef' tending to strive for innovation and 'the cook' emphasizing tradition). Of course, supermarkets are never on these shopping itineraries. Instead, their encounters with foodsellers are highly interactive social experiences in which they (and the audience) are informed by the expertise of local producers and market stall owners and where the produce gets handled and often tasted before it is bought.

Likewise, rather than being shot in the sterile world of the professional kitchen, the show (produced by the Australian public broadcaster, the ABC) is filmed in Beer's 'country kitchen' at her property in the scenic Barossa Valley in South Australia, something we are continually reminded of as Beer waxes lyrical about olives or herbs gathered directly from her garden and as we are treated to shots of her and her family dining *al fresco* in their olive grove.

In sharp contrast to the increasing scientization and technologization of food, the show is centrally concerned with conveying an essentially slow food philosophy, emphasizing local, traditional food sourced and prepared in ways that are connected to the land, a point underscored by Beer's encouraging the audience 'to always use what's fresh and nearest to your doorstep'. The food tourism genre thus presents a strong counterdiscourse to industrialized foodways and globalized agriculture, inviting viewers to think and buy locally and to reconnect their own food practices to family, to community, to a lifestyle that emphasizes social ties and connections rather than abstract rationality.

Cookery programmes and TV chefs, however, have a complex and contradictory relationship with the largely globalized, commodified, and rationalized nature of today's food culture. They can be seen to offer forms of escapism from that culture—both through an emphasis on pleasure and style and by providing viewers with apparently alternative visions of food production and consumption practices. Although culinary TV both reinforces and is thoroughly embedded in 'the global political economy of food' (Miller 2007: 117), its 'alternative' perspective on food often assumes the same idealized, self-directed consumer addressed by figures such as Holford. Thus, while an implicit concern underpinning many lifestyle-oriented cooking shows relates to the perceived evils of food rationalization and industrialism, rather than highlighting the global realities of multinational, industrial food production and trade, the moralization of food 'choice' can be seen to reinforce a profoundly apolitical 'doctrine of personal responsibility' (Miller, 2007: 120).

Jamie Oliver: From lifestyle chef to food activist

In this last section I want to discuss some of the ways in which these structural contradictions within food TV are embodied in the figure of the lifestyle chef, focusing on that ultimate pinup of lifestyle-oriented cookery, UK chef Jamie Oliver—a figure whose recent career turn as a food activist marks the complexity of lifestyle media's relationship to 'public service' issues. Jamie Oliver first appeared on TV screens in *The Naked Chef* (filmed in 1998) after being 'discovered' by BBC television producer Patricia Llewellyn when she saw him in a documentary on the famous London restaurant the River Café. Having much in common with a spate of other new cooking shows, *The Naked Chef* saw an emphasis on Jamie as an entertaining TV personality. It also, as in his numerous subsequent series, was and is marked by a clear concern with passing on bourgeois knowledge and expertise to a mass audience. While Jamie is clearly a mediator of middle class taste and style— particularly in *The Naked Chef*, in which his mod sensibility and self-conscious 'new lad' persona were dished up as part of a lifestyle package (Hollows 2003)— his popularity has also been strongly tied to his status as a kind of everyman. Like Lagasse and Ramsay, Jamie represents a figure of mobility—appealing to both working class and aspirational viewers as well as middle class consumers, while also addressing a broader demographic in terms of youth and gender.

One of the qualities that has granted Jamie this flexibility in terms of mode of address while also helping him to stand out in a crowd of new lifestyled chefs is his physical appearance and persona. As a young, blonde, good-looking 'lad' who wears his hair a little long and is softly spoken, but who also self-consciously has adopted a kind of performative cockney persona (or 'mockney' as his critics note), his self-presentation embodies the upwardly mobile 'lifestyled' male consumer while also attempting to negotiate some notion of an 'authentic' working class identity. This hybrid identity both allows him to appeal to a broad audience and creates tensions around his middle class expertise and taste and his claims to working class credibility—tensions that are evident in the level of criticism and 'hate press' that Jamie has received over the years.

While these contradictions in the Jamie persona are largely played out at the level of style and aesthetics in shows such as *The Naked Chef* (Hollows 2003), the association between his TV personality and a masculine aspirational lifestyle aesthetic has become complicated somewhat as Oliver's career has progressed (and he has married and had children). Matching his own changing life experience, his role as a lifestyle expert has expanded to include a growing focus on the healthy eating practices of families and children as well as tackling issues related to social disadvantage. In his show on reforming British school dinners, *Jamie's School Dinners*, in which he attempts to single-handedly 'make over' the British school dinner system, which provides food to state-run schools, we see Oliver using his food expertise and celebrity status to engage in a more traditional public service role. Shocked at what he sees as the poor dietary habits of working class kids, he takes on the task of improving the state of the British school dinner system while also attempting to change the eating and cooking practices of kids and their families.

As with Oliver's experiences attempting to 'transform' fifteen teenagers from the wrong side of the tracks into accomplished chefs, what makes *Jamie's School Dinners* such fascinating viewing are the tensions between the logic of lifestyle programming, with its focus on instant fixes, and the actual constraints and complexities of people's lives. And, of course, a central logic that drives the show's narrative (as is often the case on British lifestyle TV) is the gap between the bourgeois models of taste, health, and lifestyle embodied by the celebrity chef and the very different food and eating habits of the working class children, dinner ladies, and parents he encounters during his attempt to 'renovate' the prescribed school dinner menu. Jamie attempts to deal with this by continually denying the 'poshness' of the dishes on his shows, citing his cooking as being about appreciating good, healthy food, and making cooking easy, everyday, and fun.

While on *Jamie's School Dinners* he cites health as his main concern, Jamie is also clearly invested in issues of food presentation and aesthetics, emphasizing the importance of teaching children how to appreciate both the look and taste of good food. The bourgeois nature of the food knowledges and practices he attempts to impart are reflected in the horrified faces of the working class school dinner ladies forced to come to terms with preparing Oliver's rocket- and basil-laden creations. And here the show moves somewhat awkwardly between the classic makeover show format (one of the earlier and weirder of the episodes has the dinner ladies attending a boot camp in which they are taught to cook 'properly' by Jamie) and a more complex negotiation of the social issues at play.

The show, for instance, does attempt at some level to engage with more systematic and structural issues. While healthy food is constructed as a 'given', something that everyone can learn how to access and prepare regardless of their social background, the show also attempts to move beyond an individualist focus on lifestyle. A central theme on the programme, for instance, is Jamie's often-caustic critique of commercial food culture. He is regularly shown rallying against the influence of fast and pre-prepared food on children—Jamie's *bête noire*, the 'turkey twizzler', comes in for a particular amount of flack and was subsequently withdrawn from supermarkets—while lamenting the lack of raw foods in the diets of the kids he meets. This is spelled out in a particularly effective scene in which Jamie has a show-and-tell session with a bunch of children in which he demonstrates that, while they all recognize the logos of fast food outlets such as McDonald's, they have a much harder time naming the various commonplace vegetables he has brought into the classroom. The series that follows is thus transparently moralistic and pedagogical in focus, with Jamie depicted as a kind of food evangelist remonstrating with everyone from parents to teachers to food producers about the state of the diets of British children.

The type of expertise embodied by Jamie here, then, is complex and hybrid, combining a focus on individual lifestyle consumption and entertainment with a more traditional focus on food as a site of public educational and social reform. While Jamie has been hailed by many as a hero in Britain, where his efforts have led to increased government spending on school dinners, his hybridized identity as a celebrity chef cum public food activist has been marked by a number of contradictions, tensions that also mark the broader role of expertise in an increasingly complex food culture. For instance, while Jamie (like a number of contemporary TV chefs) takes a strong moral standpoint on food, exhorting audiences to eat food that's locally sourced, healthy, and made from scratch, he can be seen, at the same time, on TVs around the world endorsing a range of pre-prepared food products, such as his 'Italian Food Range' at the upmarket UK supermarket chain Sainsbury's[1] or Pam's range of (often highly processed) food products in New Zealand. Like the new nutritional experts, the mixed mode of address of TV chefs is one that is often highly contradictory, marked as it is by a desire to escape from the dominant discourses of food rationalism and industrialism and its concomitant embeddedness in a commodified food culture, with its emphasis on discourses of individualism, health, and lifestyle consumption.

Food expertise and the politics of consumption

Late consumer societies around the world have seen an explosion of popular discourses around food, a process that has been marked by the emergence of multiple competing expert figures in the marketplace. While eating and consumption has in the past been characterized by tradition and habit, food has increasingly become 'informationalized'—a site of endless and relentless choice on behalf of the individual consumer. However, just as food has become dominated by a pressure to make informed decisions, so it has become associated with a growing sense of risk and uncertainty. It seems as if every day the public is faced with new and apparently shifting definitions of what kind of diet or food item might be healthy, toxic, risky, protective, or even carcinogenic.

While the multiplication of food expertise can be seen to contribute to this process, expert advice also potentially offers 'a sort of reassurance in a world of culinary confusion' (Warde 1997: 79). The various modes of expertise that have their roots in nutritional science, for instance, provide very explicit sets of guidelines for eating and living healthily—often in the form of rigidly defined diets and '10-point plans'. As I've noted, this approach tends to view food in a highly informational, data-driven way, with the calculative and regulatory concerns associated with nutritional science being increasingly focused on the individual. The mode of address here assumes a highly motivated enterprising mode of selfhood, with calculative food consumption seen as a strategy for optimizing one's health and life chances.

In contrast, the explosion of seductive imagery around food, or 'gastroporn' as it has been termed, alongside the enormous popularity of a host of new varieties of cooking shows, which feature everything from competitive cook-offs to culinary tourism, can be seen to represent the antithesis of such rationalist constructions of food. TV chefs such as Emeril Lagasse and Jamie Oliver offer an approach to food in which entertainment, fun, and spectacle are brought to the fore. In general, the emphasis on today's more popular cooking shows is on the pleasure and sociality of cooking and eating—with certain shows encouraging excess in the realm of consumption (as in the UK show *Two Fat Ladies* or the Australian programme *Never Trust a Skinny Cook*). In emphasizing the need to enjoy food and perhaps even be a bit 'naughty' and indulge from time to time, the TV chef offers a stark alternative to the nutritional mode of expertise and its focus on regulation and control.

While the opposition between health and indulgence can be seen as an important 'culinary antinomy' structuring popular conceptions and approaches to food, these terms are in fact mutually dependent and both can be seen as products of a wider discourse of self-regulation (Warde 1997). A study of middle class consumption in the 1980s, for instance, in which yuppies were seen to combine health consciousness with bouts of excess, characterized such behaviour as 'calculated decontrol' or 'calculated hedonism' (Featherstone cited in Warde 1997: 92), a tendency associated particularly with men. There are obvious parallels here with the way in which the more recent modes of expertise discussed in this chapter can be seen to set up a dialectical relationship between the dietary asceticism of smart food and the pleasure-seeking fantasy world of the TV chef.

Is it the case, then, that both the new nutritionist and the TV chef, while seemingly representing divergent approaches to food, address a similar lifestyle-oriented social subject? A middle class consumer freed from economic or cultural constraints and able to move readily between 'the positions of disciplined, productive self and the hedonistic, leisured self' (Hollows 2003: 240)? Certainly, the new food experts such as food coaches and nutritional therapists speak to the kind of flexible subjects who are assumed to have the economic means and cultural capital to make use of often-privatized advice and services to create their own customized lifestyle 'biography'.

Similarly, while TV chefs address a much broader range of audiences, their portrayal of cooking and shopping as labour-free leisure activities again assumes a rather privileged form of social identity. And while many contemporary cookery shows seem to offer an escape from self-regulation, the 'alternative' lifestyles offered on such shows are largely driven by bourgeois values and concerns. The good taste and aesthetic values modelled by TV chefs, for instance, can be seen as a strongly disciplinary mechanism, producing or aiming to produce a particular kind of well-mannered middle class consumer.

While it is easy to discuss contemporary food experts as merely peddling different consumer models of lifestyle, it is also important to note the way in which these new food experts straddle consumer and civic culture, often having to negotiate the tensions between their role as experts and the more commoditized aspects of their public identities. Whether in their more instructional manifestations or as entertainment-oriented lifestyle TV, cooking shows (and TV chefs) have always been and continue to be concerned with issues around the family, nutrition, and public health. While these concerns have been recently repackaged in various ways on television via formats such as reality-based makeover shows, programmes such as *Jamie's School Dinners* are not only marked by commercial entertainment-oriented imperatives but are also concerned with 'empowering' the public through providing them with information and advice.

As noted, the discourse of the informed consumer-citizen often merely shores up a fairly banal and individualized model of lifestyle consumption; however, it can also provide significant points of contestation around ethico-political models of consumption. Figures such as Jamie, I would suggest, can be seen to embody these tensions. Sacked from the BBC because of his involvement as a spokesperson for UK supermarket chain Sainsbury's, on his own shows Jamie is ironically only ever depicted shopping in local produce markets or picking his own raw produce in the countryside. Jamie's various manifestations as organic food evangelist, fast food critic, food and public health activist, and celebrity endorser of processed supermarket lines have seen him attempting to juggle a number of seemingly contradictory roles. What such hybridized modes of expertise suggest is that while questions of citizenship and civic culture today are often framed within the 'logic' of consumer culture, at the same time people's everyday consumer practices are increasingly the focus of public scrutiny and (at times anti-consumerist) moral critique. This kind of moral or ethical turn within civic culture around questions of consumption is evidenced by the heated debates that occurred in the UK around and following the airing of *Jamie's School Dinners* over the role of commercial providers for school lunches and the social responsibility of food corporations to provide healthier products. The highly contested nature of food culture today and in particular the growing role of the popular food expert, then, can be seen as exemplifying a complex interplay of questions around informed citizenship, consumer rights and choice, corporate responsibility, social inequities, and the public good, with the seemingly banal discourse of 'lifestyle' increasingly marking a set of crucial negotiations within late modern consumer societies over the relationship between state, civic, and marketized space.

Note

1   Despite fronting their advertising campaign in 2005 (at the same time as *Jamie's School Dinners* was airing in the UK), Jamie publicly criticized Sainsbury's for stocking unhealthy food for children, namely, the aforementioned turkey twizzlers.

Chapter 3

'He needs to face his fears with these five queers!'
Queer Eye for the Straight Guy, makeover TV, and the lifestyle expert

Building a better straight man is really about a lifestyle makeover.
(Jai Rodriguez, 'culture expert' and Fab Five member on *Queer Eye for the Straight Guy*)

Move over Trinny and Susannah, the new queens of the makeover have arrived.
(Shrimsley 2003: 17)

In the opening scene of the lifestyle makeover show *Queer Eye for the Straight Guy*, the audience is presented with an emblematic snapshot of contemporary television. Here, to the sound of the show's pulsing dance track, we are treated to the sight of five gay men clambering into that most suburban (and supremely straight) of vehicles, the family-sized SUV, with the goal of cruising the streets of urban New York in pursuit of the show's eponymous 'straight guys'. As we follow the 'reality TV' gaze of the handheld camera into the interior of the Fab Five's style mobile, the Five present a run down, complete with witty quips and puns, of the biography of the life-challenged straight man to be made over in this week's episode. In two minutes or less we are given a potted history of 'the straight guy', highlighting, in often humiliating detail, his personal shortcomings and fears as communicated to the Fab Five by family and friends. The solution to these problems? An emergency makeover by our queer rescue team, each of whom is presented here as a specialist in inducting the 'aberrant' male (and, of course, the consuming audience) into the joys of stylish living.

So how might we understand this representation of a group of gay men on TV as 'life specialists' (as one website refers to the lifestyle experts on the makeover show *The Swan*)? Or the depiction of straight men who have 'let themselves go' as socially deviant and in need of expert intervention? One way of locating this kind of 'moment' within television is to see it as part of a broader focus within late modernity on 'makeover culture'. Numerous contemporary social theorists have suggested that what distinguishes identity in late modernity is a heightened sense of individualization and 'reflexivity' (Giddens 1991; Beck 1992), with the responsibility for dealing with the complexities of everyday life increasingly lying with the 'enterprising' self and the privatized, 'informed' citizen (Bauman 1991; Rose 1996). Beck (1992, 1994), for instance, makes the claim that we now live in a post-traditional world where identities are increasingly 'made' rather than 'ascribed'. People's sense of selfhood today, he contends, is increasingly disconnected from fixed categories of social identity such as social class, family, gender, or occupation, so that instead 'individuals must produce, stage and cobble together their biographies themselves' (Beck 1994: 13). Choice (or at least the rhetoric of choice) thus becomes pivotal to people's lives as their identities are increasingly formed through lifestyle-oriented decision making.

Related to this voluntarist, choice-based notion of social identity is the idea that we as individuals can be reduced to a mappable set of 'problems' that can be addressed through recourse to various types of expertise, and in turn can be made 'better' through the makeover process. Our everyday lives thus become seen as a therapeutic self-help 'project' to be worked upon, while enterprising individuals are exhorted to 'empower' themselves by finding better and smarter ways of living (Becker 2005). The rise of makeover culture and the emergence of the lifestyle expert can be seen to be inextricably linked, then, to this reflexive, 'DIY' conception of contemporary identity. Perhaps the most exemplary type of life specialist or lifestyle expert associated with this DIY culture is the one found on 'makeover' television or more specifically *personal* makeover shows—that is, makeover programmes where the transformation of the self is the central concern. As I discuss in this chapter, makeover television documents a shift to an ideology of selfhood that is both individualized and self-managing at the same time as it is increasingly reliant on the figure of the lifestyle expert and associated forms of 'everyday' expertise.

Queer Eye for the Straight Guy, a high-rating US show that has also had success in numerous international TV markets including the UK and Australia,[1] represents perhaps the archetypal personal makeover show and will form the backbone of the discussion here. Scholarly discussions to date of *Queer Eye* have largely focused on the way in which it represents gay masculinities (Gallagher 2004; Hart 2004; Meyer and Kelley 2004; Pearson and Reich 2004; Clarkson 2005). While, as part of my discussion here, I necessarily touch upon the way in which *Queer Eye* depicts and makes use of queer identity, my primary concern is with examining the broader role of the makeover expert in fashioning new modes of reflexive selfhood. The figure of the life specialist is, of course, integral to *Queer Eye*; this self-improvement show is centrally structured around the notion of lifestyle expertise, with the five presenters offering specialist knowledge on cooking, interior design, fashion, personal grooming, and 'culture' (with the latter category including anything from Bikram yoga to planning a marriage proposal). While the Fab Five are themselves designated as experts, they also often act as intermediaries between the show's participants and a range of other experts whose knowledge may lie outside their fields of speciality (such as Feng Shui hairdressers, antique specialists, and organic butchers). In this way, the life and selfhood of the flawed individual at the centre of the show's narrative is seen to be divided into sets of problems that are then targeted and solved by specific forms of expert knowledge.

What I want to examine here are the specific ways in which a broader shift to a rationalized, reflexive mode of selfhood are played out in the familiar yet off-centre world of *Queer Eye*. How does the show negotiate the tension between traditional ascribed modes of identity associated with classed and gendered social groupings and the purportedly 'post-traditional' self associated with reflexive individualization? How might *Queer Eye*'s refiguring of masculinity via the traditionally feminine realm of lifestyle and its valuing of queer identity be understood in the context of the show's concern with modelling a form of self-managing consumer–citizen? As McRobbie notes in an essay on the status of post-feminism in popular culture, the refiguring of selfhood in contemporary society can be seen as being marked by a complex 'double entanglement' (McRobbie 2004a: 255). Discourses and anxieties around contemporary self formation are characterized by 'the co-existence of neo-conservative values in relation to gender, sexuality and family life … with processes of liberalisation in regard to choice and diversity in domestic, sexual and kinship relations' (McRobbie 2004a: 256). What follows is a discussion that tries to capture this sense of 'double entanglement', the complex and often nuanced ways in which various modalities of selfhood and citizenship—narcissistic and communal, consumerist and traditional, reflexive yet classed and gendered—are played out in *Queer Eye* through the makeover process and via the mediating figure of the queer lifestyle expert.

Situating makeover television

As I noted in the introduction to this book, shows such as *Queer Eye* have emerged as part of a broader transformation of prime time television. While on any one night on UK, Australian, or US television you were once likely to encounter a mix of soaps, police procedurals, sports shows, quiz shows, and sit-coms, in recent years viewers have found themselves faced with an array of 'new' TV offerings, a situation TV journalists and media critics have attempted to sum up with the coverall term 'reality TV'. Particularly associated with blockbuster, globally franchised shows such as *Big Brother*, *Pop Idol*, and *Survivor*, the term 'reality TV' captures the recent obsession with fly-on-the-wall, 'live' television.[2] While the term obviously has much descriptive value, it is insufficient for capturing some of the dramatic developments that have occurred on prime time TV, from the growth of hybrid forms of television shows to the significant refiguring of television's mode of address to its audience that has marked the 'feminization' of prime time viewing (Brunsdon et al. 2001).

The rising popularity of the makeover show, itself a sub-variant of what has been termed 'lifestyle television', has had much less attention paid to it than, say, docu-soap or docu-drama or the reality game show format of *Big Brother*. While makeover TV often borrows stylistically from the reality TV format and shares a focus on 'interrogations of self under the pressures of particular conditions' (Wood and Skeggs 2004), the two genres also have distinct histories, with makeover television borrowing from the feminine culture of 'before and after' transformations found in women's magazines and on daytime TV (Moseley 2000).

In Britain, the United States, and Australia (as well as in many other parts of the international TV market), instructional, DIY modes of lifestyle television have been marked by a range of innovations in the areas of mode of address and genre. These in part can be linked to a series of broader shifts in the industry brought about by the pressures of working in an increasingly competitive and deregulated environment, with the early 1990s in particular marking an important time of transition to more reality-based makeover-oriented forms of advice-based TV. The makeover format has been associated in particular with the rise in the UK in the 1990s of a series of new hybridized reality–lifestyle formats, the 'first phase' of which included renovation shows such as *Changing Rooms* and *Ground Force* (O'Sullivan 2005: 31). The makeover format has since become thoroughly internationalized, with the genre proliferating into a variety of different forms, with a growing focus on making over ordinary people themselves and, more recently, on the kind of surveillance-oriented, 'social experiment' television discussed in Chapter 4.

A recent survey of the major makeover shows shown on US TV indicates the pervasiveness and the diversity of the genre, where the notion of the makeover is applied to anything from the transformation of the physical exteriorized self through plastic surgery (*Extreme Makeover, The Swan*), the surprise redesign of one's domestic space or garden (*Surprise by Design, While You Were Out, Ground Force*), to the customization of one's car (*Pimp My Ride, Overhaulin'*). While the style, mode of address, and audience for these shows vary considerably, all of these makeover programmes rely heavily on the figure of the expert. Usually a charismatic TV personality type, who may or may not be an 'expert' in their own right outside of the show's context, the makeover guru provides advice and guidance to the show's participant(s) and in turn to the audience, while often also acting as an intermediary between guest experts, participants, and the TV viewer.

While all of the various makeover shows discussed above are concerned to some extent with the issue of self-presentation, the focus of this discussion is primarily on the sub-variant of the makeover genre that addresses the self (rather than the car or home) as a site of potential transformation. It is this sub-genre that is one of the most prescient of the 'new' modes of contemporary television in terms of modelling a normative 'ethics of selfhood' (Rose 1996). Obviously shows such as *Queer Eye* do involve domestic transformations; however, they do so with an 'eye' to a broader transformation of the whole self. On *Queer Eye* every aspect of the candidate's lifestyle, from his interpersonal relationships and career development to his dietary habits and grooming techniques, are put under the microscope, with each problematic area being delegated to a particular life specialist to solve.

Personal makeover shows such as *The Swan* and *Extreme Makeover* also divide the self into a series of problems, which are then targeted by specific experts; however, these shows tend to focus primarily on the physical makeover and the dramatic transformation that can be brought about via specialist modes of expertise such as plastic surgery. What is interesting about *Queer Eye* is that, like much of lifestyle TV today, its focus is on mundane forms of expertise rather than the kinds of specialized credentialism associated with surgery or medicine. While, like *The Swan* and *Extreme Makeover*, its primary narrative pleasure lies in the process of transformation and 'the reveal', *Queer Eye* is also centrally concerned with highlighting techniques of *self*-management that can be adopted by ordinary people in their everyday lives—a process that is mediated via the figure of the life expert. What is of interest here is the way in which the show's concern with a pedagogy of autonomous selfhood involves a significant revaluing of what gets counted as expert knowledge as well as what kinds of figures might be seen to embody that knowledge.

From eggheads to style gurus

Lifestyle and domestic advisors have only recently made the transition from the relative margins of mainstream popular culture to centre stage; television has played a particularly powerful role in this shift, seamlessly articulating the figure of the life specialist into domestic, privatized space and into the collective imaginings of mediated communities. As Hartley argues (1999: 42), television, along with the family, the school, the church, and the state, can be thought of as an institution that contributes to the 'systematic teaching of "selfhood"'. The modes of authority and types of knowledge associated with TV, however, derive less from these official cultural institutions than from the vernacular cultures of the everyday. The forms of expertise that TV specializes in teaching are the kinds of everyday knowledge and skills associated with managing daily life—expert advice on food and cooking, care of the body, the home and home maintenance, managing money, looking after pets, planning travel, and conducting relationships. The mode of selfhood modelled here by the style guru is thus one in which the everyday practices of individuals are integrated and rationalized within a reflexive, entrepreneurial frame.

These ordinary modes of expertise have increasingly become foregrounded on television—as evidenced by the recent explosion of shows about cooking, gardening, home improvement, and, of course, personal makeovers. Partly this has been due to the granting of prime time status to modes of TV once associated with the domesticated realm of women's culture, a process Moseley describes as the 'daytime-ization' of prime time TV (Brunsdon et al. 2001: 32). This daytime-ization trend, however, has involved more than simply shifting women's programming into a different part of the TV schedule—it has crucially also been marked by a repackaging of feminine expertise under the sign of 'lifestyle TV'.

The mainstreaming of lifestyle TV and with it the 'soft' expertise of the life specialist, for instance, can be seen as an instance of a broader 'democratization' of TV. At its most basic level this is reflected in the content of television becoming increasingly concerned with everyday life, a shift that is marked by the sheer numbers of ordinary people who now feature on TV (Bonner 2003). But this process has also seen an expansion and diversification of what kinds of knowledge get valued on TV and a relative destabilization of the boundaries and hierarchies between experts and ordinary people.

This is not to suggest that versions of the older style of expert no longer feature on television or that they no longer hold any cultural authority. For instance, the lineage of popular contemporary TV experts such as the UK historian Simon Schama or the Australian-born art critic Robert Hughes, both still notably male, is clearly apparent in their 1950s TV ancestor, the talking (egg)head. However, as I have argued elsewhere about Hughes, their status as much publicized 'celebrity intellectuals' rather than as dispassionate talking heads suggests some shift in the cultural connotations of the authoritative male on TV (Lewis 2001). The broader point here is that the field of contemporary expertise on TV today is now a much more diffuse one, one in which ordinary expertise sits next to and often overshadows more traditionally credentialed modes of authority. This point is far from abstract: on TV programmes such as the US show *Extreme Makeover*, lifestyle experts, including fashion stylists and exercise trainers, literally work side by side with plastic surgeons as part of a team of credentialed makeover experts. Even in those corners of the televisual world traditionally associated with educational, 'public service' models of programming we are seeing a pluralization of forms of expertise:[3] in the UK, the BBC's championing of lifestyle TV, for instance, has seen fashion stylists, real estate experts, and home décor specialists jostling for screen time with history boffins and other more traditional BBC experts.

Such a shift has not necessarily been universally celebrated. British commentators, for instance, holding on to a rather limited view of what might constitute public service television, have been quick to label the rise of lifestyle TV and its embrace of ordinary expertise as marking the decline of television's educational role (Brunsdon 2003). However, as my argument in this book concerning the increasingly governmental role of television suggests, television is in fact becoming *more* educational. If TV represents an extension of the state and civic institutions that shape us as citizens, the rise of the lifestyle expert on prime time TV can be seen as marking the growing role of mediated expertise in the everyday lives of ordinary people. At the same time, through its dissemination of expert knowledge about the everyday and its depiction of ordinary people, television adopts a mode of pedagogy that is at once less apparent and more pervasive than earlier public service modes of education. As the content of television increasingly both draws upon and colonizes people's everyday lives, the nature, performance, and presentation of expertise and modes of authority on television are being reworked.

In the realm of lifestyle TV, these shifts are being articulated in a number of complex ways. The growing ordinariness of TV is marked in part by the breaking down of gender hierarchies around expertise and the mixture of male and female presenters on lifestyle TV. Moseley (2000: 309, for instance, cites the inclusion of male 'talent' as well as a mixture of male and female experts on daytime advice shows such as *Style Challenge*, and the emergence of new modes of prime time expertise as represented by softly masculine figures such as Jamie Oliver, as 'indicative of more general cultural shifts around gendered expertise'). Discussing the role of expert–personalities in UK gardening lifestyle shows, Taylor also notes the breaking down of distinctions between masculine and feminine domains of knowledge on lifestyle TV (2002). Class distinctions have also seemingly become softened by the growing number of regional accents on British TV (Jamie Oliver again being a case in point), although, by and large, British lifestyle TV and its values still tend to be resolutely middle class. What, then, is the role of the expert on lifestyle TV within the context of this relatively democratized space? What is the basis of his or her claims to expertise? If lifestyle TV is still overwhelmingly concerned with teaching the public about better ways of living, how might the life specialist's claims to expertise be presented and positioned in relation to the audience?

'Playing' the expert

While Moseley's and Taylor's comments here are directed at British lifestyle television, similar shifts are being played out in the US context where the makeover sub-genre of lifestyle TV has been immensely popular. The enormity of the US TV market means there are a tremendous range of makeover shows, often targeting markedly different audiences (e.g., *The Swan*'s 'soapy', 'daytime TV' mode of address versus MTV's *Pimp Your Ride*, with its audience demographic firmly located within hip-hop youth culture). While *Queer Eye* is not necessarily representative of all makeover shows, this very popular programme (shown initially in the United States on the cable channel Bravo before being subsequently rebroadcast on network television) does offer a particularly generative example for thinking through the various ways in which the nature of TV expertise has been transfigured within the contemporary lifestyle format.

What is especially interesting about *Queer Eye* is that—perhaps more than any other lifestyle programme—it is marked by a central tension around the role and status of the TV expert. The show's highly camp tone suggests that one cannot be 'instructional' on TV today without to some degree ironicizing or 'queering' one's mode of address. From the outset, *Queer Eye* is offered up to the audience as a makeover programme that self-consciously distances itself from 'straighter', more didactic versions of the lifestyle genre. While the show is actually underpinned by a strongly instructional, therapeutic, and moralistic ethos, this is largely backgrounded or rendered more palatable (particularly to a male audience) by a highly playful and self-knowing style of presentation. Thus the show's 'mission statement' on the Bravo website suggests a thoroughly tongue-in-cheek approach to the role of the lifestyle expert, mocking the current obsession with makeover culture despite operating within its logic.

> Five gay men, out to make over the world—one straight guy at a time. They are the Fab Five: an elite team of gay men dedicated to extolling the simple virtues of style, taste and class. Each week their mission is to transform a style-deficient and culture-deprived straight man from drab to fab in each of their respective categories: fashion, food & wine, interior design, grooming and culture. (BravoTV 2005)

The show's concerns with instructing both the straight guy and the audience about better ways to live are disguised here or at least undercut by a playfully self-conscious mode of address. This parodic and self-knowing approach is carried through into the aesthetic of the show itself, with its shlocky, cartoonish opening titles where the Fab Five converge superhero-like from Gay to Straight Street to rescue whatever gormless straight man might have fallen by the wayside. Drawing upon a range of popular intertextual references from *Batman* to *Reservoir Dogs*, the titles address the *Queer Eye* viewer (with a nudge and a wink) as a savvy consumer of pop culture. Continuing in this mode, the show's titles introduce us to each member of the Fab Five through freeze frames in which we are informed of their area of expertise. Like a group of superheroes or the members of a crack spy team, each member of the queer eye team is shown in these playful stills holding whatever tool of the trade is associated with his specialist knowledge. Thus, Ted, our food and wine specialist, is shown brandishing a whisk, while Kyan, our expert in 'grooming', is depicted poised with a blowdryer held gun-like in his hands.

This light-hearted undercutting of the show's instructional concerns continues throughout the programme in terms of both its aesthetic and its content. In presentation and style it borrows heavily from the reality TV genre while also referencing other TV formats, in particular crime shows. Working hard to distance itself from both traditional forms of educational programming as well as more feminized, studio-based advice shows, *Queer Eye* employs a fast-paced, fly-on-the-wall approach. The Fab Five are never depicted as static talking heads; quite the opposite, they are continually on the move throughout the show, whether driving around New York in their customized black SUV or frantically running, with straight guy in tow, from clothes shops to hair salons. This frenetic pace is associated with the makeover genre more generally, with its focus on the relatively labour-free, almost magical quality of the TV transformation (Bonner 2003). In *Queer Eye* it also serves to distance the programme from more contemplative, deliberative modes of DIY television, highlighting instead the zany, fun aspects of the makeover process.

This is nowhere more apparent than in the show's depiction of the Fab Five entering the home of the straight guy at the beginning of the programme. This segment again is highly playful and self-referential—as the Fab Five burst through the straight guy's door we are reminded of rough-and-ready real-life crime shows such as *COPS*, albeit it with a rather more camp flavour. In this part of the show the five experts, having been given a short briefing on the straight guy's 'problems', go to the 'scene of the crime' to check out for themselves just how socially aberrant their straight guy of the week is. What ensues is a frantic, chaotic, and at times carnivalesque romp through the domestic space of the 'guy' in question; here the Fab Five engage with their straight guy's 'life problems' by variously dressing up in his (or his girlfriend's) clothes, mocking his taste in furniture (and sometimes deliberately destroying certain 'pieces'), and rampaging through his kitchen and bathroom under the guise of 'assessing' the status of his diet and grooming.

While these scenes in which the Fab Five and the audience are brought into the domestic space of the straight guy are fast paced and entertaining, they are at the same time constantly intercut with the show's instructional concerns. The hectic tempo of these opening scenes is punctuated, for example, by freeze-frame images similar to those shown in the show's titles, reminding the viewer of each of the Fab Five's areas of expertise and identifying the straight guy who is the target of their makeover skills. As the Fab Five move tornado-like through the straight guy's domestic space looking for 'clues', each member of the Fab Five sums up the victim's major deficiencies, whether it is an overdose of plaid or polyester in his wardrobe, an unhealthy diet ('Is it not manly enough for cops to eat salads?'), or a lack of taste in furniture and décor ('You need Apartment 101!'). The show's instructional concerns are thus playfully inserted into the makeover narrative while the authoritative claims of the Fab Five's expertise are diffused by the use of punning and aphorisms as well as visual jokes (e.g., where Kyan is shown inspecting toothbrushes with a magnifying glass or pretending to take a swab of a straight guy's feet). Through this jokey queering of expert authority the Fab Five are thus able both to assert their authority as makeover experts and to distance themselves from the more serious implications of the transformation process.

Styling up the metrosexual

These parodic strategies represent more than just a means of distancing the Fab Five from the figure of the 'too serious' expert: they also reflect an attempt at negotiating the issues of gender, and—to a lesser extent—sexuality, raised by the show's embrace and apparent celebration of queer expertise. Among the more obvious pleasures for the *Queer Eye* viewer, male and female alike, is the way in which the show quite deliberately engages with masculinity as a performed mode of identity. The provocative title of the show, the marketing that surrounded it when it first came out, and the kind of advertising that has tended to be packaged with the show all play rather reflexively with contemporary notions of gender, evoking in particular images of the new metrosexual man (Miller 2005).[4] But what exactly is the role of the Fab Five and their queer expertise here? Are they here merely as camped-up representatives of feminine lifestyle issues? Or does their central and authoritative role on the show represent a valuing of queer knowledge for its own sake?

Among the critical scholarly responses to *Queer Eye* there have been a range of reactions to its depiction of gay identity and in particular its pairing of queerness with consumer culture and style expertise. Positive takes on the programme have suggested that it 'consistently offers the most positive representation of gay men on U.S. television that has been made' (Hart 2004: 241–242) and that its focus on gay–straight camaraderie 'is remarkable, progressive, and worth championing' (Gallagher 2004: 225). Other scholarly commentators have argued in contrast that the queerness reified in the show represents a narrowly consumerist, heterosexist, and white version of gay identity (Allatson 2004; Meyer and Kelley 2004).

Within the context of lifestyle TV, there has been a relative opening up of modes of representation around gender and sexuality, with many home renovation shows, for instance, featuring gay or effeminate men both as home experts and as contestants (Attwood 2005). As Attwood notes in an article on the UK lifestyle show *Home Front*, however, 'the balancing act carried out in the representation of lifestyle masculinity on TV' is not an uncontested one but is marked by a sense of unease (105). The 'excessive' display of highly personal 'information', 'emotion', and 'visibility' played out in these shows can be seen to create 'a precarious balance between the status quo and its destabilising elements' (Kavka 2004: 222). Part of the work of the expert involves dealing with this tension between the potentially risky promise of self-transformation and more comfortable, mainstream community values. This tension is particularly marked in relation to *Queer Eye* and its treatment of questions of gender and sexuality. In terms of both their representation as experts and their attempts to apply that expertise to the straight guy, the Fab Five are continually juggling different modes of masculinity, with the show focusing in particular on the tension between traditional forms of maleness and 'consumer masculinity' (Clarkson 2005). One way of interpreting *Queer Eye* is to see it as marketing queerness as a lifestyle 'disarticulated from its referent and resignified as metrosexuality' (Miller 2005: 112). And certainly the show's title indicates its central concern with tapping into a broader trend towards articulating new forms of straight maleness and linking these forms to modes of lifestyle consumption once associated with queerness and/or femininity.

While the Fab Five can be seen as offering up a rather commoditized version of gay identity the show's adoption of a queer perspective does open up normative heterosexual masculinity to considerable scrutiny. For the most part, the straight guys featured on *Queer Eye* are portrayed as being deficient—socially, inter-personally, and in relation to their presentation of self. And overwhelmingly these issues are linked back to aberrant or resistant modes of masculine behaviour. As Pearson and Reich put it, *Queer Eye* 'casts straight men as knuckle-dragging Neanderthals' in need of the Fab Five's "civilizing" touch' (2004: 229). The scenes where the Fab Five first enter the home of the straight man are again crucial. As they wander wide-eyed around the domestic terrains of these straight men, the Fab Five seem like anthropologists who have stumbled across some lost tribe. They rummage through and examine the markers of these straight men's lives as though they were exotic artifacts. Mouldy bathrooms, hair-clogged drains, porn videos, ancient food items in the fridge, smelly socks, and 'Eighties' furniture are cited as evidence of the out-of-date-ness of these straight guys' style-free, rough-and-tumble modes of masculinity.

Queerness itself is depicted as a form of 'cultural expertise' (Sender 2006) or 'management consultancy' here (Miller 2005: 112)—as a means of diagnosing and subsequently making over modes of masculinity that seem out of place in the contemporary world. However, while queer expertise is used on the show to mediate the transition to new manhood, gay identity itself is by no means accepted as normative. Rather the Fab Five's flamboyantly queer self-representation can be seen to act as a kind of distancing device, marking out their extreme version of feminine masculinity as safely divergent from that of heteronormative metrosexuality.

There are a number of moments in *Queer Eye*, however, where this queer excess does threaten to challenge the boundaries of straightness, such as when the Fab Five speculate about the sexuality of the straight guys in their care or the numerous moments of unease produced by the literal proximity between homo- and heterosexual bodies, with the latter often in various states of undress. This is largely balanced out on *Queer Eye* by the show's insistent focus on the Fab Five as experts, to a certain extent disconnecting their knowledge of style and self-presentation from their queer identities. Queer or camp style becomes a form of expertise or cultural capital, then, that can be adopted by straight men without challenging their straightness.

The potentially threatening elements of queerness are also negotiated by representing the perspectives of the Fab Five as largely dovetailing with those of 'the community' and, usually by the end of the show, with those of the participant. During the makeover process the Fab Five are depicted consulting with family members (often a wife or girlfriend) in a gossipy fashion about the dire state of the straight guy's hygiene, fashion sense, and/or interpersonal communication skills. These opinions are then often brought into the makeover narrative in terms of highlighting certain problems or legitimating a particular intervention by the Fab Five. The opinions of friends, co-workers, and family are also integrated into the makeover narrative through the use of brief studio grabs in which they speak direct to camera about the straight guy's problems. Each commentator here is labelled as 'the girlfriend', 'the mother', 'the brother', 'the co-worker', and so on, a device that works to authorize the universality of the issue under discussion.

This inclusion of the voices of family and friends is in keeping with lifestyle TV's broader embrace of ordinary people and its concern with legitimating the knowledge and opinions of both experts and the public. This device also works to bring the queer perspective of the Fab Five and that of the viewing community closer together. To a certain extent, then, queerness becomes ordinary here, or at least safe, clean, and fun—'to be laughed with not at' (Miller 2005: 112). While *Queer Eye* idealizes a mode of masculinity based around savvy modes of queer consumption, '[h]eterosexuality … is not replaced as the core of hegemonic masculinity' (Clarkson 2005: 240). Quite the opposite. One of the most common rationales for the *Queer Eye* makeovers is a concern with transforming style-deficient and socially clueless single guys into dateable or marriageable propositions,[5] or, if the straight guy is married, with making sure he is correctly fulfilling his duties as a husband and father. While old modes of masculinity are challenged on *Queer Eye*, personal transformation tends to occur largely at the level of taste and style rather than challenging the underlying logic of normative heterosexuality that frames the narrative development on the show.

Negotiating femininity

Alongside its foregrounding of questions of aberrant masculinity, another central pleasure in watching *Queer Eye*, particularly for female audiences, is its embrace of skills and knowledge associated not only with queerness but also with femininity. As in the makeover genre more broadly, there is a concern in *Queer Eye* with valuing the forms of expertise associated with feminine homemaking and presentational aesthetics (Attwood 2005). Recognizing these feminine skills, the various women involved in the lives of the aberrant men on the show are regularly consulted by the Fab Five for their views on style, cookery, and relationship issues.

A central aspect of the show involves watching the straight men being inducted into these feminine skills (via the Fab Five and sometimes other intermediary experts), whether this involves learning how to style their hair or attempting to improve their interpersonal skills. At the same time, the show uses a number of strategies to neutralize the more excessively feminine elements of the makeover process. First, the show's playful, zany style attempts to make light of the intermixing of lifestyle and masculinity, refiguring 'the drudgery of housework and home remodelling as festive, stimulating labor' (Gallagher 2004: 223). While the use of a camp aesthetic can be seen to mark a positive revaluation of the feminine in lifestyle television (Attwood 2005), on *Queer Eye*, I would suggest, it also works to make the feminine more palatable and less threatening to a mainstream audience.

Second, the shopping process so central to the *Queer Eye* makeover is also reworked for a male audience—the overwhelming femininity of shop space (particularly in relation to fashion) is neutralized by intercutting the interior shopping scenes with rapidly edited sequences of the Fab Five running or driving through masculine-coded street space. The potentially emasculating shopping experience is further mediated by the figure of the expert, with either one of the Fab Five or an intermediary expert there on hand to translate the shopping experience into a streamlined process of information gathering and calculative choice. The feminine pleasures of distraction, window shopping, shopping for shopping's sake are downplayed here, with the focus instead being on shopping as part of an action-oriented, makeover mission. The makeover experience is recast here along more masculine lines as a kind of self-knowing, ironicized boy's-own adventure. More broadly, then, the constant genre shifting and intertextual referencing of *Queer Eye* can be seen as an attempt to move the show away from, or at least diffuse, the feminized mode of address associated with lifestyle TV—to rearticulate the process of making over the self not just to a rational–calculative agenda but also to a more masculine postmodern space of play and performance.

The relationship between queerness and femininity, then, is a fraught one on *Queer Eye*. On the one hand, the modes of reflexive identity explored on the show draw heavily upon both femininity and queerness as privileged sites of knowledge about the presentation and management of the self in everyday life. At the same time, the rapprochement between queer identity, masculinity, and the feminine is a contradictory one. One way in which the show attempts to ameliorate this tension is through resignifying feminine knowledge here as a form of queer male expertise. As on many lifestyle and makeover shows aimed at 'mainstream' audiences that adopt the increasingly generic figure of the feminized male lifestyle expert, the Fab Five and their queered masculinity function to mediate, negotiate, and, most important, colonize the feminine realm traditionally associated with lifestyle issues while tending to reduce queerness to a question of style and taste. The recurrence of this hybridized figure on lifestyle TV indicates a complex and contested reconfiguration of gender in relation to TV's modes of address and its forms of expertise, one marked by both a reworking and a persistence of conceptions of domestic and lifestyle skills as primarily feminine and therefore culturally devalued or marginalized.

A middle class eye … expertise, cultural capital, and reflexive selves

While the process of instructing straight guys on how to live more stylish lives is largely framed as a set of queer knowledges that can be repackaged and passed on (in a diluted, de-queered form) to the straight man, the notion of lifestyle identity modelled on the show can also be seen as representing a distinct set of class values. In the context of lifestyle television, class distinctions are often characterized not so much in economic terms as in terms of one's possession of what Bourdieu, in his work on taste and distinction, has termed 'cultural capital' (1984). The notion of cultural capital points to the more intangible dimensions of classed identity, in particular the cultural or symbolic competencies around aesthetics and taste associated with class position. One of the central concerns of makeover television is with passing on certain types of cultural capital to the makeover-ee and audience, providing personal transformations through training ordinary people in the tenets of style and good taste. While on television 'style' is presented as a consumption-based mode of expertise or life skill, the aesthetic values and taste preferences offered by lifestyle experts tend to privilege certain class-based competencies over others.

As Featherstone puts it, '[T]he question [arises] of whether the concern for style and individuality itself reflect more the predispositions of a particular class fraction concerned with legitimating its own particular constellation of tastes as the *tastes* of the social, rather than the actual social itself' (1991: 87). As we see on *Queer Eye*, lifestyle consumption itself is not necessarily valued for its own sake (as the Fab Five's attacks on plaid shirts, hair gel, and other taste-challenged commodities suggests); rather, a particular kind of lifestyle connected to certain normative notions of identity is what is put on display throughout the makeover process. The new ideal of manhood sold to us on *Queer Eye* is one marked by 'an involvement in high culture' and 'a fluency in a wide variety of class-inflected taste categories' (Clarkson 2005: 239).

But what does this mean for claims around TV and its ordinariness? Without doubt the rise of lifestyle TV has involved a degree of democratization of television's mode of address, hence the concerns in the press about the 'dumbing down' of television. As noted, there are now more ordinary people on TV than ever, while the gap between experts and 'members of the public' is far less marked than it once was. And while feminine and queer expertise is often coopted on lifestyle TV to fairly normative agendas, the valuing of these knowledges does suggest some degree of expansion and diversification of television's definition of the ordinary. At the same time, these 'new experts in presentation' are now playing a central role in performing and legitimating certain normative conceptions of ordinariness— norms that tend to be closely tied to middle class forms of taste and style (Palmer 2004: 178). As Palmer argues, this new cadre of cultural intermediaries can be seen to translate the cultural capital of the traditional middle class into a series of easily adopted 'styling tips' for the aspiring petit-bourgeoisie (189).

Central to the logic of the makeover narrative, then, is the passing of this cultural capital on to the ordinary people who feature on lifestyle TV. The viewing pleasures associated with the makeover transformation on shows such as *Queer Eye*, however, emerge not only from watching inept participants acquiring some degree of style nous but also from those moments when they resist or just 'don't get' the aesthetic offerings of the Fab Five. When Thom incredulously asks a straight guy, 'But can't you see the problem with your décor?', there is an assumption that the middle class forms of taste peddled on the show represent universal markers of stylishness — in other words, that the Fab Five's definition of taste is natural and a given.

The straight guys on *Queer Eye* are drawn from a range of class backgrounds— although there is a particular focus on men from aspiring, lower-middle class backgrounds—with occupations from struggling artists and musicians to cops and small business owners represented on the show. Class, while forming the subtext of much of the show, is largely disavowed—'deficiencies' in taste and style are, instead, discussed in terms of individual flaws or are portrayed as remnants of outmoded forms of masculinity. Taste and style are thus presented not so much as markers of middle class-ness but in terms of an updating or renovation of masculine identity, a process that in turn emphasizes a highly moralized, 'redemptive narrative' of duty and ethical selfhood (Wood and Skeggs 2004) as well as the more rational and utilitarian aspects of taste acquisition.

The kinds of tastes and values upheld on *Queer Eye*, nevertheless, tend to be resolutely bourgeois. While the clothes and furnishings purchased on the show are 'matched' to the lifestyles and personalities of the individual straight guys, the emphasis tends to be on high-quality, rather expensive, and at times 'designer' items, often out of the reach of the income of the straight guy. While these items are often discussed on the show in terms of their utilitarian qualities, the underlying concern is with teaching the straight guy to recognize and embrace these objects as markers of good taste and as extensions of the self.

Stylishness here is also associated with a certain set of middle class skills around self-presentation and demeanour, or more broadly with what Bourdieu refers to as 'habitus'—where class position is played out not only through the external markers of one's social status and lifestyle but also through more nuanced discriminations in deportment, bodily management, and social etiquette. The show's focus on habitus is marked not only by a concern with the detachable markers of classed identity, then, but also through a relentless focus on *embodied* modes of class identity, on grooming, bodily hygiene, fitness, body language, and interpersonal skills.

The straight men thus undergo instruction on appropriate techniques for grooming (poor shaving technique is the *bête noire* of the Fab Five) and disciplining their bodies (through exercise regimes, organic low-fat diets, etc.), while also learning to give over their bodies to other experts for medical treatment as well as more feminine-coded activities such as tanning, exfoliation, and waxing. The makeover transformation thus involves not only instantly repackaging the straight guy as a stylish new man but also promoting the notion of the body and identity as a site of productive labour and perfectibility—the straight guy here learns to internalize the bourgeois gaze of the 'queer eye' in the name of a middle class project of self-management and self-improvement.

Learning to (lifestyle) shop

Pivotal to the process of becoming a self-managing subject on *Queer Eye* is learning how to shop. From its opening credits, with their images of dull-looking straight men in shop windows and on billboards being instantly converted into colourful, stylish consumers, it is apparent that a consumerist logic lies at the heart of the show's content and narrative structure. It also provides the economic base for the programme (Allatson 2004). Part of a broader shift towards the inclusion of advertising and commodities within TV content itself, or 'below-the-line' advertising as it is known in the industry, *Queer Eye*, like other consumer-advice-oriented formats, works 'to alert viewers to the existence of more products and services for their utility in the endless project of the self' (Bonner 2003: 104). And, as a recent story in *Fortune* magazine suggests, this process of selling commodities as part of a broader self-improvement/lifestyle package has proved extremely effective in the case of *Queer Eye* (Florian 2004).

The *Fortune* story, for instance, cites multiple examples of increased sales following the appearance of particular commodities on the show, including a settee, dubbed the 'chofa' by *Queer Eye* (because it is a chair and a sofa). While *Queer Eye* initially featured commodities free of charge, the success of the show means that companies such as *Oral-B* began to pay up to $20,000 to feature their toothbrushes and other products (although the show's producers stress the role of the Fab Five in actively choosing the products featured on *Queer Eye*). A central aspect of the 'hyperconsumption' encouraged by the show is, as I have suggested, its focus on 'consumer masculinity', whereby straight men are repackaged as metrosexuals and modelled on the advertising industry's conception of the gay male market as highly savvy consumers (Clarkson 2005: 235). *Fortune* magazine confirms *Queer Eye*'s success in addressing the male audience as lifestyle-conscious consumers, citing a study that found that on the day following an episode men were five times more likely to go shopping than women. 'Who knew that guys getting girlie would be such a boon to business?', the magazine quipped (Florian 2004: 38).

Ironically, however, this throw-away line highlights the fact that consumption (at least in the symbolic realm of *Fortune* magazine) continues to be largely coded as feminine, with men still tending to be associated with the world of production. By contrast, *Queer Eye* presents the audience with a world where these kinds of oppositions are increasingly anachronistic. Thus, the domestic spaces of many of the straight guys on the show are depicted simultaneously as sites of work, leisure, and family life, that is, as marked by a blend of consumption and production (one show, for example, focuses on a straight guy who runs a small business with his wife-to-be from their home). Nevertheless, consumption still tends to be seen as a rather 'girly' activity—hence, lifestyle TV's concern with rearticulating lifestyle shopping to other logics and modes of selfhood. On *Queer Eye*, where the straight guys in question are clearly seen as socially aberrant because of their lack of ability to shop (as evidenced by the show's concern at the surfeit of polyester and disintegrating underwear in their wardrobes and the lack of furniture in their homes), one of the central strategies adopted to get them shopping is to reframe the act of consumption through the lens of reflexive selfhood. The concern with the presentation of self and with self-improvement central to lifestyle and makeover culture becomes linked to a self-regulatory, neoliberal model of 'entrepreneurial' identity through what Rose refers to as 'a seductive ethics of the self' (1996: 153). The logic of consumer capitalism is central to this conception of selfhood where questions of social position and inequity are effaced by a discourse of endless self-shaping. Here the consumer–citizen is thus constructed as transcending gender (or social class, sexuality, etc.) and assumed instead to be an autonomous rational–calculative actor making considered lifestyle choices through the (now supposedly neutral) act of consumption.

A central feature of this refiguring of lifestyle consumption as reflexive and calculative is the focus on consumption as a form of knowledge acquisition. As Bonner notes, borrowing Freud's term 'epistemophilia', part of the pleasure of watching television is the gaining of knowledge itself (2003: 102). The popularity of cooking shows, for instance, at a time when people are increasingly eating out rather than preparing food at home lends some weight to this argument, as does the growing branding and commoditization of popular experts. The celebrity status of Martha Stewart or Jamie Oliver can be seen as an extension of epistemophilia, with the concern here lying as much with the consumption of expertise and the image of the experts themselves as with the actual act of cooking, shopping, or renovating.

The pleasures associated with consuming knowledge are also central to the *Queer Eye* makeover narrative, which, in the process of interpolating the straight guy as a commodity consumer, works to emphasize the importance of acquiring information and forms of expertise about everyday life skills. In part, this combining of consumption with a kind of informationalism can be seen as the show once again attempting to recode the shopping experience along more masculine lines. Thus, whenever a new commodity is presented on *Queer Eye* (whether a couch or a pair of shoes) it tends to be framed, as I have noted, not only in terms of its aesthetic qualities and its ability to enhance one's presentation of self but also in terms of its utility. When Carson purchases expensive designer sportswear on behalf of one of the straight guys, he tells him that cotton and other 'natural fabrics' are best because they breathe. When the audience is shown the design makeover carried out by Thom, labels pop up on the screen reminding us of the everyday utility of each new piece of furniture and design choice (e.g., 'make better use of a small space with dual use furniture such as the storage bin that doubles as a chair'). Likewise, the straight guys are often taken by the Fab Five to specialist stores where the shop assistants are themselves presented as experts and will often give a detailed rationale for the purchase of a particular product.

The show's focus on the production process behind organic meat or on the construction materials used in a piece of furniture can be seen as another example of the way in which lifestyle TV is continually attempting to negotiate the shifting relationship between lifestyle shopping and gender. Dovetailing with this process of re-gendering or masculinizing lifestyle consumption is the way in which lifestyle TV works to juggle notions of aesthetics, and of pleasure and play, with a more rationalist focus on consumption as a detached, considered act. The consuming subject of *Queer Eye* is assumed to be both style conscious and aesthetically savvy as well as an informed rational–calculative actor who weighs up decisions about grooming, diet, and personal relationships with a view to constructing a credible and consistent 'lifestyle biography', to modify Beck's phrase 'risk biography' (1992). Commodity consumption and associated questions of style and taste are presented on *Queer Eye* largely as a mode of (intensely pleasurable and life-improving) rationality linked to the forms of consumption-based expertise held by the Fab Five and other commodity specialists, and in turn passed on to the (increasingly consumer-savvy) straight guy as well as the audience.

Rearticulating identity

Holmes and Jermyn (2004) note that the rise of reality TV (and with it lifestyle TV) has largely been talked about as a side effect of broad economic shifts in TV production, a process I discussed briefly in the introductory chapter. As cheap programming that is readily franchised, reality TV is seen as a development produced by increasing competition and deregulation of the TV market. Here I do not want to dismiss such an approach—an economic analysis is certainly central not only to the production aspects of these relatively inexpensive and readily franchised TV formats but also to an analysis of their content, given that, as I have noted, this is a mode of television that tends to address both its participants and its audience first and foremost as consumers.

However, both the economic (and cultural) context out of which these new formats have arisen is much more complex than just a question of 'cheap economics of scale' (Holmes and Jermyn 2004: 15).[6] And plainly anyone who has given lifestyle TV more than a passing glance can see that a purely economic analysis is at risk of failing to capture the complex ways in which these shows are articulated to larger socio-cultural trends, which I have identified here in terms of an intensified interest in the question of lifestyle and a related shift towards a culture of reflexivity and transformation. One of the central markers of this shift is the rise over the past decade of this new figure of expertise, the life specialist. From charismatic, celebrity figures such as the Fab Five to the myriad less brand-worthy experts found on lifestyle TV, there is a sense that the gaze of the expert has penetrated all aspects of daily life while targeting everybody as potentially DIY subjects.

The way in which this process is played out via *Queer Eye*'s new lifestyled version of masculinity, however, is not necessarily straightforward. Reflexive, new modes of DIY identity are certainly on display here, but lifestyle TV also continues to be marked by an ongoing negotiation with traditional categories of identity, with lifestyle and consumption continuing to be strongly linked to social class and gender (Tomlinson 2003). The association of lifestyle skills with feminized and queered modes of identity, for instance, complicates the relationship between the lifestyle expert and new 'post-traditional' modes of self-governance. The narrative offered up by figures such as Beck and Giddens of a neat shift from ascribed to free-floating forms of social identity clearly does not capture the full complexity of identity formation under contemporary consumer capitalism. At the same time, it is apparent that makeover television is doing more than just reaffirming traditional forms of identity. *Queer Eye* can certainly be read purely as rearticulating (or appropriating) feminine lifestyle skills (via the figure of the queer expert) to an essentially middle class, masculinist model of self-managing identity. But the potential meanings of the relationship between the new metrosexuality, the 'mainstreamed' queer expertise of the Fab Five, and the entrepreneurial mode of citizenship on display in the show are not so easily foreclosed. Here again we are reminded of the complexity of the double entanglement highlighted by McRobbie between neo-conservative and liberalized modes of selfhood in popular consumer culture. When we start to think through the cultural role of the lifestyle expert, it is important to attune ourselves both to the normative dimensions of this figure and to the ways they mark the negotiated, contradictory, and shifting nature of the relationship between ordinary, everyday culture and public life, and between traditional selves and enterprising subjects in late modern culture.

Notes

1   *Queer Eye* premiered on the cable channel Bravo in July 2003, earning the channel the highest ratings in its history. Its parent company, the NBC network, subsequently rebroadcast the show a month later, drawing 8 million viewers and tying with CBS for attracting the highest number of adult (aged 18–49) viewers (Rogers 2003). The show, which ran until 2007, has spawned a spin-off series called *Queer Eye for the Straight Girl* featuring a lesbian lifestyle expert, Honey Labrador. *Queer Eye* has been popular internationally, with rights to the show having been sold in thirty countries. Foreign versions of the show have not fared so well, however, with Living TV's UK version receiving a lukewarm response early on in the series (although they went on to make a second series and the show has aired in the United States) and Australia's Channel 10 dropping its local version after airing only three episodes.

2   John Corner (2004: 290) notes that the term 'reality TV' arguably emerged from the United States and is specifically associated with actuality-based footage, of the kind associated, for instance, with reality crime shows.

3   Indeed, as I discuss further in Chapter 4, the BBC has played a pivotal role in producing new, 'democratized', and hybridized forms of lifestyle television that attempt to combine an entertainment-oriented approach with public educational goals.

4   In Australia, for instance, the first series of *Queer Eye* was sponsored by a new Coca-Cola product, Coke with Lime, the promotion of which involved a series of tongue-in-cheek (if rather lame) advertisements that attempted to play with the notion of the new masculinity by featuring males as muscle-bound, pretty boys objectified in various ways by the women in the advertisements. In the United States, interestingly, the Bravo network also ran advertisements specifically targeting a gay male audience, briefly featuring a commercial for Interactive Male, a gay phone chat service (Wilke 2003).

5   Indeed, in one episode the show deviated from its traditional format so that the Fab Five could organize a wedding for a young couple.

6   As Holmes and Jermyn (2004) point out, the assumption that reality TV formats are cheap involves conflating these shows with other modes of 'live footage' reality programming such as 'real crime' TV, ignoring, for instance, the fact that the kind of 'event' television associated with shows such as *Big Brother* comes with a very large price tag attached (15), an assumption, as they note, embedded in value-based judgments about what constitutes 'quality' versus 'trash' television (9).

Chapter 4

Honey We're Killing the Kids
Producing lifestyle TV in Australia

The television programme *Honey We're Killing the Kids* focuses on 'making over' families, and in particular children who have a combination of health and/or behavioural problems, with a view to improving their potential future health and well-being. It is an instructive example of a reality-lifestyle format with educational concerns that is centred around a more 'traditional' model of expertise, in the Australian case a child development specialist.[1] The series was first produced by the BBC for their youth-focused digital channel BBC Three in 2005 (under their Documentaries and Arts category); its popularity saw it subsequently moved to BBC 1.[2] Local versions of *Honey We're Killing the Kids*[3] were also produced in the United States in 2006 for the cable channel TLC (The Learning Channel) and in Australia, where it was shown in a prime time spot on the free-to-air commercial television channel Network Ten (the same channel on which Australia's long-running version of *Big Brother* also airs). This chapter discusses the Australian version of *Honey* based on interviews carried out with television personnel at Freehand TV (the company that produced the programme for Network Ten) and observations of shoots at the Entertainment Quarter in Sydney.

In discussing the role of popular expertise in lifestyle media so far I have drawn upon a range of approaches, from textual analysis of specific TV programmes to case studies of particular lifestyle experts. In contrast, this chapter on *Honey* is interested in foregrounding an industry perspective on lifestyle programming and popular expertise; what follows is a small-scale case study of this programme. In undertaking this research my interest was in capturing a sense of the reflexive and/or critical perspectives and role played by TV personnel in producing and shaping the meanings of popular factual formats. While there is much talk in TV scholarship of the way in which TV hosts and experts function as 'cultural intermediaries' for certain normative models of taste and value, there is less focus on the behind-the-scenes role of the TV producers who shape these programmes. Here, for instance, I was particularly interested in the processes of dialogue and translation that occurred between the different modes of televisual and 'lifestyle-oriented' expertise at work on this show.

All of the *Honey* production staff I talked to had experience working on reality and lifestyle formats. Key figures such as Peter Abbott, the show's executive producer, and Tim Clucas, the then head of Production and Development at Network Ten, have also played a role in shaping the historical development of infotainment, lifestyle, and reality television in Australia. Nevertheless, my focus was concerned less with a meta-analysis of the state of popular factual television than with the more material and conceptual concerns and constraints that came into play when producing a specific programme. As Peter Abbott commented in relation to his own critical perspective on the social role of TV: 'I come at it from inside the washing machine. There's this stuff swirling around so what it looks like from above I don't know.'

My interest, then, was in getting a perspective from 'inside the washing machine', that is, in viewing *Honey* as a messy microcosm of lifestyle TV production that might offer some insights into the complex relationships between production processes, conceptions of audiences, local/national TV culture, and TV's role as a social institution promoting and shaping, in the case of popular educational formats such as *Honey*, conceptions of 'good' citizenship and responsibility to community.

Dr Spock for the reality generation:
The recent rise of parenting programmes

While reality-based parenting shows such as *Honey* are relatively new to Australian audiences, this is by no means a new format. Over the past few years we have seen the lifestyle makeover genre shift from a primary concern with home and garden renovations to a growing focus on personal makeovers, from renovating people's finances, fashion sense, and relationships to more extreme personal interventions involving surgical transformations. More recently, the personal makeover format itself has shifted from a primary focus on individuals to embracing the family unit as a whole. Against the backdrop of growing general concerns within the United States, the United Kingdom, and Australia about childhood obesity and children's health, we are starting to see the emergence of reality-style makeover shows that focus not only on unhealthy children but also on parenting and family dynamics. What is interesting in relation to the concerns of this book around popular expertise is that all these shows are marked by a strongly instructional and educational focus; they draw upon a variety of types of 'expert' knowledge, from the 'commonsense' approach offered on the highly popular *Supernanny* to the more credentialed expertise featured on shows such as *Honey*. All are delivered in highly accessible ways via a reality TV format that links 'expert' knowledge to the everyday experiences of 'ordinary' families and that educates the audience through modulating between overtly didactic modes of address and more experiential modes of learning, as audiences witness the families attempting to implement various lifestyle changes.

As with the genre of popular factual entertainment more broadly, British TV has played a leading role in developing this type of programming, and the past couple of years have seen a variety of shows emerge out of the UK around the intersection of health, lifestyle, and parenting issues. As I have noted, while reality TV has links with a range of 'low' and popular TV traditions from US 'tabloid TV' to soap (Hill 2005), in the British context, reality-based lifestyle programming can also be seen to emerge out of, at the same time as it radically reworks, earlier public service–oriented documentary traditions (Kilborn 2003; Corner 2004; Biressi and Nunn 2005).

One of the most successful of the new parental/family makeover shows has been *Supernanny*, a programme in which professional nanny Jo Frost visits families in their homes and, after a period of 'observation', attempts to help parents to transform their children's 'problem behaviour' using various techniques and props such as the now infamous 'naughty room'.[4] First produced for Channel Four by Ricochet Ltd in 2004 and now into its third series, *Supernanny* has been the most popular parenting show to come out of Britain and has seen a highly successful US version of the format (*Supernanny USA*, which also stars Jo Frost) aired on ABC in the United States and also shown on British TV.[5]

A number of other shows have emerged from the UK that feature more 'traditional' figures of expertise such as doctors and psychologists. In Britain in 2005, for instance, ITV showed the series *Driving Mum and Dad Mad*, a reality show that follows five families with 'tantrum-throwing children' as they undertake an intensive and systematic parenting programme under the watchful eye of Dr Matthew Saunders, an Australian child behaviour specialist and professor of clinical psychology at the University of Queensland. Interestingly, when this series was first aired, an online university–led study called 'The Great Parenting Experiment' was run along with the show. UK parents were invited to join the study, which encouraged them to examine their own parenting practices and to try out the positive parenting strategies shown on the programme—a process followed up in the study via 'before and after' questionnaires.

While *Driving Mum and Dad Mad* was aired on a commercial channel, this explicit concern with educating the public through the use of the popular 'social experiment' format has (in keeping with the public service ethos) been more particularly associated with the BBC's contribution to the family makeover genre. In 2004 they produced the first reality-based instructional parenting show, *Little Angels*, which, through the use of hidden cameras and microphones, followed the lives of four families experiencing difficulty with their children. After an initial period of observation, the show's main expert, clinical psychologist Dr Tanya Byron, steps in to give the parents advice and techniques to improve their parenting skills. The audience then gets to watch the parents put these into action while they continue to be given professional advice via an earpiece.

The popularity of *Little Angels* saw two more series produced, with Dr Tanya Byron becoming a major household name and publishing a self-help manual named after the series. Byron has since gone on to host two other parenting programmes for the BBC, *Teen Angels*, where along with another clinical psychologist she devises techniques for managing unruly teenagers, and *The House of Tiny Tearaways*. The latter format, first aired in 2005, was a particularly innovative one, combining the instructional, docu-soap elements of *Little Angels* with a kind of *Big Brother* setup. Hosted by Byron and UK TV presenter Claudia Winkleman, *The House of Tiny Tearaways* brings three families into a house built for the show, where they are monitored and helped for a week. As on *Big Brother* all the rooms are wired for sound and vision, with the audience being shown edited highlights of a particular day. While Byron is clearly the source of expert advice on the show, what is distinctive about the programme is that it also focuses on the communal, mutually supportive role played by the families.

The BBC's educational push here is part of a broader thematic focus over the past couple of years on parenting issues.[6] These shows have thus aired alongside a number of other less explicitly educational reality-based programmes about parenting, including 'real-life soap opera' *He's Having a Baby*. Hosted by UK *Big Brother* presenter Davina McCall and using a similar combination of fly-on-the-wall documentary format and weekly studio-based interviews with the dads as well as commentary from friends and family, the show aired in 2005 on BBC 1 but failed to rate and was subsequently shifted to BBC 3. Despite its more entertainment-oriented reality TV format, the show, which followed eight men about to become first-time fathers over ten weeks, also included an instructional element, with the fathers-to-be being put through various 'Dad Assignments' created to give them firsthand experience of fatherhood.[7]

In 2004 BBC 3 also showed *Who Rules the Roost?*, a programme that involves parents making a radical change in their lives over a four-week period, with the mother and father taking it in turns to give up work and look after their children full time. As the BBC website notes, the parents have to make a decision about whether either of them will leave work permanently at the end of the 'experiment'. While produced by Ricochet, the same company who made *Supernanny*, this parenting show is not as overtly educational; it does not focus on behavioural problems or feature an 'expert' or presenter intervening in the families' lives. The fact that the show raises the issue of full-time working couples as a social problem, however, does suggest a broad social educational element (with strong moral overtones) to the show. It also again foregrounds the way in which television is increasingly playing a governmental role, focusing on (and often intervening in) people's ordinary domestic lives while also contributing to 'normative' conceptions of ethical selfhood and appropriate conduct.[8]

While the BBC has traditionally been driven by a strongly educational, public service orientation, over recent years it has shifted to more entertainment-oriented programming, with traditional informational and expert-driven modes of programming being replaced by popular factual or 'lifestyle' formats. This reformulation of the 'social issues' focus of the BBC's informational programming is also reflected on its website, where consumer advice programmes, health, gardening, and holiday shows as well as parenting are grouped under lifestyle. These programmes' hybrid lifestyle/educational formats, then, can be seen to represent a concern with both providing high-rating populist entertainment aimed at as wide a demographic as possible and attempting to hold on to a public education agenda. While the BBC has played a leading role in producing this kind of cross-over educational television, as I have noted these formats have also been produced by commercial channels in Britain, and many of them have travelled well internationally, indicating a global market for modes of television that merge lifestyle entertainment, reality TV, and expert/instructional advice.

From the BBC to Network Ten

In Australia the context for the production, programming, and audience reception of shows such as *Honey* is rather different from the UK context. While Australia has embraced a variety of shows popularly referred to as reality television—*Big Brother*, *Australian Idol*, *Survivor*, and many similar competitive, game-doc formats are all familiar to and popular with Australian audiences[9]—the more educationally oriented observational documentary formats discussed above have not been so prevalent on Australian TV screens. Infotainment programmes concerned with health and lifestyle in Australia to date have tended to be dominated by magazine-style formats and oriented more towards middle-aged audiences. However, a few months before *Honey* was aired in Australia, the Australian version of *The Biggest Loser* received high ratings on Network Ten (traditionally a channel associated with a 16- to 39-year-old demographic), while *Supernanny*, a show that obviously targets younger parents with small children, was also very popular with Australian audiences (there has been talk of making an Australian version). Some personal lifestyle makeover formats, including of course *Queer Eye* (whose popularity, as discussed in Chapter 3, led to a local spin-off), have also been previously shown in Australia. However, Australia has had nothing like the number of parenting/family makeover shows seen by UK audiences. Before the launch of *Honey*, then, Australian audiences' main 'training' in viewing such formats was through exposure to some of these less overtly 'educational', lifestyle makeover formats.

Australia also has a rather different televisual landscape in terms of the nature and impact of public versus commercial broadcasters and the relative lack of competition from pay TV and digital television, which have for various reasons been slow to take off. Compared with the multi-channel environments of the UK and the US, the Australian TV market is still largely dominated by free-to-air networks. There are three commercial networks, Seven, Nine, and Ten, which tend to dominate audience share, and two publicly subsidized channels, the ABC (Australian Broadcasting Corporation) and SBS (Special Broadcasting Service). The ABC, which has continued to adhere to a fairly traditional 'public service' model, is an embattled and chronically under-funded public institution and a relatively minor player in terms of audience share. With the exception of some lifestyle-oriented cooking shows, the recent low-budget makeover show *Agony Aunt*, and some early lifestyle magazine formats, most of the recent reality/lifestyle formats have appeared on commercial networks.[10] While Channels Nine and Seven, which aim by and large for an older demographic, have aired some reality formats (Channel Nine's *The Block* and Channel Seven's *My Restaurant Rules* were both highly successful, home-grown formats), their instructional lifestyle programming has tended to fall into the more traditional magazine-style infotainment category, as reflected in shows such as *The Great Outdoors* and *What's Good for You*.

Network Ten, which aims at a younger demographic, similar to that of Britain's Channel Four, has been the leader in the Australian market in terms of airing reality-based shows, both international and locally made formats including lifestyle makeover shows such as *The Biggest Loser* and *Queer Eye*. In the Australian context, *Honey* was made for a young, commercial audience highly attuned to the conventions of reality-based formats.[11] Scheduled in a prime time 7:30 p.m. slot on Wednesdays (initially following on from the daily screening at 7:00 p.m. of *Big*

Brother) and screened just after the finish of the first Australian series of *The Biggest Loser*, *Honey* was clearly being positioned for the audience as a reality makeover show first, with its 'educational' elements kept relatively in the background (as was evidenced in the *Big Brother*–style promotional ads for *Honey*, which emphasized the drama and emotion rather than the informational elements of the show).

From casting to shooting

While the industrial context in which *Honey* was produced, marketed, and shown on Australian television was rather different from in the UK, Network Ten had nevertheless purchased a set format from the BBC, and for the most part Ten and Freehand stuck to this blueprint in making the show.[12] As my interviews with the production team indicate, however, there were certain significant differences in emphasis in the Australian version in keeping with perceived differences between UK and Australian audiences. The reality-based nature of the format also meant that the programme's content was, of course, greatly shaped (and localized) by the casting, in relation to both the choice of the central expert/host (in the Australian case a highly qualified child development specialist, Dr Anne Purcell) and, more important, the choice of the families featured on the show.

My interviewees maintained that in casting *Honey*, the focus was very much on the educational dimensions of the show and on recruiting families who were motivated by the health concerns promoted by the programme rather than just wanting 'to be on television'. At the same time, Freehand and Ten were hoping to attract significant interest in the show so that they could recruit families from a range of social backgrounds. As the series producer, Matt Scully, commented, 'We were looking for variety. You've got a broadcast audience so you're wanting to increase the likelihood that someone will identify with the families you're choosing.'

Casting for the show proved to be more difficult than anticipated. Initially Freehand used a strategy similar to the BBC's and attempted to recruit through schools by sending fliers home with school children. While this strategy had worked well in the UK, in Australia it yielded a poor response, and the production team ended up attempting to recruit families through a television advertisement aired by Network Ten. While they received 4,000 calls from families interested in being on the show, relatively few of these were motivated by the programme's health focus. They also had difficulty casting families from a diversity of backgrounds. For instance, they were keen to attract families from more upper-middle class backgrounds but found that few families from higher socio-economic groupings were willing to volunteer, and that those who did did not have the appropriate combination of health and behavioural problems to qualify for the show. In the end they found six appropriate families to participate in the show, representing a mixture of working class and solidly middle class families.

Once chosen, the final six families were put through a series of medical assessments by Good Health Solutions (GHS), a private health company that principally provides health profiles for the corporate world and whose various experts also briefly feature as part of the mise-en-scène of *Honey* (for instance, in one episode the GHS dietician is seen in one of the family's homes teaching them how to make healthy meals). During the family's initial assessment, the GHS team ran a battery of health tests from physical health tests, to an assessment of the children's diets (the family was required to keep a food diary for a week), to a psychological assessment, including tests of their self-perception and self-esteem, 'to inform us what areas to target and to check that they are going to be up to the experience'. This culminated in GHS creating a health profile for each child, with information from this used to construct a morphed image of how the children might look at 40 if they continued with their current diet and lifestyle.

Drawing upon the conventions of makeover television, with its concern with visible transformations, the morphs play a central and distinctive role in *Honey* (at the end of the show the parents are also shown morphs of their children as they would look if they continued to adhere to the show's lifestyle rules). While it is clearly not possible to actually determine what a person will look like in the future, through giving a visible, embodied form to otherwise abstract issues about the potential impact of health and lifestyle on their children, the morphs act as a powerful warning and motivator for the parents (as well as, of course, a potential source of guilt and anxiety).

Following the assessments with GHS, each of the six families was then filmed for a month in their homes while they followed a three-week programme specifically constructed for them in which they were asked to implement a number of often dramatic lifestyle changes, including changes to their diet, family routine, exercise regime, and interpersonal relationships. This portion of the filming included periods of fly-on-the-wall observation and also moments of 'intervention' when an expert went into the house to help the family. It also included four visits to the studio based in the Entertainment Quarter (EQ) in Sydney, where the parents underwent a kind of family therapy session with the show's host–expert Anne Purcell. These sessions took place in the rather daunting White Room, a space resembling a cross between a *Big Brother*–style confessional room and an interrogation cell, complete with blinding white lights and a large plasma screen on which the families (and the audience) were shown the weekly rules via distinctive sets of pictograms.

The first White Room sessions were a rather charged affair, as this was when Anne would present the parents with the (often rather shocking) morphed images of their children's potential 'futures'. After this rather dramatic wake-up call, the families were given a makeover regime billed as enabling them to 'change the face of that future', consisting of a weekly manual with hints, strategies, and recipes along with three new 'rules' to follow every week (from 'No More Lollies' to 'Be Respectful'). They were then filmed over the remaining three weeks of their lifestyle makeover, with the closing credits of the programme showing images of the 'new and improved' version of the family after completing the set regime.

Behind the scenes of *Honey*

While the audience gets to view each family's experiences in the highly condensed form of a fast-paced, slickly packaged one-hour episode, which includes numerous ad breaks and frequent repeated footage, what they do not see, of course, is the 130 or more hours of filming and the complex off-screen processes and interactions that go into making a reality-based, educational format. During April and May 2006 I conducted interviews with members of the production team at the Freehand offices, including Peter Abbott, one of the directors at Freehand and the executive producer of *Honey*; Matt Scully, the series producer; and Susie Jones, the science associate producer. I also interviewed Tim Clucas from Network Ten and Dr Anne Purcell, the host–expert on *Honey*.[13]

I observed two days of shooting for the White Room sessions of *Honey* at the EQ studio. While I was unable to observe the on-location shoots of the families, watching the White Room shoots provided some useful insights into the behind-the-scenes processes and tensions involved in working on a reality-based makeover format. Both of my days at the EQ studio began with a script meeting where Anne Purcell would talk through the guidelines and suggestions presented in that week's White Room script outline with the show's science producer and executive and series producers, often with the on-location producer sitting in and giving specific feedback from the field. This was a crucial process to watch in terms of seeing the degree to which Anne shaped the content and approach of the show and also observing the way in which the team and Anne worked together to translate Anne's expert advice around behaviour, diet, and health into more 'commonsense' language (e.g., seeing Anne's comments that the children in one family needed to learn 'negotiation and social skills' translated into a scene where the children organize a barbecue for family and friends as part of one week's goal).

Different levels of negotiation were also continually played out in the White Room shoots themselves, which were a complex mix of 'private' therapy sessions between Anne and the family and interaction between the production team and Anne—with the team's various suggestions being fed to Anne (who was wearing an earpiece during the shooting) via the science producer. Here there was a particularly interesting interplay between the crew's concern with capturing the kinds of 'authentic' emotional responses that make 'good telly' and their sense of a 'duty of care' to the families concerned in terms of providing them with a supportive, therapeutic experience. In one situation, for instance, where a mother was particularly upset by the morphed images of her children, there was extensive discussion in the production room about the importance of 'doing good by these families' and the need to go 'softly, softly'. This 'duty of care' issue was also played out in relation to what Anne and the production team included in the realm of issues to be dealt with on the show. Sometimes, for instance, problems were revealed to the crew that had not come up in the initial assessment (and had not been 'caught' on film) but that after discussion, in particular with Anne, were often deemed inappropriate to be aired on the show. As my later discussion of the interviews emphasizes, this duty of care cropped up repeatedly, and there were regular debates among the crew about the show's ethical obligations towards the families.

A different issue that was foregrounded (and again this relates to some of these tensions between the entertainment-oriented and the therapeutic dimensions of a show such as *Honey*) was the element of unpredictability associated with reality-based formats. *Honey* is obviously a highly structured, rule-based format with some scripted elements. And for the production team there was, not surprisingly, a strong concern with presenting the audience with a coherent narrative demonstrating a clear process of transformation over the period of the show. The families' own concerns and actions, however, did not always neatly fit with the interests of narrative television, as in one situation where a parent 'jumped the gun' and attempted to introduce a health initiative before it was scheduled in the show. The production team had to exhibit a fair degree of flexibility and imaginative capacity therefore in terms of negotiating between the various families' desires and emotional responses and the concerns of the narrative. From the perspective of an observer watching the production team watch the families, some of the more interesting 'dramatic moments' occurred in those behind-the-scenes dimensions of the show that were ultimately not seen by the TV audience.

'Its only the media that says it's a reality show': *Honey* and the question of genre

Honey was described in much of the Australian press as an educational reality show, referred to as a 'lifestyle show' by the BBC, and characterized by one Australian TV reviewer as 'the bastard progeny of *The Biggest Loser* and *Supernanny*' (Molitorisz 2006). Part of what defines new formats such as *Honey* is their very refusal to fit into neat generic categories. Drawing elements from a range of TV formats, including the social observational documentary, reality TV, infotainment, and the makeover show, *Honey* represents an innovative hybrid of generic conventions. While it may be futile to attempt definitively to categorize shows such as *Honey*, questions of genre are obviously still important here as they frame the critical reception of TV shows and have been central to debates over reality television. Accordingly, I was interested in how much questions of genre and format shaped the approach and concerns of the *Honey* production team. How did they situate *Honey* within broader shifts around new factual and lifestyle-oriented formats?

Aside from questions of genre in relation to *Honey*, one point to note here is that issues of genre and format do play a significant role at an industry level in terms of employment of production staff and their 'history' in the industry.[14] When I talked to the production team, the junior staff commented in particular on their current relative employability owing to their previous work on reality formats as compared with colleagues with a background in drama, which in Australia has seen its funding cut in half since 2000 (Mangan 2004).

Thus, the staff I talked to had all worked across a range of formats similar to *Honey* and had all also worked overseas on lifestyle/reality formats. As I have noted, more senior figures such as Clucas and Abbott have played an important role in paving the way for the reception of shows such as *Honey*, having helped shape the development of infotainment and lifestyle formats in Australia (and having also made some contribution to the infotainment genre internationally) and having worked on reality shows such as *Big Brother*.[15] The more junior staff had collectively worked across a range of reality and lifestyle/makeover formats, including UK Channel Four's observational documentary *Boys Alone* (2002) and the second series of the US show *Survivor: The Australian Outback*, shot in Australia in 2000. *Honey*'s series producer, Matt Scully, had come to the show after working in the same role on the long-running Australian lifestyle magazine show *Better Homes and Gardens*.

While they readily used terms such as reality TV, infotainment, and lifestyle format (although often with gestured scare quotes), the production staff all talked about the difficulty of defining *Honey* in terms of one generic category. The senior players in particular were critical of attempts by journalists to categorize shows such as *Honey* according to a one-size-fits-all label and talked about the limited nature of generic terms for capturing the specifics of individual TV shows.

> They're only useful for the press to use as pigeon holes because it makes things easier for them. Journalists ring up and say 'reality shows like *Big Brother* and *Idol*' and I say what's the connection between those 2 shows—it's just journalistic laziness. What it does point to is the problem for anyone trying to pigeon hole television in terms of genres—it doesn't work like that anymore. It's the same in publishing, in magazines, the lines are so blurred in the genres, they're all just TV shows, some have more information, some have less, some have real people, some have actors. An information-based show that uses actors to reenact a scene—is that a drama now? It's just silly for people to desperately try

to pigeon hole things because it's irrelevant … How does the show work? Who's it aimed at? How long does it run? How much does it cost? Those are the important things for us—not which pigeon hole we are going to put it in. (Tim Clucas)

Likewise, Peter Abbott noted the difficulty of reducing television's flexible, innovative approaches to format to set generic categories:

I don't think the form matters a bit, I think you could make an educational sitcom if you wanted to, it's all just packaging for an idea … There's this kind of simplistic notion—that documentary shows are factual and that magazine shows are how you do lifestyle television.

This sense of a growing fluidity and play around generic categories marks the new 'factual' formats such as *Honey* in particular—evidenced in the difficulty one member of the production team had in defining the show:

Honey's a funny one, usually you can say what concisely the show is—I find myself saying it's an observational documentary, it's a reality TV show … I guess I'm only just starting to distinguish between the reality and the educational kind, between the entertainment of *Big Brother* and this show's concern with health … it shares some things with *The Swan* and *Extreme Makeover* … *Supernanny* is the one most like it … it's the basic makeover but dressed up with more information, more facts. (Susie Jones, science associate producer)

While critical of attempts to confine a show to one genre, the more senior producers did talk in broad-brushstroke terms about where *Honey* might be located in relation to wider shifts in informational programming and formats. In defining what kind of informational format *Honey* might be associated with, however, the emphasis was strongly on questions of audience address rather than formal distinctions.[16]

Situating *Honey* within the broader context of new approaches to educational television, for instance, Peter Abbott argues that reality shows like *Wife Swap* and *Brat Camp* operate as Trojan horses smuggling in educational messages, whereas *Honey* is more overt about its educational goal:

I think these two programmes [*Wife Swap* and *Brat Camp*] are a bit postmodern as you academics would say. They've got no structured outcome. The audience can make up their minds as to what they want to take out of it and I'm sure they do take quite different things from it. Whereas *Honey* is a little bit more didactic in the sense that the rules are quite clear.

Nevertheless *Honey* is seen by Abbott and the other interviewees as marking a radical shift away from earlier informational programming such as the magazine-style lifestyle format where the viewer could passively sit disengaged from the programme and was not called upon to participate in the show or indeed to do any of the things demonstrated on the show. While television's transformational power often has a magical, labour-free quality, acting as a kind of 'fairy godmother' (Bonner 2003: 127), in certain ways formats such as *Honey*, with their focus on the labour, sacrifice, and pain involved in the makeover process, are marked by a relative realism, albeit a realism framed by a three-week timeline and complete with on-call camera crew and lifestyle expert. As many of the production team pointed out, the challenging nature of the makeover 'journey' is a central part of the appeal and effectiveness of the show.

As Matt Scully comments, comparing *Honey* with *Queer Eye for the Straight Guy*:

> that's a different genre, that's the dream come true show and that's something this show isn't. You don't get the cash prize, you don't get the dream come true, you have to work hard and to take the responsibility to make this happen yourself.

Likewise, comparing the emotional pull of the newer information-based entertainment shows with older magazine-style formats, Tim Clucas notes:

> They work in a completely different way to shows like *Honey*. *Honey* is an example of a show where you have to take someone through the very painful steps to get the result. And to some extent the entertainment is in watching the journey. The show wouldn't work if you said here's how your kids will look at 40, here's how you can change that, we'll come back in 6 months and see how you've gone. What you want to see is the children throwing the vegetables at the mum and dad, you want to see the pain in the parents' faces when they have to tell the kids to turn the telly off and go to bed 'but mum we never go to bed at this time', tantrum ensues …

> So it's a very different scenario from magazine shows where you're not going on a journey, you're in your armchair—you're not feeling any emotion when you're watching those shows. With *Honey* you cannot help feel something when you watch the show. You cannot help but think 'what did I put in the kids lunchbox yesterday?' So they're completely different experiences and our audience [Network Ten's 16–39 demographic] demands to be involved … They feel emotionally invested in the show. They want to see how it turns out for the family.

'It's quite an Australian show': Indigenizing international formats

Given the emphasis placed by the production team on the role of the audience, one important question that arises with formats, including *Honey*, that are sold on to international markets is how they fare in different national contexts. While Australian television audiences are adept at interpreting and assimilating British and US programming, social observational formats such as *Honey* would seem to exhibit a good deal of national specificity in terms of their everyday, domestic concerns and the kinds of 'ordinary' people who populate these shows (Bonner 2005: 37).

Given the importance of audience identification (and in particular of appealing to the 'average Australian') highlighted by the production staff in relation to *Honey*, featuring Australian families on the show was obviously crucial, as was tying the families' health, behavioural, and relationship issues to Australian concerns through the use of national health statistics (as well as running a Parenting Survey in parallel with the show). In terms of translating and localizing imported formats such as *Honey*, a number of interviewees pointed to the fact that Australian audiences have been raised on a rather different diet of informational/lifestyle TV. As Peter Abbott comments in relation to questions of national specificity: 'I don't think anyone's gone as mad on magazine shows as we [Australians] have, and probably no one's gone as mad on ob-doc "construct" TV as the UK has.'

Linked to these differences in generic traditions, a number of interviewees also pointed to the rather different ways in which British and Australian observational formats cast and portray the 'members of the public' that feature on these shows. While shows such as *Wife Swap* were often cited as sophisticated and groundbreaking examples of the genre, in general the perspective was that British observational TV tends to be more concerned with playing on class differences and focusing on what one interviewee described as 'extreme characters':

> That's why a lot of this stuff doesn't translate, a lot of the drama of UK TV is underpinned by class struggle or, for me, a disconnect between the viewer and the people on the show. There's a lot more 'oh these are people you can laugh at 'cos they're not like us'. There's a certain meanness in that to me. (Peter Abbott)

In contrast, most of the production team argued that Australian audiences are more interested in seeing people like themselves on television, in being shown images of 'average' Aussie families or at least what they imagine average families to be:

> To show really poverty line families is so out of the Australian way of thinking. It does exist but it's not something we identify with … Even though we've got elements of that [British class difference] and you could paint a similar picture. We don't recognize it. (Matt Scully)

While Tim Clucas notes that audiences no doubt derive some pleasure from seeing other families in chaos and therefore 'feeling better about themselves as parents', in general his and others' comments were about the sense in which Australian versions of 'reality' work more on the level of audience identification than through humiliating the people featured in these shows. All in all, they were largely of the view that conflict was less central to the dramatic narrative of

Australian reality programming than to US and UK versions. As one member of the production team commented about the *Honey* format:

> In a way I think it's quite an Australian show. It doesn't end up victimizing people and it has a happy ending, which I think Australians want to see. They want some positive element—it's like on Australian *Big Brother* where the nasty housemates always get voted out first—whereas in other countries that doesn't happen.

'Education by stealth': Lifestyle TV and teaching the audience

While there has been much commentary in the UK on the decline of the educational genres (in particular 'serious' social documentary) traditionally associated with public service models of television, as I have been discussing in this book, there has also been growing interest in the pedagogical and governmental role of new factual formats such as makeover and lifestyle shows. With its focus on national health statistics and concerns such as childhood obesity and its raising of questions of social responsibility in relation to personal health, *Honey* clearly taps into a wider public educational agenda, although in a way that I would argue tends to overly reduce such concerns to the level of the privatized self. As neoliberal governments focus increasingly on devolving responsibility for issues such as health to the individual and the family, television has come to play a growing role in teaching us how to 'conduct ourselves in the diverse spheres of our lives', that is, in steering the population towards becoming 'good' citizens (Palmer 2003: 1).

When I discussed these issues with the production team, many commented on the way in which shows such as *Honey* seem to be filling a gap in the public's knowledge and expressed surprise at the lack of 'life skills' exhibited by the people shown on similar reality formats. Noting the range and type of health and relationship advice provided on *Honey*, one person commented, for instance: 'It's funny as the lessons on the show are all easy to achieve, it's all very basic lifestyle stuff ... it's a real comment on where people are at if they don't even know how to construct a good meal'.

Also noting this gap in people's life skills, Anne offers a broader take on the appeal of shows like *Honey*:

> It fills that human need to be disciplined, a lot of families they lap it all up straight away. And you think why can't you do this of your own accord? Maybe because we're all so institutionalized from a young age, we need teachers ... television's taking up that role of the educator, the disciplinarian.

While shows like *Honey* can be seen as playing a role as educator, they are certainly a far cry from traditional educational television or indeed the usual mode of infotainment fare popular on Australian TV screens. As Susie Jones, science associate producer, notes, what distinguishes *Honey* from traditional educational or informational formats is that

> [p]eople who wouldn't sit down to watch a documentary on health might sit down to watch this. Perhaps it's not as thorough or informative but you do get an education without even noticing it. Like the ABC's 'arts by stealth' [the official policy of former ABC TV head Sandra Levy]—so it's almost education by stealth I guess.

While *Honey* does have a clear didactic element with the health and relationship advice and strategies offered to the families also being directed to the audience (via pop-up fact screens, voiceover commentary, and more interactive modes such as the parenting survey and the show's website), for the production team much of the show's effectiveness comes from this ability to 'smuggle' educational concerns into a largely entertainment-oriented format. The show's emphasis on drama and emotionality, for instance, can be seen to play an important if submerged educational role, with the docu-soap elements of the show educating the public about not only everyday life skills but also moral and social issues around self-worth, sociability, and mutual respect. As one member of the production team commented, 'The real feel-good element of the show is not so much teaching the kids not to eat badly but seeing the families treat each other with more respect … that's the real clincher of the show.'

The other way in which *Honey* packages its educational message in entertainment terms is through its use of conventions taken from the makeover format. Each week the show sees a family transformed following the 'problem, intervention, resolution' narrative central to the makeover. While the drama of the show changes each week as we get to meet a new family with a new set of 'issues', the narrative structure is highly repetitive and structured in ways that reinforce the educational elements of the show. As series producer Matt Scully argues in relation to the rules given to the family by Anne each week (which are also signalled to the audience via pop-up graphic images):

> The rules that are applied are quite repetitive because the nature of the show in my opinion is that it's repetitive learning for the audience, they'll get that message. There's some variety in there as well but there are certain rules that come up over and over again—healthy food, structured exercise, structured activity, mum and dad time, things like that that people may be forgetting is part of a balanced family life.

Perhaps one of the more powerful as well as problematic elements of the show is its use of the morphed images of the children showing their projected potential future at age 40 given their current health profiles. This has not surprisingly been one of the more controversial aspects of the *Honey* format, with critics expressing concern at the show's claims to predict future appearance, including such subjective elements as hairstyle and emotional expression (while the morphs do also have an unfortunate generic resemblance to criminal mug shots). The use of images of visual transformation here obviously draws strongly on the conventions of more traditional makeover shows. In particular, the morph resembles the pivotal moment of the 'reveal' in terms of its shock value and seemingly 'magical' quality, although of course in *Honey* the morph is shown at the outset of the show, with the (it is hoped) positive transformation revealed at the climax.

Discussing the morphs with members of the production team revealed some mixed feelings about the use of this strategy given uncertainty about just how 'factual' any such imagery might be and the potential impact on the children concerned if they were to subsequently see the images on TV (much effort is made to ensure they do not see them during the shoot). At the same time, the morphs were seen as being particularly effective at grabbing the attention of viewers and switching them on to the show's health message:

> A show like this needs something a little bit sensational for the average mainstream audience. It would be a bit dry without it. It would turn more into a standard documentary. It offers the kind of wow factor that these shows seem to need. (Susie Jones)

In relation to the potency of the morphed images, a number of interviewees talked about the broadly educational potential of televisual 'messages':

> No other medium does it better than TV. TV can call people to action better than any other medium. I think a lot of health professionals—Good Health Solutions included— recognize that for the sensitive issues of ethics and duty of care associated with the show—if we can be careful about those things then the powerful message that goes out has the opportunity to motivate an awful lot of people. (Matt Scully)

And, as Matt Scully goes on to note, this potential educational impact is heightened in reality formats:

> It's a combination of the way people learn, there's audible learning, there's visual learning. Television combines those different forms of receiving information and it has a compounding effect, much more impact than just reading or just listening. Build into that the emotional and you've got a very powerful communicating tool.

'You need an informed host ... rather than just a face': The role of the expert–presenter

Central to the educational dimension of *Honey* is the role of Anne Purcell, who both fronts the show and acts as the show's main expert, observing the families in their homes and providing them with feedback and advice in the White Room space of the studio. Anne's role as a host *and* an expert reflects some of the tensions around a show such as *Honey*, which, although it is primarily concerned with entertaining the audience, is also playing a public educational role in the areas of child health and development and modelling 'good' family dynamics. Linked to this recognition of the potential impact of the show's 'message', a central theme emerging from the interview participants was the role played by Anne (as well as the experts from Good Health Solutions) in providing the show with legitimacy and accuracy. As executive producer Peter Abbott put it, 'If we are going to get up and preach (although I hate the word preach) let's make sure that whoever we've got has the intellectual credibility to be able to speak with authority.'

While Anne's knowledge and authority as a child development specialist were obviously important to the show in relation to her ability to provide expert assessment, management strategies, and counselling to the families involved, her extensive credentials as a child development specialist were seen in many ways as having more relevance to potentially hostile media critics than to the audience at large, as the following comments suggest:

> It will be interesting to see how the public react to Anne as she isn't a TV character. She is the real deal as opposed to on a show like *You Are What You Eat*, where I don't think the presenter has qualifications. In the end though the expert's credentials are more important for the media than the audience because if the media has a bone to pick with you that's where they will look. (Member of production team)

> I fear it's easy to sell expertise to the audience. If you say this is a fashion expert, I don't think people examine that that closely. I think the media will look more closely and try to undermine the expertise if there's something there to undermine. (Matt Scully)

As I've noted in relation to lifestyle TV, authority and credibility are not necessarily tied to traditional notions of expertise but are increasingly linked to the ordinary and the everyday. Peter Abbott, for instance, notes the decline of expert authority more broadly:

> Talking socially and not just in terms of TV I think authority and expertise have largely become commodified. I mean do we believe in any of our politicians any more? Do we believe in reporters as much as we did? Do we believe in the newsreader as much as we did? No. Isn't that part of postmodernism? I think we've deconstructed all that. They're just one of us really.

Credibility for TV audiences, then, is as likely to be linked to issues such as life experience as it is to more formal credentials. For instance, as Abbott notes about AJ, the host of the Australian version of *The Biggest Loser*, 'her qualifications are that she's lost a lot of weight herself, which gives her a level of personal credibility with the contestants and perhaps with the audience'.

Likewise, Matt Scully notes that part of Anne's credibility on *Honey* is the fact that she is a mother and we can 'introduce her as Anne Purcell, child development specialist and mother of two'. She is accordingly able to present herself as both an expert and as an ordinary person with 'real-life' experience.

Even though she is a credentialed expert, a central part of Anne's credibility also lies in her ability to *perform* the authoritative role of the expert. As Matt Scully notes, 'It's almost like they have got to play the character part of the expert as well.' While she may represent someone the audience can relate to as an attractive TV personality and a mother,

> Anne's persona is pretty imposing, she's not a person that you'd just go up and give a hug … and I think you need that kind of persona because we are setting rules. She's different from the Fab Five [on *Queer Eye*] because they take on almost a buddy role whereas she's more schoolmistressy … I think we are very much working off the BBC model. Anne does portray a similar character to Kris Murrin, who has a kind of tough but fair approach, and then comes across as a bit gentle at the end. (Susie Jones)

While she performs the somewhat cool and distanced persona of the traditional expert, what marks Anne out from most talking heads on TV is that, like the other lifestyle experts discussed in this book, she represents a kind of hybridized figure blending expertise with the facilitatory role of host–personality. As Susie Jones puts it:

> It is a new breed of hosts. Obviously previously in documentaries you had experts being interviewed but that was in a very dry, piece to camera way. This is a good way of making it more digestible for people … There is a growing trend towards these people being pulled from their areas into TV. I think it's probably a good thing for the industry. I find the role of a TV host who's nothing more than a pretty talking face a bit frustrating so I like having people with actual knowledge on TV rather than just actors. I think the more you can have the actual face of the show informed the better. It makes it a bit more genuine I think.

In her role as the 'face of the show', Anne expressed some surprise, however, at how much input she ended up having:

> I think it's a question of power and I had no idea about the power that the host might hold. When I first started I thought I'd be handed a script and maybe an auto cue and I would be a talking head. As time's gone on I've understood how much they're relying on me and how much of an influence I have.

At the same time, she points out the big difference between her power as the expert and host versus the power of the show's producers. While she has some input into shaping the show's content, as she notes:

I don't know how much of my input will end up on the cutting room floor … what I see as therapeutically beneficial may not necessarily be what the network sees as ratings material … if there was to be a next series I would find it beneficial for me, as the host, to be a part of the editing process because I think that's where the story unfolds and you can have a say in what ends up on the floor and what ends up in a take.

'Television's a team sport': Negotiating expertise within the lifestyle format

The hybrid figure of the host–expert is one way in which the lifestyle format attempts to negotiate the tension between its educational claims and its role as entertaining TV. In the interviews I conducted with Anne and the production team, there was much commentary on the way in which these issues were negotiated behind the scenes in the day-to-day production of the show. While Anne represents the main public face of the show's claims to educational and expert legitimacy, clearly the populist format of the show and the industrial and formal constraints of television mean that the form and content of the educational messages promoted and the kinds of processes and strategies developed for dealing with the families' health and relationship issues could not simply be dictated by Anne and the experts at Good Health Solutions. At the same time, the experts used on *Honey* were not just there to provide the show with a veneer of legitimacy without having any input into its content or development. From the interviews I conducted with Anne and the production team, and through observing the script meetings between Anne and members of the team and the White Room shoots, it was evident that the show's educational 'message' was produced through considerable dialogue between Anne and the production team. There was also substantial input from the experts from Good Health Solutions not only at the assessment phase but also in terms of script development. Peter Abbott notes, for instance: 'Good Health Solutions said we'd like to approve the script and I said no it's worse than that. I want you to look at the show and tell me that you're comfortable with everything we're saying.' As Susie Jones describes the relationship:

There is an ongoing connection with GHS. As we come up with rules, if there's something we're uncertain about we'll ring for advice so it's an ongoing consultancy but as we get more confident it gets less and less. Specifically when there are kids and families who are problematic—I'm sure we'll be checking how best to deal with the [X] family. And this is where having a host who's informed is a real aid too because she knows the family—she's been dealing with them and she can advise us.

This process of consultation with the experts involved a continual process of translation—in terms of making their advice and suggested strategies fit within the logic of television and also translating expert knowledge into laypersons' terms. As Matt Scully's comment illustrates:

> We get the GHS people to assess the family and give us a whole raft of advice that's targeted at the level of this program. So it's not prescribing drugs … it's at a much simpler level. Say, it would be great for dad to spend some time with his son doing a physical activity. In terms of my input into it, I think, rock climbing is good because there's a level of trust. So I'm applying my level of logic to it and checking it with our host who is a child development specialist and checking it with the medical experts. OK you recommended this so we're going to do it like that because we reckon its good TV, its colourful—what do you think?

Anne also foregrounded the important role of translation in working on *Honey*, discussing some of the tensions involved in balancing her role as expert advisor with the show's more populist aspirations. She commented, for instance, on her concerns regarding her peers' potential negative reaction to aspects of *Honey* such as the use of morphing technology and 'sensationalist' statements made on the UK version of the show such as 'Kris Murrin [the show's equivalent of Anne] has the power to see into the future'. At the same time, she notes that she was committed to making complex ideas available to the public. As she comments:

> On the show they've said things like 'don't use such big words'. You could call that dumbing down and that was my initial knee jerk reaction but at the same time this is about making information accessible, palatable, because this is not just everyman but every child, 11 yr olds, etc. How do you get to a market that wide without talking a common language? So for me the issue is how to take my education in this area and make that concise enough to disseminate it to that wide target audience … it's a challenge.

'We have a duty of care': The ethics of observational TV

In discussing the way in which popular factual TV shows are increasingly attempting to educate people about 'the society in which they live' (Bignell 2005: 49) at the same time as entertaining them, Bignell notes '[t]he tensions that can arise in this hybrid form with hybrid aims' (50). A central concern on social observational formats such as *Honey* is how these productions balance a focus on ratings with their (in this case therapeutic) responsibility to the unpaid non-actors who have volunteered to be on the show. While media coverage of reality TV often tends to foreground its lack of ethics, Hill (2005: 132–133), discussing the way in which lifestyle TV encourages viewers 'to learn about an ethics of care', argues that broad ethical considerations 'are at the heart of reality programming'.

On *Honey*, issues around the ethics of representing the private lives and concerns of the families on the show in particular were continually raised not just during my interviews with the production team but also during script meetings and shoots. Both Anne and the team regularly debated questions about what aspects of the families' lives were appropriate to show to the audience, while as Anne notes above there was also concern with making sure that the show's interventions not only resulted in good dramatic televisual narratives but were also 'therapeutically beneficial'.

In my interviews with the production team a wide range of ethical concerns were raised, particularly with respect to the impact of reality formats on the people who take part in these shows. While *Honey* was viewed as a potentially beneficial show, for instance, people generally expressed surprise at the public's willingness to be on reality TV:

> Given how savvy people are about reality and lifestyle shows—I mean there's no one now who can't know what happens—I find it amazing that people still actually want to go on TV. I'm intrigued by the psychology of why they do it. Particularly something like *Extreme Makeover*, to go through that in public! (Susie Jones)

In discussing their concerns about the potential impact of the reality format, as I've noted a number of my interviewees used the term 'duty of care' to describe their sense of moral responsibility to the families on *Honey*. This consciousness of a duty of care was discussed, for instance, in relation to the recruitment process. While they were seeking families who would 'make good TV', they were also concerned with the potential negative effects on certain families. As Matt Scully notes:

> We had a number of families who we thought would be good but we thought let's get some independent advice. For instance, if we were concerned about a little boy we'd ask our medical advisers to go out and interview this family and tell us if we would be endangering his well-being by putting him on the show.

As discussed above, they were also reluctant to cast families whose primary concern seemed to be celebrity rather than health:

> In some senses they're very keen to be on television and that is not the motivation we want. The motivation has to be the love of their kids and desire to do something for them, that's really the criteria we were after. (Matt Scully)

While the families who took part in the show had been assessed as being 'robust enough' to withstand the effects of being in the public gaze, there was still considerable ambivalence about the process of publicizing people's private lives and problems. Thus, while they all felt the show had significant benefits for both the families involved and the public, there were still ongoing concerns about the ethics of using certain families, and in particular children, as examples of poor health and parenting, as the following two comments illustrate:

[With this] format there are no bells and whistles, prize money and razzle dazzle. It is genuinely concerned with improving people's self-esteem. Where on *The Biggest Loser* people end up losing weight but along the way everyone is completely humiliated for entertainment value. The down side of this show though is there will be some of that. People will watch and think oh my God their diet is horrendous or look at their parenting skills. (Member of production team)

I think this show has a great message and I hope that it will be largely a much more positive thing than a negative thing but I do worry about the effect it will have on the kids in the show. Hopefully it will be one of those experiences that you don't enjoy at the time but does bring about positive changes. The people who watch it get educated through being drip fed information via entertainment. But being one of the children, to be held up as an example, the ramifications of being on TV. I do worry about that … but I hope it will do more good than it does bad. (Susie Jones)

Learning from lifestyle television

In their introduction to the edited collection *Reality TV: Remaking Television Culture*, Murray and Ouellette make a distinction between unscripted reality-oriented programming and its concern with 'dramatic uncertainty, voyeurism and popular pleasure' and traditional information formats, such as news and documentaries, 'whose truth claims are explicitly tied to the residual goals and understandings of the classic public service tradition' (2004: 2–3). While some reality programming may have educational elements, they argue that in celebrating 'the real as a selling point, reality TV distances itself from the deliberation of veracity and the ethical concerns over human subjects that characterize documentary programming in its idealized modernist form' (3).

Obviously, reality and infotainment formats do represent a dramatic shift away from the serious, dry social documentary or educational formats associated particularly with traditional conceptions of public broadcasting. At the same time, I would argue that the rise of educational lifestyle formats such as *Honey* complicates the opposition between what Murray and Ouellette call 'sanctioned information formats' and new forms of popular factual programming (2–3). As I have outlined here, *Honey* is one of a range of shows that have come out of the UK in particular that have been concerned with educating the public about child health and behaviour issues and that are part of a broader rise in popular factual programming. While these shows are typically populist in focus and aimed at as wide a demographic as possible, they also tap into a public service tradition of social observation and education, albeit in *Honey*'s case adopting a rather paternalistic mode of address. What marks these shows out as particularly interesting, then, is the way in which they continually breach the boundaries between the traditional domains of serious, bourgeois 'quality' television and the ratings-oriented realm of commercial TV with its focus on 'popular pleasures'.

As I have noted, in negotiating these shifts between commercial concerns and 'the public interest' and in taking on an increasingly governmental role, popular factual formats raise a number of ethical issues. However, rather than being distanced from 'the ethical concerns over human subjects' that underpin public service TV, as my discussion of *Honey* suggests these issues are at the fore not just of public debate and media criticism but also in the minds of those in the 'front line' of TV production. Part of my concern with discussing these issues in relation to *Honey* is to suggest that rather than dismissing reality TV as commercial, populist, and therefore somehow an ethics-free zone we need to develop a more nuanced and multi-factorial understanding of television that goes beyond class-riven oppositions between 'quality' and mass programming (Holmes and Jermyn 2004: 8–10).

Finally, I was also, of course, particularly interested in the specifics of the role played by experts and expert knowledge on a show such as *Honey*, a format in which the central host–expert exhibits a considerably more authoritative mode of expertise than the more personality-driven lifestyle experts discussed in this book. What was particularly interesting about this in relation to *Honey* was the degree to which the professional knowledge, authority, and status of experts was drawn upon in shaping the content and approach of the show—while keeping in mind Anne's caveat that the ultimate power here lay in the hands of the producers. What was also particularly apparent in observing the making of *Honey* was the way in which the translation and popularization of expertise was a collective process, framed by industrial and televisual concerns and filtered through the experiences and cultural values of the production team. The notion, central to his book, of the lifestyle expert as a mediator of middle class taste and values, then, might be usefully expanded here in recognition of the role played by media personnel in TV and other lifestyle media as often hidden but no less potent 'cultural intermediaries'.

Notes

1   In the UK version, the host, Kris Murrin, was billed as a 'child psychology expert', and the host–expert on the US version was a nutritionist, Dr Lisa Hark.

2   At the time of writing, a second series was being aired in the UK on BBC 3.

3   From now on referred to as *Honey*.

4   Frost creates official 'timeout' spaces within the homes she visits, designating them the 'naughty room' or the 'naughty step'.

5   Both the UK and US versions have been aired to high ratings in Australia, and local versions of the format have also been produced in Germany, France, Argentina, and Brazil.

6   This focus mirrored that of the Labour government in the UK, which over recent years has laid out a range of plans to deal with 'social exclusion' and 'anti-social behaviour' through targeting parents and families in 'at-risk' communities. One initiative involved a plan to send an army of 'supernannies' to help parents living in deprived areas with 'problem kids', an approach that has earned the government the title of the 'supernanny state' (Weaver 2006).

7   A book advertising itself as 'the complete guide to fatherhood' was also published out of the show.

8   The BBC's broader social pedagogical concerns here are reflected in their parenting website, which features links to all their parenting shows, with each programme's website often offering expert advice related to the issues dealt with on the show concerned (as in the link to Tanya's Top Tips on the *Little Angels* site). The website also features links to external government websites as well as links to their own BBC-authored websites, with information on issues such as becoming a step-parent and tips for encouraging children to play outdoors. Under the heading 'talk', it also links to an online chat space for parenting issues, just one of a number of the BBC's 'lifestyle message boards' where people can 'swap advice'.

9   As are earlier versions of reality TV, such as the very popular 'real-life' soap *Sylvania Waters*, first aired in the early 1990s.

10   Although SBS, Australia's 'multicultural' channel, which is also known for producing public educational television alongside more niche and cutting-edge programming, has aired some rather left-field reality lifestyle formats. Most recently, for instance, they showed a two-part series called *The Lifestyle Experts*, which was unusual in its focus both on the families and individuals being coached and on the lives of the lifestyle experts themselves as well as a rather more critically reflexive take on 'the makeover' experience. SBS also ran a popular spoof of magazine-style shows called *Life Support*, which featured various experts offering highly dubious forms of lifestyle advice, and has recently aired an educational lifestyle show complete with 'eco coach' called *Eco House Challenge*.

11   In OzTAM's ratings for the *Honey* premiere the show won the largest percentage of viewers (38.8%) out of the commercial channels in the 16–39 age group in its timeslot (against Channel Seven's magazine-style science show *Beyond Tomorrow* with 38.1% viewer share and local drama *McLeod's Daughters* with 23.1%) (sourced from Network Ten).

12   While Freehand was given a degree of freedom to 'indigenize' the format, they regularly made contact with the BBC to get advice at different points of the show's production, and at one point a BBC representative visited Freehand to check on their compliance with the format.

13   The interviews were semi-structured, addressing a range of issues, including how questions of genre and genre-crossing frame the production of specific formats; the role of the audience in these new formats; how TV personnel conceptualize and negotiate the educational, ethical, and social issues raised by social observational formats; what role experts and expert knowledge play in such formats; and how expert and educational concerns are brought together with the aesthetic concerns, narrative conventions, and populist imperatives of commercial TV.

14   The diversity of this work experience (as well as working overseas, most production staff had worked across public and commercial broadcasting) is no doubt partly due to a deregulated work environment in which members of production teams are increasingly freelance workers who are contracted for varying (often very short) periods of time depending on their job title.

15   In relation to specific programmes, their involvement has ranged from the groundbreaking science and technology show *Beyond 2000* (which debuted on the ABC in 1981 as *Towards 2000* with Peter Abbott as executive producer) to later infotainment and 'lifestyled' formats in the 1990s such as *The Great Outdoors* (1992), *Better Homes and Gardens* (1995), *Sex* (1991), and *Money* (1993), the latter two shows being produced by Clucas.

16   Although clearly issues of format and mode of address are interlinked.

Chapter 5

DIY lifestyles?
Health, lifestyle media, and the reflexive consumer

In examining the contemporary role and status of popular expertise and lifestyle media, this book has adopted a range of approaches, from mapping a history of print-based lifestyle advice to discussing the part played by TV producers in shaping the values and concerns of educational lifestyle programming. What has been missing so far is an examination of the ways in which audiences make use of and negotiate lifestyle media and expertise. A central theme in this book is the way in which knowledge and expertise have become relatively democratized, with consumption-based models of agency in particular emphasizing the role of 'laypeople' not only as informed consumers but as 'experts' in their own right. One area where this process has been particularly marked is in the area of health.

This chapter discusses how young people use the internet to access health-related material. In looking at the experiences of young internet users, I am interested in examining a range of commonsense assumptions surrounding advice-based media today concerning processes of media consumption and, in particular, the notion that media users can be 'empowered' through information, access, and choice. I want to complicate individualistic conceptions of lifestyle consumption and choice by highlighting the ways in which 'traditional' questions of social identity (in particular class) continue to play an important role in shaping people's experiences and perceptions of health and self-care.

At the same time, I want to discuss the specific role of health within lifestyle discourse, in particular its relationship to self-governing or DIY models of citizenship. Health figures in this chapter, then, both as a site of information and consumer choice around discourses concerned with the body and personal well-being and as a broader marker of the growing focus on individual lifestyle choice as a site of moral responsibility to nation and community. I want to set to scene for a discussion of online health consumption by mapping some of the wider shifts in the social meanings of health and lifestyle and briefly noting some recent trends within popular lifestyle media in relation to health and fitness.

Lifestyling health

Health clearly is a central feature of contemporary lifestyle media and culture. From magazine shows to lifestyle makeovers, today's lifestyle experts are as concerned with questions of the body, the psyche, and the soul as they are with fashion, home furnishings, travel, and other more overtly consumerist pursuits. Indeed, it is increasingly hard to distinguish between medical and health and fitness advice and other lifestyle-oriented information from beauty, grooming, and bodily maintenance to advice on 'balancing' work, home life, and relationships. While traditionally in medical and public health circles the term 'lifestyle' has been rather narrowly associated with people's habits and behaviours in relation to diet, exercise, and other 'lifestyle factors' such as smoking, the realm of popular expertise now tends to operate within an 'expanded concept of health' in which health concerns are seen to converge with broader issues of social identity (O'Brien 1995). In particular, the term 'lifestyle' here marks a shift whereby questions of health and well-being increasingly overlap with a broader 'stylization of life' (Featherstone 1991: 86).

Dovetailing with this stylization of everyday life has been a growing emphasis on health and lifestyle as questions of individual consumer choice. Despite evidence that people's lifestyles continue to be strongly determined by social position (Chaney 1996; Skeggs 2002; Tomlinson 2003), this individualized conception of lifestyle as a site where ordinary citizens can exercise choice and control not only circulates as a dominant discourse within consumer culture but also now plays an increasingly dominant role within neoliberal government policy, particularly in the area of public health and health promotion (Lupton 1995; Petersen 1997; Higgs 1998).

Supporting Beck and Giddens' arguments concerning the growing role within late modernity of 'reflexive' rather than traditional modes of identity, public health and health promotion have increasingly refigured health issues in DIY terms, with individuals being seen as constructing and managing their own 'health biographies'. The price to pay for the 'new public health' is that its rights and 'freedoms' around lifestyle come with a set of personal duties and responsibilities (Petersen 1997). The contemporary understanding of lifestyle and its merger with consumption practices is not just about the stylization of health, then, but also involves a growing focus on the *ethical* dimensions of consumer–citizenship (Lupton 1995). If lifestyle discourse in the 1980s and 1990s could be broadly characterized as emphasizing postmodern 'play' and self-styling, what marks out contemporary lifestyle culture is a growing focus on the way in which identity choices and individual biographies are linked to moral questions around citizenship and responsibility to family, community, and nation. And this is nowhere more apparent than in the realm of personal health.

Healthy, Wealthy and Wise:[1] Health advice in the media

In the context of the shift to an increasingly devolved welfare state marked by an intensified focus on the responsible informed consumer, the popular media is taking on a central role in both representing, mediating, and translating medical, health, and lifestyle issues for the 'lay public' and in popularizing and legitimating a kind of 'just-do-it' politics of privatized self-care around public health concerns.

Women's magazines have a long history of providing laypeople with accessible forms of health information and of linking personal and family stories and experiences around health and illness with community and national health concerns (Bonner et al. 1998). In their study of Australia's highest-selling magazine, the *Australian Women's Weekly*, Bonner et al. found that the magazine's coverage of health and well-being increased over the years 'from slight to so substantial that by the end of the 1980s researchers found that magazines were the principal source of health information for Australian women' (1998: 154), with health columns in the 1990s increasingly focused on the self rather than the family (159).

This large growth of interest in and popularization of health issues has occurred not only in the pages of women's magazines; as health has been relatively de-feminized as an issue in recent times and tied to more masculine entrepreneurial modes of personal development and investment in the self, we have also seen the growing role of health in men's magazines (Mechling 2003: 15). The rise of health as a site of individualized consumption has been accompanied by the emergence of a range of niche, lifestyle-oriented magazines dealing with everything from alternative medicine and body building to vegetarianism and yoga.

While magazines have traditionally dominated as sources of popular health advice, television has also played an important role in translating expert medical knowledge for lay audiences (Corner 1999: 118). While TV's focus on health has often been associated with information about medical breakthroughs, as featured, for instance, in science and technology shows or on TV drama (Bonner 2003: 114–115), health has also been one of the core concerns of more 'ordinary' forms of TV, from daytime chat shows to magazine-style advice programmes (98).

More recently, innovations within lifestyle TV have seen a renewed focus on health within prime time TV, marked by the emergence of a host of reality-based lifestyle makeover and observational documentary–style shows centred broadly on health concerns. Focusing on a range of health-related issues, from parenting practices and child health to diet and weight loss, medical and health expertise is framed and drawn upon in a variety of ways in these formats. Like mass-market magazines such as the *Australian Women's Weekly*, many of these new formats bring together traditional forms of expert advice and the voices and stories of laypeople, with the focus of these formats being on the emotional journeys undergone by the ordinary people featuring on the show.

These formats are marked by a range of different modes of address in terms of the way they target health issues and how they position the experts and the lay people involved in the show. While makeover shows like *Queer Eye* offer a playful, camp mode of address, undercutting the instructional role of the expert, educational lifestyle programmes such as *Honey We're Killing the Kids* are more openly didactic and expert-driven with a clearly normative public health message around childhood obesity, behavioural issues, and parental responsibility. While, like *Queer Eye*, these shows can be read as directing people to becoming responsible self-managing subjects, *Honey* is more heavy-handed in its focus on normative social identity and behaviour and its policing of the often working class participants on the show—the healthy self converges here with a strongly self-surveillant mode of subjectivity, with, as Ouellette puts it, TV playing the role of social worker (2006).

The Biggest Loser is another health-oriented makeover format, although one distinguished by a *Survivor*-style competitive game show structure where two teams of obese adults compete for prize money and status as 'the biggest loser'. While, like *Honey*, this show can be seen as addressing the contestants and the audience within a framework of self-surveillance and normative social values around health and bodily maintenance, the mode of address here is more democratized. The people on the show are once again 'on display' as markers of social deficiency or aberrance (and this is no more evident than during the often humiliating weigh-ins). However, compared with *Honey*, their voices and stories are brought much more to the fore in the narrative, taking up as much space as those of the experts (in particular the fitness coaches who 'lead' each team) and indeed often dominating and driving the narrative.[2] While, as I previously noted, the makeover format in *Honey* can be linked back to a more traditional public service documentary mode of TV, *The Biggest Loser* arguably owes its heritage to a populist tradition of talk show television where the personal confessions and emotional outbursts of ordinary people are privileged over rational 'balanced' discourse (Livingstone and Lunt 1994).

The growing focus within lifestyle media on personal health and fitness marks at once a popularization and democratization of medical and health knowledge and a reconfiguration of once public health concerns as privatized, consumer issues. Such shifts can also be seen to tie into broader neoliberal governmental approaches to health and lifestyle, with formats such as *Honey* in particular addressing audiences in terms of a discourse of individual self-governance. Shows such as *The Biggest Loser*, while certainly marked by an ethos of (competitive) individualism and a relentless focus on self-improvement, are also tied into other 'affective' logics of social connection and solidarity forged around sharing the personal experiences of ordinary people. The rise of lifestyle-oriented health expertise in the popular media, then, occurs within the context of a complex wider set of social and political concerns around health and obesity, with public health issues increasingly framed in voluntarist and individualized terms as a question of 'choice'. These concerns around personal health and self-care, however, are enacted in a range of ways within popular media sites, marked by both discourses of informed consumption and more didactic modes of expertise as well as by softer forms of governance linked to experiential modes of learning and shared identification.

Seeking health information on the internet

Alongside these more traditional forms of lifestyle media, there has been much recent discussion in the press and in particular the medical literature around the role of the internet as a growing source of health and lifestyle expertise (Jahad and Gagliardi 1998; Lindberg and Humphreys 1998; Cline and Haynes 2001; BBC 2002; Baker et al. 2003; Bee 2004). The internet would seem to represent an exemplary medium for the kind of proactive health-oriented mode of citizenship currently being championed within public health and the popular media. More than any other media technology, the internet can be seen to speak to the user as an individualized, DIY subject, providing targeted health information in the service of broader goals of self-improvement and personal life management.

Despite attempts to create a sense of dialogue with viewers/audiences (via interactive websites, viewer phone-ins, readers' letters, and so on), broadcast and print media continue to represent (to use the language of 'push' and 'pull') predominantly push modes of media. The web, in contrast, is a medium where lifestyle consumers can pull down whatever information they want whenever they want—sourcing just-in-time personalized advice about everything from diet and exercise to online spiritual guidance. While magazines and TV select and frame what health concerns are presented to their audiences, the internet appears to represent the ultimate personalized and democratized media technology, enabling users to piece together their own health and lifestyle solutions. Furthermore, the medium offers a space that moves beyond the confines of push–pull media to a greater potential for interactivity and sharing of knowledge. The content available is relatively unregulated, and while advice and expertise around health and lifestyle are dominated by commercial websites and institutional sources such as medical and government websites, for lay users and content creators the internet also provides a potential global space or 'commons' for sharing health information and experiences through personal websites, blogs, chat rooms, and so forth.

Despite this distinction between the internet and more mass-oriented modes of media, in reality the relationship between these new and old media forms is rather more converged, complementary, and co-dependent than such an account would suggest. The health information available on the web is often, for instance, one part of a broader media experience or brand package. The highly popular website www.oprah.com is a classic case in point—providing a regularly changing array of information on health and well-being for those web users who want to pursue particular topics, spruiking the contents of the current issue of *O, The Oprah Magazine*, and enabling users to interact with Oprah's TV show through viewer feedback and embedded clips of 'today's show' (allowing them to view, for instance, on the day I accessed the site, Dr Oz as 'he answers your most embarrassing questions').

What the 'Oprah experience' also points to is the limitations of talking about media use and access purely in terms of information. Health messages on many websites are presented as part of a broader approach to lifestyle, with health and medical information mixed seamlessly with advice on beauty products and healthy skin, as well as self-help expertise and pop psychology more broadly. As with TV and magazines, health- and lifestyle-related advice is often packaged in experiential terms through narratives of transformation and personal growth, addressing audiences not only as informed consumers but also as members of an emotional or affective community, making it hard to define these media experiences and exchanges in purely instrumental, informational terms.

Keeping in mind the limitations of a purely 'informational' approach to internet consumption, we can say that the web nevertheless has emerged as a major source of expertise and advice around health in recent years. There has now been a considerable amount of research conducted into laypeople's use of online health information, with much of it consisting of large quantitative surveys of US users. A recent report conducted by the Pew Internet & American Life Project, for instance, indicates that 80% of US web users had accessed information about one of the seventeen health topics listed in the Pew survey (Pew 2006), while another recent survey by the market research company Datamonitor of more than 4,500 adults in France, Germany, Italy, Spain, the United Kingdom, and the United States, found that 57 percent of respondents had consulted internet sources when looking for health information (BBC 2002).

While these large-scale quantitative surveys are useful in terms of mapping trends in internet consumption, raw statistics give little sense of the way in which people make use of the internet in their daily lives and the way in which their social identities—their beliefs, values, and life experiences—impact upon and are in turn shaped by their media consumption. I want to turn now to a research project I conducted looking at how young people use the internet for health information, which attempted to address some of these questions about media consumption. My study looked at a number of issues and themes around health consumption, but here I want to focus on two specific issues relevant to the broader concerns of this book.

First, in light of debates over the role of the informed consumer, I want to focus on questions around the democratization of health expertise and the role of audience or consumer agency. Second, and related, given the growing emphasis on health and lifestyle as sites of individual choice and responsibility, I want to examine how social identity and social location, that is, people's life opportunities, experiences, and values and beliefs, impinge on their conceptions of and approaches to managing their own health. Drawing upon Bourdieu's concept of habitus, I have coined the term 'health habitus' to examine the ways in which contemporary ideals around 'reflexive' or DIY modes of identity might not necessarily be experienced evenly or in the same manner across different social groups. What role, I ask, might the social dispositions or habitus associated with different social backgrounds play in framing young people's perceptions and experiences of health consumption?

Lifestyle choice or a bad attack of cyberchondria?

Despite the prominence of notions of informed consumption and choice in contemporary culture, public debates over media consumption are often marked by concerns about the competency and capacity of audiences. That is, the same media that address their readers as savvy DIY selves, providing them with daily advice and expertise on how to manage themselves and their lives, also regularly run panic campaigns about the potential for ordinary people to be overwhelmed by too much information or to be duped by misinformation.

It is not perhaps completely surprising that debates in the medical literature over online health consumption, despite some discussion of the role of the empowered and informed health consumer (Ferguson 2000; D'Alessandro and

Dosa 2001; Craan and Oleske 2002), have been overwhelmingly concerned with protecting users from misinformation or 'cyberquackery'. While Mullner (2002: 491–492), for instance, agrees that the internet provides consumers with 'information empowering them to make more informed and sophisticated choices', he paints a picture of the web as a potential source of risk and disease, arguing that it promotes 'unhealthy activities such as the use of illicit drugs, gambling, and risky sexual behaviour' (citing as evidence one outbreak of syphilis linked to an internet chat room!).

One of the common ways in which people's internet use is characterized, then, in both the medical literature and the wider press, is as a disease or pathology. As Reed notes (2002), during the late 1990s the US media even promulgated the notion that the population was at risk of developing a new psychological illness, 'internet addiction disorder'. Likewise many of the discussions of online health consumption have been framed by disease metaphors. For instance, an article in the *British Medical Journal* on health information on the internet used the language of contagion to ask, 'Are we witnessing the beginning of an epidemic of misinformation' (Coiera 1998: 1469), while a more recent article in the British newspaper the *Independent* subtitled 'Confessions of a cyberchondriac' labelled the current obsession with researching one's symptoms on the web as 'the internet disease' or 'printout syndrome' (Bee 2004).

In these depictions of online health consumption, the web is portrayed as a risky and potentially dangerous space. Lacking the regulatory and gate-keeping mechanisms of traditional media or the evidence base and legitimacy of the medical profession, the internet is depicted as an informational quagmire, and the layperson is characterized not as an empowered health consumer but as a potential victim, at risk of being misled by dubious forms of health advice, of being encouraged to engage in 'unhealthy behaviours' and/or of developing some kind of compulsive, health-seeking addiction.

Online health consumption: A web user's perspective

There is obviously some validity to medical and media concerns regarding the quality of the material available on the web, and in particular concerns about the need to regulate commercial interests on the web. In my research, however, I was interested in both moving beyond the discourse of 'panic' that often frames accounts of audiences in relation to health and media and, at the same time, complicating conceptions of audiences that overemphasize 'informed' and 'empowered' models of consumption. My concern was to offer a more nuanced picture of online health consumption that was grounded in empirical research on people's everyday use, perceptions, and beliefs surrounding web-based health advice and expertise, and that in turn linked questions of media use to social identity and 'health habitus'.

From mid-2003 to mid-2004 I conducted in-depth, one-on-one interviews with nineteen young people aged between 17 and 25. To incorporate contrasting social backgrounds into the study, I drew roughly half of my sample from the University of Melbourne undergraduate student population and the other half from a city branch of the Melbourne Citymission.[3] The interviews focused on a number of topics both in relation to the use of the internet for accessing health and lifestyle advice and around personal health more broadly; the object of the study was to capture a sense of the major discourses participants drew upon in narrativizing their approaches to health maintenance in their daily lives.

First, of course, I was interested in whether the study participants were actually using the web to find health-related material and if so what kind of information they were interested in. Despite issues of access for some of the Citymission participants, all of the interviewees described themselves as regular internet users, and most of them had looked up health information on the internet at some point (with six out of the nineteen young people describing themselves as regularly using the web for health advice). In terms of the type of health-related material they accessed, I deliberately avoided setting up a rigid definition of 'health' and instead was interested in what the study participants included under this broad umbrella term. The wide range of answers they gave indicated a variety of definitions, from more narrowly medical understandings to much broader 'lifestyle' approaches to health. The types of medical information participants had accessed included everything from treatments for diseases such as hepatitis C and checking out the potential side effects of medications to looking up symptoms and differential diagnoses before going to the doctor.

Contradicting the image of the cyberchondriac obsessed with disease, however, many of the young people looked up types of health material that could be seen as part of a broader concern with 'lifestyle' issues, well-being, and illness prevention. These included everything from seeking advice on body building, to looking up the benefits of vitamins and finding healthy vegetarian recipes, to checking out the potential health risks of body modification (e.g., tattooing and piercing). While the notion of health information discussed in the medical literature tends to see health as something that can be divided off from other aspects of everyday life, for many of the study participants it was hard to separate out knowledge about health issues from their broader everyday lives. Thus, for instance, one boy talked about his investment in martial arts not just as a sport but as a way of life, with health issues such as choosing to be vegetarian being just one aspect of this 'lifestyle choice'.

While the interviewees spoke about health issues in a variety of ways, as a broad generalization the university students by and large looked up information related to body maintenance and body image, particularly information about nutrition and exercise. There was also a marked gender difference among the university students, with girls tending to look up information on diet and boys tending to be more concerned with exercise. Derek, a 21-year-old education student, for instance, described using the web to access the exercise regime of his favourite Australian rules football team.

> Well actually [my concept of health] … it's more again about fitness, I've looked up. I follow Essendon in the footy and I looked up their website and they actually put up, their fitness coach puts up their pre-season, everything that they do, so I've actually printed that out to sort of look at it and try to do some of that … it was interesting to know the amount of stuff they do but also see how much I could do.

In contrast, the young people from the Citymission tended to be more concerned with becoming informed about specific medical issues such as diseases or medications. They accessed forms of information associated more narrowly with a biomedical rather than a broader preventive model of health. This response from Jane, a 17-year-old girl from the Citymission, for instance, reflected a common concern with potential disease risk—in this case blood born infectious diseases:

> Yeah I always use the internet 'cos like I've lost a few of my mates … like a lot of my mates did stupid things and ended up getting … unwanted things. Like one of my mates ended up with AIDS and died … so a few of my mates also have hep B so we were like curious so we hopped on the Net on the library and looked up all stuff on that and found out a lot of stuff 'cos the doctor wouldn't explain to us.

'You can't take it as a 100% factual':
Web users' perceptions of credibility of online health material

A central issue examined in the study was how web users perceived health information on the internet and how they conceived of themselves as online health consumers. In contrast to dominant conceptions in the press and medical literature about online health consumption, the participants in my study presented, for the most part, as fairly discriminatory users of the internet.[4] From the outset, people were sceptical about the information on the web because 'just anyone' can put their opinions out there. They rarely treated the information they found at face value but would often compare and contrast it with other material, as this quote from Daniel, a 19-year-old at the Citymission, suggests:

> [I]f I'm on the internet and say I'm looking up [X's] health products, looking up their website about a health issue I've got and they've specified this new vitamin and mineral supplement pill to take that will keep me healthier I'll do a bit of a search and see what articles there are. Both good and bad articles if there are both and just get a general feel for what other people have had to say about it.

At the same time, their approaches to web-based health material were strongly informed by prevailing community conceptions of the internet as not being a completely reliable source of information and of media audiences as potential victims of misinformation. They also tended to privilege forms of expertise associated with biomedical models of health. Thus, despite fears among the medical profession that people are likely to be duped by lay knowledges and cyberquackery, only a couple of the young people in the study actually wanted to be able to access laypeople's health experiences on the web. Most instead spoke of concerns about the legitimacy of web-based health information and expressed a desire for access to expert knowledge, which they associated with trustworthiness, factuality, and objectivity. The following comment from Rachel, a 21-year-old media and communications student, was typical: 'I think you have to be careful 'cos anyone can write stuff and put it on the internet and it'll come up in a search engine so we would have to be careful what we read and what we take to heart and follow.'

However, while respondents were largely concerned with accessing expert medical advice on the web, they didn't necessarily accept such advice uncritically—as the following comment from Luke, a 22-year-old man from the Citymission, indicates:

> There's too much broad ranging information for hep C and it's too controversial … you can read through an article on one website and then go to another website and it'll say the entirely opposite … you've got to go through like 500 sites to get a decent perspective on it … I just go through and read things up and think OK this has got this and this from here and there and this one's got some references to this site … Comparing information and trials and stuff like that.

Tellingly, while study participants saw themselves largely as cautious, sceptical users of the internet, they would often comment on their concerns about other people being able to access any health information on the web. As Paul, a 21-year-old education student who was actively into managing his own health and saw himself as a bit of a 'health expert', put it:

> I'm a little concerned about all the information on the internet about medicines and that sort of stuff 'cos people look at it and go yeah I know everything about it without consulting a doctor or a pharmacist. 'Cos people look at it and they try and self diagnose and they go to the doctor and say oh my god I have this nasty disease when they've probably got a cold.

Thus, while most of the young people in the study saw themselves as being more than capable of discriminating between different kinds of health information, in tune with the medical and press debates over online health consumption they tended to regard the wider public as potential victims of misinformation, suggesting the continuing dominance within the 'public' mind of a 'hypodermic' model of media consumption.

DIY selves?

As I've argued, more than any other media form, the internet offers the possibility of accessing highly specific, personalized, and often specialized knowledge about health issues. This mode of media consumption seems particularly attuned to DIY models of health management, although as a recent Pew survey has shown (Pew 2006), people use the web not just for self-management but also to access information for relatives and friends, a theme that also emerged in my study. As Pew's associate director, Susannah Fox, put it, 'These days, internet users bring the gift of information to a bedside, along with flowers and best wishes' (Pew 2006).

While such developments can be seen as reflecting a democratization of access to health and medical advice, the preoccupation with managing and optimizing personal health through acquiring the latest online information can also be seen as the triumph of privatized models of public health. In my study, many of the interviewees exhibited a strong awareness of discourses of health promotion, often linking their own personal health to community health issues such as obesity (a topic that had recently had a large amount of coverage in the Australian media). There was a pervasive sense of measuring oneself against a healthy ideal to which many of the young people saw themselves as not matching up. When asked whether she was healthy, Joanna, a 19-year-old female science student who described herself as looking up information on healthy eating and exercise on the internet once a week, reading regularly about health issues in magazines and newspapers, and regularly taking vitamins, commented: 'Um I don't think I'm healthy, I'm not sure but I don't think I'm healthy … Maybe I may lack some nutrition … my nutrition may be not balanced.'

It was in comparing themselves with community ideals around healthy living that clear distinctions started to form between the two groups of young people in relation to their values and perceptions of health norms and what they considered to be 'rational' health behaviour. Like Joanna, most of the university students talked about health maintenance in terms of monitoring their exercise regimes and dietary intake. Keeping slim and fit was seen not merely in terms of body image—although that was a major driver—but also as an investment in one's future health, as this comment from Diane, a 20-year-old arts student, illustrates:

> I think it's important to eat well and exercise … I've got a friend who doesn't do anything, doesn't do exercise, she's not overweight or anything so it's not a big issue now but I was reading in a magazine or a newspaper article or something that not doing exercise can equate to the same as having cancer in terms of how bad it is for your body.

Study participants at the Citymission were also generally aware of public debates around health and diet and often talked of the problems associated with junk food and the need to keep fit. However, the ways in which they defined a 'healthy' diet or what it might mean to be 'fit' often clashed with more normative community ideals. Many, for instance, described themselves as being 'fit and healthy' at the same time as they admitted to being regular smokers (one young woman who was an overweight smoker described herself as a 'health freak').

Specifying reflexivity

Central to the shift to more 'reflexive' or choice-based modes of selfhood is a growing awareness of external risks and hazards. In a discussion of risk and reflexivity, Giddens (1991) argues that people who indulge in risky behaviours despite knowing the potentially negative results of such actions are often living out the notion of lifestyle as a package of risks. For these individuals, risky behaviour is tolerable within an overall set of lifestyle choices; such risk behaviour, according to Giddens, is underpinned by a reflexive awareness that they are refusing to adapt to what might be seen as a risk-reduction lifestyle. The assumption here is that individuals are fully conscious and in control of their decision-making processes; DIY health is seen as a process of considered reflection where an array of life choices are weighed up against each other and where 'risk' is something external and objective rather than being influenced by one's social identity.

For many of the Citymission youth in my study, however, there was a lack of fit between these discourses of autonomy, choice, and control and their own personal experiences and life circumstances. By and large, these models of responsible, healthy selfhood sat rather uncomfortably with life narratives that were often marked by a sense of unmanageable risk and lack of control over both oneself and one's environment. A classic example came from Joe, an 18-year-old who had developed an eating disorder brought on by the stress of living in a very chaotic home situation. In describing his problems with eating, Joe tended to use the language of self-actualization to both narrativize and take control of his situation:

> After my 17th birthday, I mean only a year and a bit ago, I sat down and thought to myself this isn't going to be easy but I have to do something. I'm not happy with my … emotional or physical self, I've got to do something. So I did a chart—this is what I eat, this is what I don't eat, this is how much I eat.

For Joe, attempting to frame himself within the model of the self-monitoring healthy subject seemed to offer a way of managing the chaos of his life. However, Joe found himself increasingly losing control over his weight as he oscillated between bouts of overeating and periods of anorexia. Rather than empowering him to deal with a rather dire social situation, the ideal of reflexive identity contributed to an internalization of his broader social and family problems, here manifested as a pathological obsession with food intake. Within the framework of the DIY self, Joe is cast as a failed reflexive agent. Here we see the gap between the life experiences and values of the middle class subject—the specific form of social disposition or habitus that I would suggest underpins the notion of the reflexive self—and those of other social groups for whom questions of lifestyle 'choice' are framed by rather different sets of social, cultural and material contexts and constraints.

This sense of the way in which different life experiences and forms of what I have termed 'health habitus' produce distinct modes of reflexivity was particularly highlighted by the manner in which the study participants discussed questions of risk. The students, for instance, framed potential threats to their health largely in terms of preventable factors internal to their own lifestyles, such as diet and exercise. Thus while they went to doctors when they were sick, they talked about health largely in preventive non-medical terms, that is, as something intrinsic to their broader lifestyles and therefore primarily self-managed.

In contrast, the young people from the Citymission often spoke of risk in externalized terms: fear of illness, particularly infectious illness such as hepatitis C, of the effects of drug use, and of developing diseases that were 'in the family' such as diabetes featured strongly in their health narratives. The largely medical focus of their health concerns meant that 'taking control' of one's health tended to translate into a heavy reliance on doctors and other experts and support provided through state institutions. Paul, a 21-year-old man I interviewed at the Citymission, described his regime of bodily maintenance as follows: 'I go for check-ups every few months just make sure everything's alright. I generally go to the hospital, wait for a few hours … just standard blood tests, skin tests, dental check-ups … should I need it.'

Another example of this tendency to perceive (and experience) risk in external terms was the fact that, even though all of the people I interviewed at the Citymission were smokers (compared with none of the university students), smoking was never discussed as a health risk. While they were aware of anti-smoking health promotion discourse, most of the interviewees seemed to see their own smoking as an inevitable part of life rather than as something that could or should be managed or controlled.

This mode of 'self-care' is certainly very different from that of the middle class university student proactively monitoring his or her own diet and exercise regime. Both, of course, can be described as moments of consumer 'choice', but here we see an example of the way in which such notions gloss over the ongoing contribution played by social identity to shaping an individual's lifestyle 'preferences'. So while the young people from the Citymission were marked by a large degree of fatalism and/or habituation in relation to issues such as smoking and drug use, the university students by and large experienced themselves as being in control of both their health and their broader life biographies and seldom referred to external risks.

Complicating lifestyle consumption

Young people's online health consumption clearly does not fit easily into one simple explanatory model but is articulated in complex ways to questions of social identity and framed by the pressures and constraints of everyday life. Such findings suggest the limitations of voluntarist conceptions of health and lifestyle and the need to recognize the ongoing validity of Bourdieu's thesis that lifestyle, taste, and consumption continue to be closely articulated to social position (Tomlinson 2003).

Despite the shortcomings of lifestyle discourse, in some ways the notion of lifestyle enacted in personal makeover shows such as *Queer Eye for the Straight Guy*, with its emphasis on the connections between personal health and well-being and wider issues such as relationships and interpersonal communication, family dynamics, and career concerns, marks a gesture in popular culture towards a more holistic understanding of health, albeit within an individualized framework. And Jamie Oliver's more recent 'activist' turn in attempting to 'make over' UK school dinners can be seen as a step towards emphasizing not just the role of individuals and families in tackling public health issues but also the need to target schools, government, and the commercial sector.

Likewise, lifestyle media's focus on ordinary people's lives and personal narratives clearly cannot just be understood as promoting a middle class discourse of individualism; these popular media formats provide a space in which a range of people who might not normally be represented within public debates and discussions can achieve a degree of visibility, even if the terms of this visibility are framed by the concerns of more powerful media actors such as television producers.

While I have argued in this book that middle class taste and values are circulated, via the notion of lifestyle, as normative ideals against which citizens are increasingly measured, it is also important to note then the way in which health and lifestyle discourses in the media represent a contested social site where a range of definitions and meanings of 'acceptable' bodies and selves compete and where ordinary people are variously addressed and positioned as social subjects. As a source of popular pleasures and various forms of social identification and comparison, the lifestyling of health cannot be seen as producing just one mode of citizenship. My focus on questions of health habitus here aims, then, to capture the way in which, despite strongly normative pressures concerning definitions of healthy citizenship, differences in social experience and identity continue to produce a range of meanings and experiences of health and lifestyle, which are in turn reflected in the diversity of people we encounter in our everyday engagements with popular media forms.

Notes

1   *Healthy, Wealthy and Wise* was an early groundbreaking Australian magazine-style lifestyle TV show shown on Network Ten that featured a range of resident lifestyle experts including a naturopath.

2   This relative lack of hierarchy between the experts and 'the cast' is also played out in *The Biggest Loser* spin-off book, which focuses strongly on the personal experiences of, and features numerous tips and personal quotes from, the show's participants alongside advice from the various 'experts' associated with the show.

3   The University of Melbourne is a prestigious university located in an inner-urban area of the city and has traditionally drawn its student base from an educated middle class elite largely based in the affluent eastern suburbs of Melbourne. Over more recent years, this student demographic has shifted somewhat to incorporate full-fee-paying international (particularly South-East Asian) students. The Melbourne Citymission is a charitable organization that through its 'Frontyard' youth services provides help to young people who are homeless or in need of support. Given the issue of low internet access for the Citymission group, who were often either homeless or living in squats or transitional housing, I specifically recruited people to the study who were using a free internet service offered daily during the working week by the Frontyard service. The internet service was offered as a drop-in service and was completely voluntary. Young people would often come to the Citymission to use the range of services on offer, from health care and dental care to legal advice, and would also check their e-mail and surf the internet while they were there. Of the nine young people I recruited through the Citymission, five of the participants were male and four were female. All were Australian born from Anglo-European backgrounds. The Melbourne University group consisted of six females and four males. They were all full-time undergraduate students undertaking a range of majors. While four people in the group were born overseas (two were from Malaysia, one was Indonesian, and one was born in Germany), they had all lived for significant periods in Australia. The rest were Australian born and of Anglo-European ethnicity.

4   These observations were limited by what was obviously a potentially significant gap between people's perceptions and reporting of their online health consumption and their actual patterns of web use. My study sample here is also clearly not a representative one; the 2006 Pew survey, for instance, found that only 15% of users consistently check the source of online health information, a significant drop from their previous survey in 2001, although they also note that most users visit two or more websites during a search (Fox 2006).

Chapter 6

Lifestyle Inc.:
Celebrity, branding, and ordinary expertise

The 'know-business' is getting more like 'show-business.'

(Hartley 1999: 5)

Recent times have seen the rise of a small but prominent number of celebrities whose fame has emerged out of their roles as lifestyle experts. In the case of figures such as Martha Stewart, Nigella Lawson, and Jamie Oliver they have attained enough celebrity status both within their countries of origin and (to varying degrees) internationally to be known simply as Martha, Nigella, and Jamie. This 'first-name fame' has seen their lifestyle expertise in turn become thoroughly commodified and merchandized, a process most spectacularly played out through the figure of 'the human brand', Martha Stewart.

There is an extensive literature on the role of celebrities as pre-eminent cultural authorities today (Marshall 1997; Couldry 2000; Turner et al. 2000; Corner and Pels 2003; Turner 2004; Evans and Hesmondhalgh 2005), much of which also discusses the way in which other representatives of authority such as experts and intellectuals have been relatively marginalized by celebrity but have also to a certain degree become caught up in its logic. This process has seen the emergence of a range of hybridized public identities, and there has been some critical analysis of this process, including my own earlier work on celebrity intellectuals and expert–personalities on TV (Lewis 2001, 2004). While numerous scholars have turned their analytic gaze to the figure of the lifestyle expert, particularly on television, the part played by celebrity in relation to the role and status of the lifestyle guru is relatively uncharted territory.

In this final chapter I begin to explore some of this territory by bringing together a range of previously disparate literatures on intellectuals, celebrity and ordinariness, privatized citizenship, and branding. I discuss the ways in which the celebritization of expertise (via the figure of the lifestyle guru) can be seen as a marker of a growing convergence between a public sphere of commodity production and spectacle and an 'intimate' private sphere of consumption and everyday life. The increasingly central role played by branding and lifestyle consumption within the logic of popular expertise is central to my argument here; in particular, I am concerned with highlighting the mutually dependent relationship between branded celebrity experts as lifestyle role models and the consumer imaginary in a context where information, entertainment, privatized lifestyle consumption, and ethical modes of citizenship have become increasingly interconnected.

In mapping the role of the lifestyle expert in relation to these complex shifts in informational and commodity culture, the chapter is structured as follows: discussing the historical background to the rise of the celebrity expert, I first examine the growing role of media culture in flattening out and reconfiguring distinctions between expert and ordinary discourse through processes of celebritization. I then connect these processes to broader shifts around the domestication and privatization of public culture and citizenship, in turn linking the foregrounding of ordinary people's intimate lives to shifts in commodity culture and a growing emphasis on the consumption of lifestyle-related advice, goods, and services.

The second half of the chapter then turns to examine the specific role of lifestyle experts in this process, discussing (via case studies) the increasingly common phenomenon of the celebrity expert as product endorser as well as the growing role of the branded expert. Here I locate the lifestyle expert within a broader brand culture increasingly concerned with the informational dimensions of consumption. The chapter concludes with a discussion of the way in which the celebritization and branding of lifestyle expertise—that is, of modes of knowledge and ways of being that are intimately linked to the domestic lives of ordinary people—can be seen as part of a broader shift towards an informational capitalism marked by an increasing colonization of the social imaginary.

Celebrities as experts, experts as celebrities: The shifting ground of cultural authority

In this book I have talked about style and makeover gurus primarily as experts. As I've suggested, though, it is becoming increasingly difficult to make neat distinctions between the figure of the expert and other 'personalities' within the media. In this first section of the chapter I complicate the notion of expertise by discussing the growing role of celebrities as markers of cultural authority and knowledge as well as focusing on the increasing celebritization of expertise itself. Before doing so I want to set the rise of the celebrity expert within a broader socio-historical context.

Traditionally, we have thought of experts and celebrities as existing in markedly different spheres of public life and as linked to very different sets of values and logics. Like the figure of the intellectual, experts (at least in the conventional sense of expertise) are associated with high culture as well as with the modes of rational knowledge and techniques of social organization that accompanied the rise of the modern state. In contrast, celebrity is often equated with popular and consumer culture, with 'a mediatized public sphere where entertainment is privileged over information, affect over meaning' (Lewis 2001: 234).

Despite this seeming opposition, these figures are historically linked to the rise of modernity as well as to a series of tensions within modernity around questions of power, social status, and democratization. Garnham (1995) notes, for instance, that the intellectual (and the expert) has from the outset been marked by this central contradiction; while modernity has provided the basis for the democratization of knowledge, it has also historically put control of that knowledge into the hands of an elite few. Likewise, in mapping out the historical emergence of 'the public individual', Marshall (1997) associates the birth of the celebrity with the emergence of modernity and its twin discourses of capitalism and democracy. Like the figure of the expert/intellectual, the celebrity 'has come to embody the ambiguity of public forms of subjectivity under capitalism' (Marshall 1997: 4). That is, while celebrity is marked by privilege, at the same time 'celebrity status invokes the message of possibility of a democratic age' (6).

In representing two rather different types of cultural authority, the expert and the celebrity are both nevertheless characterized by a similar tension between a claim to exceptional or elite status and a kind of public representativeness. However, while the public sphere has classically been the site where experts and intellectuals have reigned, the processes of populist 'democratization' and mediatization that have accompanied its growing commercialization have seen the authority of traditional experts become relatively weakened as more fashionable figures of authority such as the celebrity take centre stage.

One way in which Frith and Savage (1998) contextualize the declining cultural influence of intellectuals and experts (and as a corollary the growing power of celebrities) is in relation to the increasing role of populism in the politics of the public sphere. Discussing in particular the seismic cultural shifts that took place in the UK under Thatcherism in the 1980s, they argue that popular culture became the pre-eminent site where the politics of citizenship and civic issues played out.

During this period the popular media gained power, with the press working to construct the 'people ... as a mythical site of authority' (Frith and Savage 1998: 11). This populist push saw a shift in commonsense understandings of political and cultural power and influence. As they put it, 'In broader cultural terms, the effect has been to elevate the authority of experience (valorized in much feminist and pop writing) over the authority of the intellect, and subtly to change what is meant by knowledge' (13).

While marking a very specific moment in recent UK history, the social and political shift mapped by Frith and Savage has considerable relevance to contemporary Anglo-American political and cultural life under neoliberalism. Distinctions today between the state and commercial/popular culture have become increasingly fraught as the popular media sphere and the realm of lifestyle consumption become pre-eminent sites for the rehearsal of questions of politics and citizenship. In this populist setting, traditional figures of authority and/or expertise have found themselves competing for media airtime with a range of other figures who have as much or more authority within the media sphere. Celebrities especially have become increasingly ubiquitous and influential. As figures whose logic of identity is tied to the commercial fortunes of popular media and whose popularity is often strongly linked to the biographical and the experiential, it is not surprising that celebrities have in many ways taken centre stage as the 'new popular heroes' of contemporary consumer culture (Featherstone 1995: 69).

While celebrities have arguably always played an important role in public life, what is perhaps rather different today is the way in which they can be seen to 'move between' spheres traditionally associated with fame (such as acting, modelling, and sport) and those associated with other forms of authority or expertise (such as politics). It is increasingly commonplace to see celebrities such as UK rock star Bono representing various global 'causes' and meeting with prominent leaders on the world stage or even, like Arnold Schwarzenegger, moving into the world of politics itself. Within the hyper-mediatized public sphere, the 'sign' of cultural authority can be seen to have developed a degree of equivalency and exchangeability. As Turner et al. argue in *Fame Games* (2000: 11), 'the distinction between celebrity and other kinds of social or political elite status is becoming less clear as the signs of celebrity drive out less powerful alternatives'.

If celebrities now reign supreme, where does this leave the figure of the expert in modern life? How, for instance, does this explain the growing role of popular expertise as represented by the lifestyle advice gurus discussed in this book? Bauman (1987) has famously argued that more traditional forms of 'legislative' knowledge and expertise have lost their potency in contemporary culture, while Garnham (1995: 380) suggests that 'the figure of the expert is now a deeply ambivalent one in our culture'. This does not mean, however, that experts no longer have currency today. Rather, as I have argued in this book, what we are seeing, particularly in the realm of lifestyle media, is the reconfiguration of expertise along more popular (and putatively democratic) lines.[1]

In this process the relationship between the celebrity and the expert is no longer necessarily marked by hierarchies and distinctions of experience versus rationality, popular and consumer culture versus the professional/governmental realm (although these oppositions hold some residual power for certain sectors of the population). Rather, I would suggest that there is an increasing overlap between these figures, with expertise today increasingly caught up in the logic of celebrity. This is not to suggest that experts are now just a sub-variant of the celebrity figure—the popularity of the lifestyle expert suggests that the claim to expertise still has some credibility with media audiences—but to argue that one of the ways in which the figure of the expert has been reconfigured is through a process of celebritization.

Celebritization and ordinary expertise

While many experts continue to authorize themselves through claims to distanced rationality, the growing mediatization and commercialization of everyday life has seen expertise increasingly refigured in terms of a logic of celebrity. One obvious way in which this has occurred is through the rise of expert 'personalities', such as *What Not to Wear*'s Trinny and Susannah, who now pop up on various TV shows and at media events playing the role of well-known public personalities as much as makeover gurus. This, of course, has not only occurred within the populist realm of lifestyle advice but has also affected more traditional modes of expertise. Thus, increasingly we are seeing doctors, surgeons, marine biologists, historians, public intellectuals, and academics presented along celebrity lines as embodied, charismatic personalities (Shumway 1997; Lewis 2001).

One crucial way in which expertise has borrowed from celebrity culture is paradoxically through its growing association with the ordinary. While the combined aura of celebrity and expertise enables popular experts to possess a considerable degree of authority and influence, media celebrity also involves being presented as a kind of exemplar of 'ordinariness'. As Dyer argued in his classic work on stars (1979: 39), stardom 'combines the spectacular with the everyday, the special with the ordinary'—again reflecting the tension within popular modernity around elite versus popular, democratic culture.

The realm of the ordinary, however, is associated more with television as a media form than with the film stars discussed by Dyer (Marshall 1997). As Marshall puts it, 'Whereas the film celebrity plays with aura through the construction of distance, the television celebrity is configured around conceptions of familiarity' (1997: 119). Noting Langer's argument that television produces personalities rather than stars, Marshall argues that there is an 'intense emphasis on the familiar in television' (122), which is tied in particular to its often more commonplace mode of address.

At the risk of eliding the differences between the various forms and conventions of media fame, I would argue that this more familiar televisual mode of celebrity is playing a growing role in public life more broadly. Evans and Hesmondhalgh (2005) usefully discuss this effect in terms of 'celebritization', that is, the process whereby growing numbers of public figures today, including experts, are increasingly framed in ways that make them more accessible, more media-friendly, and crucially more 'ordinary'. Politicians today, for instance, are increasingly caught up in a process whereby, through various media techniques, their 'aura of greatness and distance' is replaced by a sense of familiarity (Evans and Hesmondhalgh 2005: 45). Contemporary media forms and conventions increasingly situate political figures in such a way as to produce a sense of closeness and engagement for audiences; that is, the politician and the audience are positioned in what Horton and Wohl (1956) term a 'para-social interaction' (cited in Evans and Hesmondhalgh 2005: 44).

Television is, however, undoubtedly the pre-eminent site where this 'ordinarization' of celebrity culture has been played out, and it is no surprise that the emergence of the ordinary experts discussed in this book is particularly associated with this sphere. As Bonner argues in *Ordinary Television* (2003: 3), much of the TV schedule is populated by shows hitherto largely ignored by critics and academics, shows that attempt to replicate the routine and familiarity of everyday life through 'direct address of the audience, the incorporation of ordinary people into the programme and the mundanity of its concerns'.

Lifestyle TV and the figure of the lifestyle expert emerge out of and borrow from the codes, conventions, and concerns of ordinary television. Many lifestyle experts might be seen as personalities rather than stars: their 'celebrity' is limited and largely tied to a specific format/programme, and their role is to produce a sense of familiarity and trust for the viewing audience (Bonner 2003: 65–66). Figures such as Jamie Oliver and Martha Stewart, however, have a broader form of celebrity, one that enables them to move across a range of TV formats and other media sites (and at times move outside of their national contexts) and that also involves a foregrounding of their personal lifestyles and biographies. Despite being charismatic and at times elite figures—and, in the case of Jamie Oliver's food activism and charity work, being perceived as 'heroic'—their brand of celebrity and of expertise is first and foremost tied to the familiar and the everyday, in terms of both presentation style and content.

This growing intersection between celebrity, expertise, and the ordinary is reflected in a recent survey conducted in Britain in which people were asked which celebrity parents they would prefer to give them parenting advice (Home-Start 2006). Jamie and Jools Oliver shared first place with the married hosts of the popular daytime magazine show *Richard & Judy* as most trusted celebrity parents, with Tony and Cherie Blair coming in third (only just ahead of Ozzie and Sharon Osborne!). Both the two top celebrity couples deemed most trustworthy here could be broadly classified as lifestyle advisors. Jamie's expertise is, of course, connected to food rather than parenting, and Richard and Judy are both actors with no particular specialist knowledge in the area. Both couples, however, are themselves parents whose personal and family lives feature centrally in their role as public identities—their expertise, then, is partly experiential, linked to lifestyles that as part of their celebrity status are a familiar feature of the British media-scape (both Jamie and Richard and Judy are regularly referred to in the UK press as national icons and/or institutions). And both sets of couples represent the more accessible end of the celebrity spectrum, through a familiar 'I'm one of you' mode of address and the domestic orientation of much of their advice. Their perceived trustworthiness and authority here, then, is linked as much to their life experience (in terms of both success and failure) and media personas as to their perceived expertise. Surveys like this do not simply suggest the growing difficulty of making meaningful distinctions between celebrity and expertise today; more crucially, they point to the way in which the authority of expertise and celebrity is increasingly tied to once private and personal sets of concerns and values around the familiar and the domestic. The celebrity lifestyle expert embodies the way in which celebritization today increasingly negotiates and reworks power and identity in terms of a seemingly democratized logic of the ordinary.

Intimate citizenship and lifestyle consumption

In his discussion of television's preoccupation with representing 'the ordinary' and the 'close-to-hand', Couldry argues that 'we have reached, it seems, the opposite of the society of the spectacle' (2002: 291). The figure of the lifestyle expert in many ways can be seen as emblematic of this shift within contemporary media culture. In contrast to the processes of distancing and alienation traditionally associated with stardom and spectacle, celebrity lifestyle experts present us with images and modes of advice embedded in rather than abstracted from everyday life. Perhaps the pinnacle of this celebration of the 'anti-spectacle' are the 'storage experts' and cleaning gurus featured on lifestyle programmes such as the UK's *How Clean Is Your House?* and *Life Laundry*, where the most banal and routine aspects of domestic life are on display. But how might we understand this relentless focus on the ordinary and the anti-spectacular—via the mediating gaze of the domestic expert? What does this reification of domestic life and practices of consumption tell us about the broader politics of contemporary culture?

Here Berlant's (1997) notion of 'the intimate public sphere' offers a useful perspective on this foregrounding of domestic, familial life and its relationship to the celebritization of public culture and the growing role of ordinary expertise.

Since the rise of Reaganite politics in the United States, there has been a dramatic shift in how conceptions of the public sphere and of citizenship are imagined. Habermas, as Berlant notes, described the 18th-century spaces of intimate, domestic life as sites 'where persons produced the sense of their own private uniqueness, a sense of self which becomes a sense of citizenship only when it was abstracted and alienated in the nondomestic public sphere of liberal capitalist culture' (1997: 4–5). Life today in the United States (and in the neoliberal West more broadly) has seen a conflation of these social spaces and of the privatized self and the citizen. The centre of political life has shifted towards the private sphere, with citizenship increasingly regarded as being 'produced by personal acts and values', a process that Berlant sees as evacuating politics of social structural considerations while '[d]ownsizing citizenship to a mode of voluntarism' (5).

It is not difficult to see how the figure of the celebrity lifestyle expert might participate in this logic of privatized citizenship. As I have discussed in this book, 'lifestyle' has become an accepted, commonsense notion in contemporary culture, reflecting a broader shift to a politics of selfhood framed in strongly voluntarist and consumer-oriented terms. In a lifestyled milieu, 'big picture' social and governmental concerns are increasingly reframed as privatized, individualized issues, with people's lifestyle 'choices' foregrounded as important sites of moral responsibility. As figures who celebrate the home as a site of creative productivity where one can improve oneself and one's lifestyle through mastering the art and aesthetics of the domestic, lifestyle experts stand as particularly prominent representatives of a politics that has seen a growing articulation and overlap between the privatized realm of taste, values, and lifestyle and public conceptions of the good citizen.

Their role as paradoxically ordinary types of celebrities, as markers of anti-spectacle and familiarity, is again central here. While media coverage of figures such as Martha, Jamie, and Nigella often discusses their public lives and woes— whether the focus is on the pressure Jamie's public work puts on his relationship with Jools or the endless jokes about how Martha might decorate her cell while in prison—these concerns are invariably linked back to the domestic, to their intimate home lives and personal concerns.

Another critical element of this foregrounding of domesticity and the privatized self is the central role of consumption in constructing models of good citizenship. Just as the social is increasingly conflated with the private, familial sphere, so too 'productive' modes of citizenship are more and more discussed in terms of personal leisure and consumption, where an investment in practices of lifestyle consumption is seen as an investment in the 'enterprise' citizen–self.

In the realm of 'ordinary television', domestic and family-oriented consumption practices are often naturalized and integrated with processes of citizen formation. As Bonner puts it (2003: 105), 'The objects and services that are the content of so much of ordinary television, then, have a prime role in identity formation and its fine-tuning, but also in the production of the ordinary, civilized individual'. Lifestyle and makeover shows—in which practical modes of expertise are internalized as 'codes of conduct' (131)—are particularly central to this process. Much of ordinary television, then, works to construct lifestyle and identity in terms of an ethics of consumption where '[t]astes, practices and possessions are all seen to reveal the self' (214).

What lifestyle programming sells to the audience are not just products but ways of living and managing one's private life. Celebrity lifestyle experts take this process one step further—embodying and enacting models of consumer–citizenship through their own much publicized and idealized domestic and personal lifestyles, which are played out across their various personas as experts, celebrities, and private selves. In relation to processes of celebrity endorsement, celebrities can be seen as 'super-consumers' (McCracken 2005: 112). As McCracken puts it, 'They are exemplary figures because they are seen to have created the clear, coherent, and powerful selves that everyone seeks' (112). But just as they are markers of trust, familiarity, and stability, they are also characterized by their 'experimentation' and capacity for 'self-invention' (111–112).

Like celebrities, lifestyle experts embody both this idealized model of selfhood and the promise of mobility and transformation. Furthermore, they represent a mode of collective identity that brings together optimal forms of consumption with a kind of rationalization or informationalization of everyday life. In this next section of the chapter I examine this convergence of consumption and information culture through a discussion of the growing phenomenon of the lifestyle expert as a product endorser and a brand. I first discuss the use of celebrity lifestyle experts for product endorsement and then move on to an examination of lifestyle experts as themselves a form of brand. US domestic guru and lifestyle entrepreneur Martha Stewart—a woman whom Klein refers to as 'one of the new breed of branded humans' (1999: 2)—provides an exemplary case study, with the discussion of Stewart foregrounding questions about what it means when information and expertise start to become branded and connected with a specific human face. Is this merely an extension of celebrity endorsement, or does the branded expert represent a new development in marketing and consumer culture? In what ways is the branding of lifestyle expertise tied to a broader refiguring of information in and through the figure of the citizen–consumer?

Celebrity endorsement and expertise

The endorsement of products by celebrities is obviously not a new phenomenon. Nor is the use of the figure of the expert—from doctors advertising cigarette smoking in the United States in the 1950s—'More doctors smoke Camels than any other brand!' (Blount 2005)—to the popular 1980s adverts in Australia for Oral-B toothbrushes featuring a faceless, silent dentist, 'Rob', cleaning his teeth in his bathroom with his bare back facing the camera. What is new is the growing use of figures who are no longer generic, anonymous representatives of 'expertise' making fleeting appearances as bespectacled talking heads or nerdy figures in white coats (such figures are now more often than not used as markers of postmodern irony in contemporary adverts). Instead, the figures of expertise used in advertising are increasingly likely to be media personalities or celebrities in their own right.

In Marshall's discussion of celebrity and power, he argues that the celebrity can be seen in semiotic terms as a kind of sign or text. 'Celebrity signs represent personalities—more specifically, personalities that are given heightened cultural significance within the social world' (Marshall 1997: 57). This intensification of meaning around the celebrity sign means that figures such as Martha, Nigella, and Jamie (whether as live embodied TV images or as printed names/faces/signatures on a product) can produce an instant set of associations.

This ability to condense a range of connotations into a specific sign enables the logic of celebrity to dovetail nicely with processes of commoditization. As Turner et al. put it (2000: 12), 'Within a highly fragmented but increasingly globalised mass market, the use of celebrities has become a very efficient method of organising cultural significance around products, services and commercially available identities.' They note, however, that there are drawbacks associated with using celebrities as marketing devices. One problem is that the very success and elite status that go with their celebrity can also mark them as somehow inauthentic (particularly in relation to the often magical, labour-free way in which they are seen as gaining success), and subsequently a source of resentment (Turner et al. 2000: 13).[2]

The use of celebrities with specific skill sets to endorse related products and brands can be seen as representing an attempt by marketers to confirm the authenticity of both the celebrity and the brand—a process marketers describe in terms of 'brand synergy'. The classic case is the massively (and mutually) lucrative sponsorship deal struck between mega-celebrity basketballer Michael Jordan and Nike in 1984. As a figure who is a celebrity but whose status is tied to his or her (apparently disinterested) specialist knowledge of everyday lifestyle needs, the lifestyle personality would seem to offer a particularly potent site for brand synergy. Not surprisingly, we are seeing growing numbers of lifestyle experts putting their names and badge of expertise to various products from homewares to wine clubs.

In Australia one of the better-known lifestyle experts to move into the realm of product endorsement has been celebrity gardener Jamie Durie. Durie, who has more recently made the leap into the US media market via a regular guest slot on

The Oprah Winfrey Show, first became known to Australian broadcast TV audiences through the garden makeover show *Backyard Blitz*.[3] Subsequently hosting the hugely popular reality show *The Block* (in which contestants competed to renovate an apartment block), Durie came to the role of popular TV expert via a background both in landscape design and horticulture and in the entertainment industry as an actor and model (and most notoriously as a member of the male stripshow Manpower). While Durie has strong expert credentials, his media persona is also very much tied to his role as an attractive and down-to-earth TV personality. His TV persona, however, is a complex one that draws upon his credentials as an entertainer and an expert but is also strongly bound to his ordinariness as a genuine 'Aussie bloke'—interviewers often note, for instance, that he hails from a rural, working class background and started off life as a carpenter.[4]

Durie's hybrid persona as expert and handyman, TV personality, and all-round good bloke has given him considerable potency as a marketing tool, and it is not surprising that he was recently signed up to front the campaign for a new line of KingGee clothing (an iconic Australian clothing line normally associated with working man's wear) called 'Worn G'. In the news section of the website of Pacific Brands (the company that owns KingGee), an article announcing the sponsorship deal points to the various synergies between Durie and the brand (PacificBrands 2006). Quoting from Durie's own personal testimony, they note that he has worn KingGee for years and 'is genuinely excited about how the range fits in with his lifestyle'.

Comments in the article made by Sonia Young, the KingGee marketing manager, about the campaign foreground the way in which the brand draws upon Durie's role as a complex celebrity–sign around which a number of diverse meanings and values have accrued, values that reinforce KingGee's existing status as an 'authentic' and 'trusted brand' while also enabling a broadening out of the brand's potential connotations in relation to class, gender, and age. Gesturing towards the brand's traditional associations with the older male generation as a kind of no-nonsense workwear, Young notes that 'Jamie personifies the honest, down-to-earth, unpretentious values of the brand'. At the same time she points to the brand's attempts to speak to a younger, socially mobile audience concerned with questions of taste and style. As she puts it, 'A landscape designer by trade, Jamie fits squarely into our target market in an aspirational, contemporary, laid back way'. Durie's status as both a working handyman and a lifestyle expert thus enable him to appeal to notions of social mobility without appearing elitist, a particularly useful quality in the Australian market, where the public prefer their celebrities and experts to be relentlessly ordinary.

While Durie's past as a model and member of a 'male dance troupe' are not featured up front as part of the marketing script, these intertextual (and subtextual) elements can also be seen as playing a role in the campaign. His version of masculinity is marked by a flexible appeal to women (as important 'influencers', as Young puts it, in the purchase of clothing for male partners) and to an unspoken gay audience, while also enabling straight 'working' men to wet their feet in the realm of fashion while still staying firmly in the territory of bloke-dom. Young summarizes this brand shift (in rather measured, conservative terms) as follows: 'The new Worn Gs range has a fashionable casual edge, and is designed to be worn at work or having a beer with your mates down at the pub, at the cricket or over a BBQ on weekends.'

The appeal of the lifestyle expert as a celebrity endorser in Durie's case is that he can be seen to 'anchor' the potentially ambiguous and free-floating meanings of celebrity to the values of 'authenticity', 'reliability', and 'trustworthiness', and, in the Australian setting, to a specific kind of blokey egalitarianism, while also enabling some broader associations for the interpretive audience around masculinity and taste. Like other lifestyle experts such as Jamie Oliver, Durie's (marketed) appeal is that of a real person rather than a 'star'. At the same time, the process of endorsement for these figures draws its power from their celebrity status and, ironically, to a certain extent from their residual association (as experts) with the seemingly objective, anti-commercial world of information and advice—the realm of anonymous, faceless doctors and dentists mentioned above.

Branding domesticity with Martha Stewart

The phenomenon of the branded lifestyle expert can be viewed in many ways as a logical extension of the process of celebrity endorsement discussed above. While a brand can be seen as purely a name or logo for a product or service, in the highly marketing-driven world of consumer culture, branding increasingly involves attempting to symbolically embody or distil a range of distinctive qualities and meanings associated with a company, product, or service. Obviously this process overlaps with and emerges out of the tradition of celebrity endorsement with its focus on processes of identification and synergy between the lifestyles of celebrities and ordinary people. However, in the discussion that follows, the focus is on the way in which branding now marks a significant shift in consumer culture to a focus on the immaterial rather than just products, on symbolic and informational processes rather than purely on traditional commodities. If celebrity endorsement attempts to construct or trade on a set of imaginary associations between products and celebrities, the brand can itself be seen as an imaginary set of social relations that takes us beyond a focus purely on commodity consumption into the realm of everyday life. It is in this context that we see the emergence of celebrity experts not just as super-consumers but as 'branded humans' (Klein 1999) who represent the complete integration of information, consumption, and lived experience.

Both Jamie Durie and Jamie Oliver, for instance, have sought to extend their credibility as experts into the commercial realm through not only endorsing other companies' products but also producing their own products and (to varying degrees) branding their own identities as celebrity experts. Like Nigella Lawson's kitchenware range (which comes complete with intimate personal quotes from Nigella about why each item is integral to her lifestyle),[5] both Jamies have produced branded 'signature' product lines, in Oliver's case cookware and in Durie's case a range of outdoor products produced by his own company and sold exclusively through Kmart, as well as another company, Jamie Durie Publishing, which produces lifestyle-oriented books.

The ultimate example of branded expertise, however, is without a doubt US lifestyle doyenne and popular cultural icon Martha Stewart. While a number of famous lifestyle experts and personalities have developed significant commercial presences around their branded products and identities, Stewart has taken the phenomenon of embodied branding to another level by building an extensive and diversified multimedia business empire around the brand name Martha Stewart Living (Omnimedia). Stewart provides an illuminating case study of the branding of domestic advice culture via the figure of the embodied celebrity expert. However, her career trajectory, characterized as it is by a relatively long-term involvement with and profile in the media industry, is not necessarily representative of that of other lifestyle experts. Stewart is a successful businesswoman and media player whose superstardom is no doubt enabled in part by the broader mainstream interest in lifestyle advice but is also due to the careful, long-term management of her celebrity image. In contrast to the almost accidental celebrity of some lifestyle experts, such as Jo Frost, the profoundly ordinary expert in *Supernanny*, Stewart is the exemplary instance of a highly managed and constructed mode of branded expertise.

While Stewart prefers to be known as 'a presence' rather than a brand (Didion 2000), in press coverage and business news alike she is continually referred to as 'Martha Stewart the brand' (with more recent coverage not surprisingly being particularly interested in the impact of Stewart's imprisonment for insider trading on the fortunes of her namesake trademark).[6] For instance, in a *Los Angeles Times* article on the poor ratings of NBC's spin-off show *The Apprentice: Martha Stewart* (aired in 2005), she is discussed almost exclusively in corporate terms (Collins 2005). Noting that her syndicated daytime show *Martha* has done much better than her version of *The Apprentice*, Collins contends that her daytime show

> … is aimed at helping sell Martha-branded products … and building that sort of market awareness is the main reason that Stewart does TV to begin with. Unlike, say, Oprah Winfrey or Ellen DeGeneres, Stewart is a merchandiser first and a television personality second (1).

While this characterization of Stewart is reductive (and, like a significant proportion of the press coverage of Stewart, somewhat negative and dismissive), it does point usefully to the way in which her identity as a celebrity lifestyle guru has become thoroughly enmeshed with her corporate identity and branding.

Stewart's status as a branded celebrity, however, has been highly contested. While the press have had a strong interest in (the highs and lows) of her corporate brand power, she is also strongly associated with the realm of the feminine and with a 'genealogy of domestic advice' that stretches back to the mid-19th century (Leavitt 2002: 4).[7] For instance, *The New York Times* once described her as 'a latter-day Mrs Beaton in Armani' (cited in Leavitt 2002: 204), while she has also been variously referred to as 'the diva of domesticity', 'the home-making diva', 'the doyenne of domesticity', 'queen of artfully distressed home furnishings', 'the princess of potpourri', 'the home-decorating czarina', 'the style maven', and 'the domestic taste maker mired in an insider trading scandal' (Stabile 2004: 323). Stewart's perceived elite 'diva' status alongside her attempts to combine hard-headed entrepreneurialism with the flowery realm of domestic expertise have opened her up to considerable criticism, much of which has been highly misogynistic in tone (Stabile 2004).[8] At the same time, much like 'domestic goddess' Nigella Lawson, Stewart is often condemned by the press and by academics for promoting what many see as a regressive model of white, elite femininity in which the domestic sphere is defined as that of the female homemaker (Leavitt 2002).

As one of America's most successful businesswomen, ranking alongside power players in the entertainment industry such as Oprah Winfrey and Madonna (Goldman and Blakeley 2007), Stewart's own identity is far from traditional, however. She started out in modelling in the 1960s and then worked as a successful New York stockbroker for seven years, with her career in domestic advice beginning in the 1970s when she left work to look after a young daughter and started a small catering business from home. Commencing with the publication of her first book, *Entertaining*, in 1982, she developed a successful publishing career over the 1980s and was subsequently offered a publishing deal with Time Warner for the magazine *Martha Stewart Living*, which first came out at the end of 1990 (Armbruster 2004). While Stewart by this time had already attained some media celebrity through various TV appearances on, for instance, *The Oprah Winfrey Show*, and as a spokesperson for Kmart, her rise to the position of celebrity icon and household brand began with a television show called *Martha Stewart Living*, which aired first on the women-oriented cable channel Lifetime in 1993 and moved to CBS in 1997, where it rated as the most popular new syndicated programme (Mason and Meyers 2001).

Part of the success of the Martha Stewart brand has been her recognition of the importance of systematically colonizing the realm of domestic advice through working across a variety of media. As Stewart has commented about her discussions with business advisor Sharon Patrick, 'We talked about how you take over an area—in my case, the home, the garden, the surroundings—and monopolize it' (cited in Smith 2000: 337–338). With this goal in mind, alongside her ventures in publishing and television, she moved into radio, newspapers, and the internet. In 1995 she started a syndicated newspaper column called *askMartha* and in 1997 started up a radio show of the same name, one week after her Martha Stewart Living Omnimedia website was launched (Mason and Meyers 2001). With each media outlet of the Omnimedia conglomerate referring to advice (and products) shown on other media segments, Martha Stewart Living Omnimedia represents a classic case study of the marketing potential of media convergence. Stewart's use of multimedia cross-promotion—she also regularly appears and presents advice (on topics that parallel current issues in her own media outlets) in other media forums such as the NBC's *Today* show—has been represented as a central strategy in the construction of a seamless branded entity. The widespread dissemination of the Stewart brand has involved not only operating through multiple media sites but also further brand extension through, for instance, the sale of Stewart's own 'home fashions line' (under the name Martha Stewart Everyday) through Kmart. The power of the Martha Stewart brand is borne out here by the fact that some business commentators analysing the 'merchandizing relationship' have started referring to the chain as 'Kmartha' (Brady 2000).

Some of the gloss was taken off this 'Martha mania' (Brady 2000), however, when Stewart was charged with insider trading in 2002 and sentenced to prison in 2004. While the press coverage, which as Stabile notes 'aggressively and delightedly chronicled [Stewart's] … serious reversal of fortune' (315), perhaps overestimated the amount of damage the prison time would do to Stewart's credibility and brand power, her namesake business did experience significant losses over the affair. One press report in 2003 noted that Brand Keys, a company that tracks customer loyalty to brands, found loyalty ratings of Stewart's brand at its lowest level ever (Li 2003). As Robert Passikoff, president of Brand Keys, commented, 'This is a textbook example of the fragility of a brand invested in a human being' (cited in Li 2003).

Since her release from prison in March 2005, however, Stewart seems to have gone from strength to strength. While her spin-off version of *The Apprentice* had poor ratings, since September 2005 she has been hosting a new daytime talk show, *Martha*, which blends interviews with celebrity guests and segments related to cooking, gardening, and interior design, and which was nominated for several Emmy awards in 2006. Her time in jail has, if anything, lifted her profile—*Time* magazine, for instance, named Stewart one of 2005's most influential people, and in September 2005 CBS aired a made-for-TV movie (starring Cybil Shepherd and titled not-so-subtly 'Martha Behind Bars') that traces her life from the time her company went public in 1999 to her release from jail. Meanwhile, not only have her business interests quickly recovered—the *Guardian* named her 'the comeback queen' (Burkeman 2006)—but she has continued to expand the reach of Omnimedia into new territory, including launching a satellite radio network on which Stewart (naturally) has a weekly show, and also producing a new magazine, *Blueprint: Design Your Life*, for women in their thirties concerned with living 'better and more gracefully' (Burkeman 2006).

New York Times journalist Katharine Seelye (2006) argues that Stewart's relative lack of presence in the *Blueprint* venture (she features in adverts in the magazine but not in the editorial or any of the columns) indicates she has taken on board criticisms 'that it was a mistake for an enterprise to become too wrapped up in the identity of one person'. Stewart's comments in an interview with *Wired* magazine in 1998 suggest, however, that much earlier she was aware of the rather fraught relationship between a company brand or logo and the status of any founder or identity associated with that company. When the interviewer asked her what would happen to her brand if she died, Stewart commented, 'I'm trying to make sure that my brand extension is broad enough that if anything happens, or I decide to check out, it can continue' (cited in Lury 2004: 81). Emphasizing a disconnect between the 'real' Martha Stewart and the branded image associated with MSL Omnimedia, she informed the interviewer that '[w]e have taken the next five years of photographs of me already, so if anything happened to me we have those closets full of photos' (81).

The notion of brand extension here implies that the Martha Stewart brand can become freed from its original connection to a real person, that photos of Stewart can somehow continue to do the work of the living and breathing, embodied Martha Stewart. The impact of Stewart's time in jail on the brand complicates this notion somewhat in the sense that the negative impact on MSL Omnimedia of what was happening in Stewart's personal life indicates that the image and lifestyle of the 'real' Martha Stewart is obviously not completely detachable from the 'meaning' of the brand. At the same time, the fact that the company and brand were able to carry on (albeit taking some losses) while Stewart was in jail might perhaps suggest that the brand had also started in a sense to take on a life of its own separate from its namesake, as a kind of self-contained 'icon' (Lury 2004: 81). Here, then, is the paradox of celebrity endorsement and human branding: while it seeks to embed its credibility and authenticity in (the lifestyle and expertise of) an actual embodied subject, the relationship between the brand as sign and its original source or 'referent' is variable and unpredictable—despite marketers' attempts at containing and managing the meaning and image associations of brands.

There is no doubt, though, that Stewart and her spin doctors are masters of brand management, knowing when to draw upon the associations of the Martha Stewart brand in more subtle ways, as in the example of *Blueprint*, as well as knowing when to link new undertakings directly to Stewart's embodied persona. In terms of the latter approach, one of the company's latest ventures into the realm of brand extension—building Martha-branded communities—indicates the robustness of the MSL brand while also confirming Stewart's status as a leading role model and authority figure in relation to taste and lifestyle. A sales launch commenced in March 2006 for plots in the first Martha community to be built in Raleigh, North Carolina, in conjunction with KB Home, an American builder. The joint team also plans 'to build 1,800 Martha-inspired homes and assorted products in the coming months' in new communities around the country (Brady 2006). As one media report notes (Brady 2006), this push to build an entire community based around Stewart's status and lifestyle as a domestic guru—the houses were inspired by Stewart's own three homes in New York, Maine, and Connecticut—represents 'a new level of branding'. While Canadian housing consultant Brethour Ron Desjardins comments in the article that Ottawans are probably not ready to move into a Martha community, he notes:

> Everything and everyone tells us that people want to buy more than a house. They want to buy a neighbourhood, a community, a lifestyle … We are moving that way—the Martha way—in small steps in new neighbourhoods that have community centres. The US is way ahead of us—partly because of its population. But maybe Martha is the next step in branding a community.

From goods to brands: The rise of informational capital

Martha Stewart obviously represents an unusually prominent and successful example of branded expertise. Like the numerous other expert–personalities who have moved into the realm of branding and celebrity endorsement, however, her success is linked in part to a range of broader trends in consumer culture today. The triumph of the Stewart brand reflects, for instance, the way in which ordinary, everyday life is becoming increasingly rationalized and colonized by modes of expertise that are inextricably linked to consumption processes. More broadly, however, it is linked to the rise of a new kind of consumer culture dominated by brand image. In this last section of the chapter I want to discuss the growing role of the brand in consumer culture as a means of contextualizing the rise of the branded expert and of examining the changing relationship between the informational realm and consumer culture. How does the branding of individuals relate to a broader extension of consumer culture into everyday lived experience? What does the formation of brand communities around figures such as Stewart suggest about the role of consumer culture in producing/facilitating new modes of social connectedness?

A number of academic and popular books on brands have pointed to the centrality of branding to contemporary culture (Klein 1999; Lury 2004; Arvidsson

2006). Discussing the growing difficulty of distinguishing between commercial interests and sponsored culture, Klein (1999: 30), for instance, notes that figures such as Martha Stewart 'now mirror the corporate structure of corporations like Nike and Gap'. The suggestion is that where there was once some ability to distinguish between the commercial world and the realm of artistic, intellectual, and expert culture, those spaces of relative autonomy have now disappeared. As Klein puts it, processes of commodification have become so ubiquitous and commonplace that '[t]he idea of unbranded space [...] has become almost unthinkable' (59).

The difficulty of finding a symbolic or cultural realm outside of the world of wall-to-wall branding is compounded by the fact that the brand, unlike physical commodities—the cars, fridges, and TVs of previous eras of consumer capitalism—itself exists in a kind of symbolic or imaginary space. While 'hard' consumer goods obviously still play a central role in consumer capitalism, the rise of a 'soft' culture of branding is linked to a growing focus on symbolic and informational processes. As Lury argues (2004: 1), the brand is to a large extent marked by its intangible, incorporeal nature—'it is *a set of relations between products or services*'.

In an era characterized by a 'transition into informationalized capitalism' (Schiller 2007: xiv), economic value increasingly emerges less from tangible commodities than from the symbolic realm structured through and around the brand. What is crucial about this shift is that this symbolic realm is not cordoned off from the remainder of the social—rather, as Klein suggests, branded culture has imperceptibly started to merge with other forms of culture. As Frow (2002) notes in his essay on the signature and the brand, commercial culture is increasingly borrowing from the logic of high culture and aesthetics today (and vice versa), with the brand mimicking the aura and authenticity of the author's/ artist's signature. We can start to see, then, why the popular expert might come to take on a particularly central role in this context. While Martha Stewart may be thoroughly corporatized, in a realm of infinite, unbounded information, figures such as Stewart bring a form of distinction to the brand that owes something to the 'disinterested culture' of the artist/intellectual (Frow 2002: 72)—that is, they embody a (commodified form of) high cultural or informational capital.

Moreover, the specific form of household-based expertise offered by lifestyle experts such as Stewart dovetails neatly with shifts in branding and marketing towards an increasing focus on 'synergy and lifestyle branding' (Klein 1999: 146), where the lifestyle brand involves 'extending the love of luxury objects' (Frow 2002: 64) and high cultural aesthetics more broadly into the space of the home. Through a convergence of media entertainment, instructional discourse, and brand management (with a particular focus on managing the lifestyle expert's persona as someone who has access to elite culture but is also somehow ordinary), domestic advice merchants come to embody particular modes of taste and lifestyle that are aimed at consumers' everyday lifestyle needs. This focus on synergy is less concerned with selling products than with matching people's individual aspirations to lifestyle brands, that is, with providing people with 'complete lifestyle packages' (Klein 1999: 149)—Martha-inspired housing communities being a particularly good example of this process.

For Klein, the ubiquity of such processes of branding—the logo-ing of lifestyle, as it were—points to a loss of critical autonomy in consumer society and the need to struggle against the constraints of, and make alternative types of spaces available within, consumer culture. Given the ubiquity of processes of branding, where might such spaces exist and how might consumers act within them? What Lury's analysis of branding points to is not only the role of marketers, media producers, and cultural intermediaries such as lifestyle experts in shoring up an informational economy but also the central role of consumer–citizens. As she notes (2004: 48), the brand functions and acquires value through its status as 'an *interface* of communication between producers and consumer'. While this interface is marked by an 'asymmetrical communication' that may not necessarily be a beneficial exchange for consumers (53), it points to the growing centrality of consumers' beliefs, values, and concerns in shaping the informational economy.

This brings us back to one of the central questions asked in this book—whether the rise of popular forms of informational/lifestyle media and the emergence of the branded lifestyle expert can be linked to a new kind of citizen–consumer. And, relatedly, whether this mode of cultural citizenship involves an evacuation of politics (as suggested by Miller 2007 and Berlant 1997) or a reconfiguration of the politics of citizenship? To address some of these concerns and conclude the chapter, I want to turn now to Arvidsson's insightful critique of brand capitalism and his discussion of the central role of consumer agency in the shift to an informational economy.

In his discussion of the brand as a dominant organizing principle in contemporary everyday life, Arvidsson's focus, like Lury's, is directed less at economic issues than at branding as a (media) cultural process. His interest lies with thinking about the brand as a critical interface between production and consumption and with examining the role played by consumers in giving brands meaning. In foregrounding the role of the consumer imaginary in producing brand identity, however, Arvidsson sets out a much more ambitious argument about what he sees as the growing role of brands as a source of shared beliefs, meanings, and social connectedness within contemporary capitalism. Brands not only merge aesthetics and economics, informational and commodity culture; they have come to play a more profound role in organizing or giving meaning to the everyday. In today's thoroughly branded existence, consumption can be seen to have taken on an enabling and productive quality, as a site or set of practices through which consumers construct 'the common social world that connects them to each other' (Arvidsson 2006: 19). At the same time, the consumer comes to play an increasingly agentic role in brand culture as, via the intellectual 'labour' of brand consumption, they can be seen to produce a kind of informational capital.

For Arvidsson, the origins of this lifestyle-oriented, informational approach to consumption can be linked back to the rise of new forms of media in the 1950s and 1960s and the beginnings of a transition away from the massified culture of Fordism, a transition that saw shifts in the practices and techniques of advertisers and marketers and the emergence of new associated forms of consumer agency. Television played a decisive early role here as the first medium to integrate consumer goods into everyday life and to enable advertisers to create 'a lifestyle format where products were linked to a particular and often imaginary form of life that consumers were invited to perform' (27). In contrast to the passive consumption associated with media in the pre-war era, in the decades that followed 'the new, more diversified media environment made a wider range of information and knowledge available and catered to an experimenting, interactive attitude' (29).

In the 1980s, in particular, consumers were increasingly addressed by advertisers in interactive terms as creative producers, working to 'complete the product themselves, either materially ... or symbolically' (29). At the same time as consumer agency was being emphasized, the impact of advertising was starting to be somewhat diluted by the multiplication and diversification of media outlets, prompting marketers and advertisers to move from a focus on image and style to a more sophisticated approach to managing customer relations. An expansion of the data collected on consumers (including a growing interest in qualitative research) saw a concern with building 'brand loyalty' through developing brand communities held together by a sense of shared consumer identity (63). In the 1990s this growing merger between branded consumer culture and the production of everyday social relations was consolidated by the convergence between media organizations and a range of other industries. Like Martha Stewart's Omnimedia empire, such processes of convergence enabled media brands to integrate with and extend into every aspect of daily existence.

Arvidsson's mapping of the historical shift within Western marketing, advertising, and media culture to an increasingly sophisticated, data-driven focus on consumer agency, interactivity, and socially embedded lifestyles sets the scene, then, for contemporary branding practices and the emergence of branded information and advice. Brand management today is increasingly concerned with the notion of value as existing at the level of the social imaginary rather than being embodied by particular products, that is, as something created by the broad set of social relationships that link a brand to particular consumers. Taking the notion of consumer interactivity and connectivity one step further, contemporary marketing recognizes that 'brand identity is only *realized* insofar as consumers are involved in its co-creation' (Arvidsson 2006: 82).

The process of human branding, and in particular the branding of specific forms of lifestyle advice via figures such as Stewart, emerges out of and contributes to this culture of creative and agentic consumption and to informational capitalism at a number of levels. First, the familiar mode of information and advice offered by lifestyle experts both implies and works to create an interactive relationship with consumers in which they are seen to engage actively with that information on the basis of their own lifestyle concerns and needs. Extending the identification process associated with celebrity, the human brand also works to create an imaginary connection that moves beyond the world of commodities and merges with other forms of sociality and community. The figure of the branded lifestyle experts thus enables people to imagine (and organize) their everyday lives and consumption practices in terms of broader shared notions of lifestyle, personal ethics, and cultural values—a process that may or may not feed back into the logic of informational capitalism in any kind of predictable or manageable fashion.

Lifestyle revisited

This final chapter has mapped the way in which the figure of the lifestyle expert is both defined by and thoroughly enmeshed in media consumer culture, from the growing overlap between celebrity and expertise to the more recent rise of the branded lifestyle expert. As my discussion of celebrity expertise shows, the hierarchies of authority that once structured the public sphere have grown increasingly complex as they have become articulated to the concerns and logics of popular media and consumer culture. Media-based modes of authority—such as the figure of the 'ordinary' expert—can be seen to produce paradoxical effects within public culture. Lifestyle gurus, celebrity chefs, and makeover experts, for instance, translate and democratize elite taste and knowledge for ordinary viewers while also representing everyday life and domestic skills as themselves forms of expertise, in the process valorizing ordinary and often feminized forms of knowledge.

The flip side of this process of democratization is that these figures can also be seen to function as agents of largely middle class, consumer-driven modes of governmentality.[9] Through both their instructional role as life teachers and their celebrity performances as exemplary consumer–citizens, they affirm particular personal values and modes of living, often framed by strongly commercial forces and imperatives. Their focus on the domestic here is not accidental. At the same time as these figures continually work to deny their own authoritative role as experts, through the intimate, domestic focus of their advice they are seen to pass on, to devolve as it were, issues of decision making and responsibility to ordinary citizens. Lifestyle media as exemplified by the figure of the lifestyle expert, then, becomes a pre-eminent site where the politics of privatized citizenship is played out—where questions of individual morality, choice, and responsibility, as performed on lifestyle TV or in the makeover sections of magazines, come to dominate and displace other potential definitions of citizenship.

Branded lifestyle expertise can be seen as a logical extension of this privatized politics, where figures such as Martha Stewart offer consumers faced with an enormous array of choices an all-encompassing lifestyle 'blueprint' (as her new magazine is entitled) that they can apply to every aspect of their lives (except perhaps the ethics of stock trading). As Lury and Arvidsson's work suggests, however, consumers are not passive in the way they make use of this kind of branded expertise in their lives. The brand–consumer relationship instead can be seen as a dynamic, interactive process where consumers not only forge the meaning of brands but also create the wider set of social relations in which brands are given value. Thus, while consumption has previously been seen as an essentially nonproductive activity, with the rise of informational capitalism we see the imaginative processes and intellectual labour associated with privatized, domestic, and everyday consumer choices and practices taking on economic value. This process is in turn valorized by lifestyle expertise with its emphasis on investing in imaginary projects of self- (and community) improvement through 'responsible' modes of consumption.

Which returns us to the question of the politics of privatized citizenship. Does this displacement of public/national concerns onto the space of private, domestic consumption represent the death of 'a common public culture', as Berlant has suggested (1997: 3)? Or rather are we seeing a more complex redefinition of the boundaries and sites of citizenship and politics? The shift to a hyper-mediatized informational capitalism has seen consumption around brand image and identity emerge as a pre-eminent site of social relations and communality. With the branding of lifestyle-oriented information and expertise—in which lessons around taste and discernment converge with issues of responsible personal conduct—we see questions of citizenship increasingly played out within the realm of lifestyle consumption.

The limitations of modes of consumer–citizenship enabled by brand capitalism are, as Arvidsson notes, reflected in the ease with which capital exploits the social relations of consumption as a form of surplus value. At the same time, he also argues that the social relations produced by the power of the consumer imaginary continually escape the bounds of regulated capitalism; that branding itself, with its increased dependence on the social as a site of productivity and value, is in fact a sign of the instability of informational capitalism and of 'a general weakness of capitalist command' (136). This may seem an overstatement given Arvidsson's own systematic mapping of the way in which brand capitalism efficiently exploits 'the productive autonomy of the social' (137). However, it does usefully highlight the way in which the power of popular lifestyle expertise and of lifestyle consumption partly emerges from its ability to engage more broadly in the production of social values—which may or may not converge with the desires of brand marketers, and may indeed provide modes of activist consumer–citizenship.

While it is perhaps hard to see where Martha's transformational aesthetics might translate into consumer activism, the many spoofs of Stewart—including Tom Connor's best-selling parodies *Is Martha Stewart Living?* and *Martha Stewart Is Better Than You at Entertaining?*—do reflect a degree of consumer scepticism about the relentless discourse of self- and home improvement (at the same time as they, of course, can be seen as a form of unofficial brand extension). Certainly the powerful response that Jamie Oliver's activism around children's diets received from the public—where he targeted not only family but also government and corporate responsibility for the poor nutrition of UK children—marks the space where the social imaginary is not always so readily tied to predictable forms of brand value. A crucial point to repeat here, however, is that the branded lifestyle expert is a product of the growing convergence of information and consumption—of the naturalization of brand culture as a site of broader modes of culture and sociality. Modes of consumer activism as well as strategies for creating imaginary sites beyond the logo will work best, then, when they construct practices and spaces that critique and defamiliarize the increasingly ubiquitous and informational logic of brand capitalism.

•   •   •

This book has sought to highlight the growing role and importance of expertise in our everyday lives. It has mapped a number of the ways in which the most private as well as the most mundane areas of daily existence have become the focus of a rapidly proliferating army of style mavens and advice merchants. While this final chapter has focused on the role of lifestyle experts as mediators of informational/consumer capitalism, the book as a whole has presented a range of different perspectives on, and put forward a variety of analytic frameworks for understanding, the contemporary role and status of popular expertise. While emphasizing the ubiquity of lifestyle expertise in contemporary everyday life, I have been most concerned with foregrounding the different ways in which popular advice is played out in a range of cultural sites, from food to celebrity to health, and in diverse media settings, with popular expertise framed by a range of different aesthetic, generic, industrial, and audience traditions. A central theme has concerned the ordinariness of these modes of expertise and media forms, reflected in their focus on the most routine habits, rhythms, and spaces of our lives. While cultures of domesticity and the everyday tend to remain marginal within academic debates, here I have sought to move such issues to centre stage. In doing so my aim was to demonstrate persuasively the ways in which seemingly mundane modes of advice culture are linked to a range of broader social and political issues concerning the relationship between self, family, and community and questions of good citizenship in an increasingly privatized, consumer-driven culture. I also hope to have contributed to a broader recognition of the critical importance of taking such developments in popular cultural and media seriously: they are not merely banal instruments of a globalizing neoliberal commercial culture but complex sites where social norms and relations are reflected upon and reproduced.

Notes

1   In using the term 'democratic' here, I am referring less, of course, to traditional notions of political process than to the growing symbolic role of the ordinary in public life and the apparent flattening out of distinctions between experts and ordinary people. See Turner's (2004) critique of the premises underpinning the 'democratainment' thesis and his counter-argument that contemporary media is marked today by a 'demotic' rather than a democratic turn.

2   These issues have been particularly evident in the case of Jamie Oliver, whose claims to ordinariness and authenticity have met with heavy criticism, although attacks on his 'mockney' persona have declined since he gained the respect of the UK public through his school dinners campaign and his involvement in the Fifteen Foundation.

3   Durie was first 'discovered' through an article in the Australian design magazine *Belle* on his landscape design business, Patio (thanks to Nicci Hartley at Jamie Durie Publishing for this information).

4   Less often mentioned is Durie's Sri Lankan background (his mother was born in Sri Lanka).

5   For instance, an advertisement for a Nigella Lawson whisk was accompanied by the following quote from Nigella: 'I cannot live without a small whisk (which can fit in my handbag!) that can get lumps out of anything. With this, I can whisk eggs, stir batters, make sauces. In fact, I can't cook without it.'

6   Dubinsky, for instance, notes that 'brand' becomes a derogatory term when linked to Martha Stewart, while Dyer contends that '[s]uch is the strength of the Martha Stewart brand, [… it has] weathered her conviction and imprisonment in 2004 for lying to investigators about a stock sale'.

7   Leavitt comments that Stewart's success comes from bringing 'domesticity out into the world' (2002: 201), noting that '[t]he image of Stewart toasting her initial public offering (IPO) at the New York Stock Exchange with fresh-squeezed orange juice and homemade brioche caught so many people's attention specifically because of the perceived clash between the public sphere of stock trading and the private sphere of the home'.

8   As Armbruster noted in 2004 (2004: 721), in the previous eight years, six books came out attacking Stewart's 'ambition and empire'. Stabile argues that the 'popular ressentiment' (2004: 315) apparent in the press coverage of Stewart's indictment and trial not only reflected her perceived elite status and mega-celebrity but was also due to the fact that her corporate approach to domestic advice was seen as violating the 'codes of femininity' (319).

9   And as Turner argues in *Understanding Celebrity* (2004), the democratizing turn here needs to be recognized as also being framed by the wider economic and industry-driven logics of media.

References

Adema, P. (2000). Vicarious consumption: Food, television and the ambiguity of modernity. *Journal of American & Comparative Cultures*, 23 (3): 113–123.

Allatson, P. (2004). Queer Eye's primping and pimping for empire et al. *Feminist Media Studies*, 4 (2): 208–211.

Andrejevic, M. (2004). *Reality TV: The work of being watched*. Lanham, MD: Rowman & Littlefield.

Armbruster, E. S. (2004). *Martha, Inc.: The incredible story of Martha Stewart Living Omnimedia*, 37 (4): 721.

Arvidsson, A. (2006). *Brands: Meaning and value in media culture*. London; New York: Routledge.

Attwood, F. (2005). Inside out: Men on the 'home front'. *Journal of Consumer Culture*, 5 (1): 87–107.

Baker, L., T. H. Wagner, S. Singer, and M. K. Bundorf. (2003). Use of the Internet and e-mail for health care information: Results from a national survey. *Journal of the American Medical Association*, 289 (18): 2400–2406.

Bauman, Z. (1987). *Legislators and interpreters: On modernity, post-modernity and intellectuals*. London: Polity.

Bauman, Z. (1991). *Modernity and ambivalence*. Cambridge, UK: Polity.

BBC. (2002). Health websites gaining popularity. 14 September. Retrieved 20 September 2004 from http://news.bbc.co.uk/2/hi/health/2249606.stm.

Beck, U. (1992). *Risk society: Towards a new modernity*. London: Sage.

Beck, U. (1994). The reinvention of politics: Towards a theory of reflexive modernization. In U. Beck, A. Giddens, and S. Lash (Eds.), *Reflexive modernization: Politics, tradition and aesthetics in the modern social order* (pp. 1–55). Cambridge, UK: Polity Press.

Becker, D. (2005). *The myth of empowerment: Women and the therapeutic culture in America*. New York: New York University Press.

Bee, P. (2004). How the internet ruined my health—Confessions of a cyberchondriac. *Independent,* 1 February: 4.

Bell, D. and J. Hollows, Eds. (2005). *Ordinary lifestyles: Popular media, consumption and taste.* Maidenhead, UK: Open University Press.

Bell, D. and J. Hollows, Eds. (2006). *Historicizing lifestyle: Mediating taste, consumption and identity from the 1900s to 1970s.* Aldershot, UK: Ashgate.

Bennett, L. (1998). The uncivic culture: Communication, identity, and the rise of lifestyle politics. *PS: Political Science and Politics,* 31 (4): 740–761.

Berlant, L. G. (1997). *The queen of America goes to Washington city: Essays on sex and citizenship.* Durham, NC: Duke University Press.

Bignell, J. (2005). *Big Brother: Reality TV in the twenty-first century.* Basingstoke, UK: Palgrave Macmillan.

Biressi, A. and H. Nunn. (2005). *Reality TV: Realism and revelation.* London: Wallflower.

Blount, K. (2005). *What's your poison: Addictive advertising of the 40s–60s.* Portland, OR: Collectors Press.

Bonner, F. (2002). Magazines. In S. Cunningham and G. Turner (Eds.), *The media & communications in Australia* (pp. 188–199). Crows Nest, NSW: Allen & Unwin.

Bonner, F. (2003). *Ordinary television: Analyzing popular TV.* London: Sage.

Bonner, F. (2005). Whose lifestyle is it anyway? In D. Bell and J. Hollows (Eds.), *Ordinary lifestyles: Popular media, consumption and taste* (pp. 35–46). Maidenhead, UK; New York: Open University Press.

Bonner, F., S. McKay, and K. Goldie. (1998). Caring for the family: Fifty years of health in the Australian women's weekly. *Journal of Australian Studies,* 59: 154–164.

Bourdieu, P. (1984). *Distinction: A social critique of the judgement of taste.* Cambridge, MA: Harvard University Press.

Brady, D. (2000). 'Kmartha' to the rescue?, *BusinessWeek Online.* 4 October. Retrieved 30 May 2006 from http://www.businessweek.com/bwdaily/dnflash/oct2000/nf2000104_588.htm.

Brady, S. (2006). The Martha factor. *Ottawa Citizen,* 18 March: I3.

BravoTV. (2005). Official website for queer eye for the straight guy. Accessed 2 February. http://www.bravotv.com/Queer_Eye_for_the_Straight_Guy/.

Brunsdon, C. (2003). Lifestyling Britain: The 8–9 slot on British television. *International Journal of Cultural Studies,* 6 (1): 5–23.

Brunsdon, C., C. Johnson, R. Moseley, and H. Wheatley. (2001). Factual entertainment on British television: The Midland's TV Research group's '8–9 Project'. *European Journal of Cultural Studies,* 4 (1): 29–62.

Burkeman, O. (2006). Comeback queen: Martha Stewart's next lifestyle launch. *Guardian,* 2 May: 14.

Business Wire. (2004). New clinical study shows walnuts protective for people with Type 2 Diabetes. *Business Wire,* Factiva, 2 December.

Chaney, D. (1996). *Lifestyles.* London; New York: Routledge.

Chaney, D. (2001). From ways of life to lifestyle: Rethinking culture as ideology and sensibility. In J. Lull (Ed.), *Culture in the communication age* (pp. 75–87). London: Routledge.

Clarkson, J. (2005). Contesting masculinity's makeover: Queer eye, consumer masculinity, and 'straight-acting' gays. *Journal of Communication Inquiry,* 29 (3): 235–255.

Cline, R. J. W. and K. M. Haynes. (2001). Consumer health information seeking on the internet: The state of the art. *Health Education Research,* 16 (6): 671–692.

Coiera, E. (1998). Information epidemics, economics, and immunity on the internet. *British Medical Journal,* 317 (7171): 1469–1470.

Collins, S. (2005). Martha is not a master of prime time. *Los Angeles Times.* Calendar section; Part E. 7 October: 1.

Coolidge-Consumerism. (2007). Notes on 'Frederick, Christine, Consumer Celebrity,' The Coolidge-Consumerism collection–US Library of Congress. http://lcweb2.loc.gov:8081/ammem/amrlhtml/coolhome.html.

Corner, J. (1999). *Critical ideas in television studies.* Oxford: Oxford University Press.

Corner, J. (2004). Afterword: Framing the new. In S. Holmes and D. Jermyn (Eds.), *Understanding reality television* (pp. 290–299). London: Routledge.

Corner, J. and D. Pels, Eds. (2003). *Media and the restyling of politics: Consumerism, celebrity, cynicism.* London: Sage.

Couldry, N. (2000). *The place of media power: Pilgrims and witnesses of the media age.* London: Routledge.

Couldry, N. (2002). Playing for celebrity: *Big Brother* as ritual event. *Television & New Media, 3* (3): 283–293.

Craan, F. and D. M. Oleske. (2002). Medical information and the internet: Do you know what you are getting? *Journal of Medical Systems, 26* (6): 511–518.

Crompton, S. (2005). The choice is yours. *The Times,* 8 January. Accessed from LexisNexis® Academic.

D'Alessandro, D. M. and N. P. Dosa. (2001). Empowering children and families with information technology. *Archives of Pediatrics & Adolescent Medicine, 155* (10): 1131–1136.

Deveny, C. (2006). Mad dogs and bogans go on telly. *The Age,* Melbourne, 4 November (Saturday edition): 56.

Didion, J. (2000). Everywoman.com: Getting out of the house with Martha Stewart. *New Yorker.* 21 February. Retrieved 10 June 2006 from http://www.newyorker.com/archive/content/?040322fr_archive01.

Dyer, R. (1979). *Stars.* London: British Film Institute.

Edwards, T. (2003). Sex, booze and fags: Masculinity, style and men's magazines. In B. Benwell (Ed.), *Masculinity and men's lifestyle magazines* (pp. 132–146). Oxford: Blackwell.

Ehrenreich, B. and D. English. (2005). *For her own good: Two centuries of the experts' advice to women.* New York: Anchor Books.

Evans, J. and D. Hesmondhalgh. (2005). *Understanding media: Inside celebrity.* Maidenhead, UK; New York: Open University Press.

Featherstone, M. (1991). *Consumer culture and postmodernism.* London: Sage.

Featherstone, M. (1995). *Undoing culture: Globalization, postmodernism and identity.* London: Sage.

Ferguson, T. (2000). Online patient-helpers and physicians working together: A new partnership for high quality health care. *British Medical Journal, 321:* 1129–1132.

Florian, E. (2004). Queer Eye makes over the economy! *Fortune, 149* (3): 38.

Thefoodcoach. (2006). The food coach website. Accessed 20 June. http://www.thefoodcoach.com.au/.

Fox, S. (2006). Online health search 2006 (Pew Internet and American Life Project). Retrieved 31 January 2007 from http://www.pewinternet.org/pdfs/PIP_Online_Health_2006.pdf.

Frederick, C. (1913). *The new housekeeping: Efficiency studies in home management.* Garden City, NY: Doubleday, Page.

Frith, S. and J. Savage. (1998). Pearls and swine: Intellectuals and the mass media. In S. Redhead, D. Wynne, and J. O'Connor (Eds.), *The clubcultures reader: Readings in popular cultural studies* (pp. 7–17). Oxford: Blackwell.

Frow, J. (2002). Signature and brand. In J. Collins (Ed.), *High-pop: Making culture into popular entertainment* (pp. 56–74). Malden, MA: Blackwell.

Gallagher, M. (2004). Queer eye for the heterosexual couple. *Feminist Media Studies,* 4 (2): 223–225.

Gallagher, M. (2004). What's so funny about Iron Chef? Japanese cooking-competition show in the global television era. *Journal of Popular Film and Television,* 31 (4): 176–184.

Garnham, N. (1995). The media and narratives of the intellectual. *Media, Culture and Society,* 17 (3): 359–383.

Gelber, S. M. (1999). *Hobbies: Leisure and the culture of work in America.* New York: Columbia University Press.

Giddens, A. (1991). *Modernity and self-identity: Self and society in the late modern age.* Cambridge: Polity.

Gill, R. (2003). Power and the production of subjects: A genealogy of the New Man and the New Lad. In B. Benwell (Ed.), *Masculinity and men's lifestyle magazines* (pp. 34–56). Oxford: Blackwell.

Goldman, L. and K. Blakeley. (2007). The 20 richest women in entertainment. 18 January. Retrieved 3 February 2007 from http://www.forbes.com/2007/01/17/richest-women-entertainment-tech-media-cz_lg_richwomen07_0118womenstars_lander.html.

Goldstein, C. (1998). *Do it yourself: Home improvement in 20th-century America.* New York: Princeton Architectural Press.

Gough-Yates, A. (2003). Understanding women's magazines. London: Routledge.

Hart, K.-P. R. (2004). We're here, we're queer and we're better than you: The representational superiority of gay men to heterosexuals on queer eye for the straight guy. *Journal of Men's Studies,* 12 (3): 241–248.

Hartley, J. (1999). *Uses of television.* London: Routledge.

Hawkes, H. (2005). Food for thought. *Vogue,* Australia: 156–158. October

Heinrichs, P. (2006). Coming clean. *Sunday Age,* Melbourne, 13 August: 15.

Higgs, P. (1998). Risk, governmentality and the reconceptualisation of citizenship. In G. Scrambler and P. Higgs (Eds.), *Modernity, medicine and health: Medical sociology towards 2000* (pp. 176–197). London: Routledge.

Hill, A. (2005). *Reality TV: Audiences and popular factual television.* London: Routledge.

Holliday, R. (2006). Home truths? In D. Bell and J. Hollows (Eds.), *Historicizing lifestyle: Mediating taste, consumption and identity from the 1900s to 1970s* (pp. 65–81). Aldershot, UK: Ashgate.

Hollows, J. (2003). Oliver's twist: Leisure, labour and domestic masculinity in *The Naked Chef. International Journal of Cultural Studies,* 6 (2): 229–248.

Holmes, S. and D. Jermyn. (2004). *Understanding reality television.* London: Routledge.

Home-Start. (2006). Jamie Oliver and Richard and Judy top Mother's Day poll, Home-Start. 21 March. Retrieved 1 February 2007 from http://www.home-start.org.uk/news/press_releases/timebank_real_celebs_release.

Horton, D. and R. R. Wohl. (1956). Mass communication and para-social interaction: Observations on intimacy at a distance. *Psychiatry,* 19 (3): 215–229.

Jahad, A. R. and A. Gagliardi. (1998). Rating health information on the internet: Navigating to knowledge or to Babel? *Journal of the American Medical Association,* 279 (8): 611–614.

Kavka, M. (2004). The queering of reality TV. *Feminist Media Studies,* 4 (2): 220–222.

Ketchum, C. (2005). The essence of cooking shows: How the food network constructs consumer fantasies. *Journal of Communication Inquiry,* 29 (3): 217–234.

Kilborn, R. W. (2003). *Staging the real: Factual TV programming in the age of Big Brother.* Manchester: Manchester University Press.

Klein, N. (1999). *No logo: Taking aim at the brand bullies.* New York: Picador.

Langland, E. (1995). *Nobody's angels: Middle class women and domestic ideology in Victorian culture.* Ithaca, NY: Cornell University Press.

Lawrence, M. and J. Germov. (1999). Future food: The politics of functional foods and health claims. In J. Germov and L. Williams (Eds.), *A sociology of food and nutrition: The social appetite* (pp. 54–76). South Melbourne, Australia: Oxford University Press.

Leavitt, S. A. (2002). *From Catharine Beecher to Martha Stewart: A cultural history of domestic advice.* Chapel Hill: University of North Carolina Press.

Lewis, T. (2001). Embodied experts: Robert Hughes, cultural studies and the celebrity intellectual. *Continuum,* 15 (2): 233–247.

Lewis, T. (2004). PIs on TV: Intellectuals, public culture and Australian television. In D. Carter (Ed.), *The ideas market: An alternative take on Australia's intellectual life* (pp. 115–132). Melbourne, Australia: Melbourne University Press.

Lewis, T. (2006). Seeking health information on the internet: Lifestyle choice or bad attack of cyberchondria? *Media, Culture & Society,* 28 (5): 521–539.

Li, K. (2003). Martha Stewart brand faces uphill battle. *Reuters News.* 6 June. Accessed from Factiva.com.

Lindberg, D. A. B. and B. L. Humphreys. (1998). Medicine and health on the internet: The good, the bad, and the ugly. *Journal of the American Medical Association,* 280 (15): 1303–1304.

Livingstone, S. M. and P. K. Lunt. (1994). *Talk on television: Audience participation and public debate.* London: Routledge.

Lupton, D. (1995). *The imperative of health: Public health and the regulated body.* London: Sage.

Lury, C. (1996). *Consumer culture.* Cambridge: Polity.

Lury, C. (2004). *Brands: The logos of the global economy.* New York: Routledge.

Lush, S. and J. Fleming. (2005). *Spotless.* Sydney, Australia: ABC books.

Lush, S. and J. Fleming. (2006). *Speed cleaning—A spotless house in just 15 minutes a day.* Sydney, Australia: ABC books.

Lynes, R. (1954). *The tastemakers.* New York: Grosset & Dunlap.

Maffesoli, M. (1996). *The time of the tribes: The decline of individualism in mass society.* London: Sage.

Magder, T. (2004). The end of TV 101: Reality television, formats and the new business of TV. In S. Murray and L. Ouellette (Eds.), *Reality TV: Remaking television culture* (pp. 137–156). New York: New York University Press.

Mangan, J. (2004). No drama. *The Age,* Melbourne, 10 Aug (A3 Section): 4.

Marshall, P. D. (1997). *Celebrity and power: Fame in contemporary culture.* Minneapolis: University of Minnesota Press.

Mason, A. and M. Meyers. (2001). Living with Martha Stewart media: Chosen domesticity in the experience of fans. *Journal of Communication,* 51 (4): 801.

McCracken, E. (1993). Decoding women's magazines. Basingstoke, Hants: Macmillan.

McCracken, G. D. (2005). *Culture and consumption II: Markets, meaning, and brand management.* Bloomington: Indiana University Press.

McRobbie, A. (2004a). Post-feminism and popular culture. *Feminist Media Studies,* 4 (3): 255–264.

McRobbie, A. (2004b). Notes on 'What Not To Wear' and post-feminist symbolic violence. *Sociological Review,* 52 (s2): 97–109.

Mechling, J. (2003). Advice literature. In B. E. Carroll (Ed.), *American masculinities: A historical encyclopedia* (pp. 13–15). London: Sage.

Mellencamp, P. (1992). *High anxiety: Catastrophe, scandal, age & comedy.* Bloomington: Indiana University Press.

Mennell, S., A. Murcott, and A. H. v. Otterloo. (1992). *The sociology of food: Eating, diet and culture*. London: Sage.

Meyer, M. D. E. and J. M. Kelley. (2004). Queering the eye? The politics of gay white men and gender (in)visibility. *Feminist Media Studies*, 4 (2): 214–217.

Miller, T. (2005). A metrosexual eye on queer guy. *GLQ: Journal of Lesbian and Gay Studies*, 11 (1): 112–117.

Miller, T. (2007). *Cultural citizenship: Cosmopolitanism, consumerism and television in a neoliberal age*. Philadelphia, PA: Temple University Press.

Miller, T. and A. McHoul. (1998). Helping the self. *Social Text*, 57: 127–155.

Molitorisz, S. (2006). Honey, we're killing the kids! *The Age*, Melbourne. 12 July. Retrieved 2 August 2006 from http://www.theage.com.au/news/tv-reviews/honey-were-killing-the-kids/2006/07/11/1152383733020.html.

Moran, A. (1998). *Copycat television: Globalisation, program formats and cultural identity*. Luton, UK: University of Luton Press.

Moran, A. and M. Keane. (2006). Cultural power in international TV format markets. *Continuum*, 20 (1): 71–86.

Mort, F. (1996). *Cultures of consumption: Masculinities and social space in the late 20th century*. London: Routledge:.

Moseley, R. (2000). Makeover takeover on British television. *Screen*, 41 (3): 299–314.

Mullner, R. M. (2002). Introduction: The internet and healthcare: Opportunities and challenges. *Journal of Medical Systems*, 26 (6): 491–493.

Murray, S. and L. Ouellette. (2004). *Reality TV: Remaking television culture*. New York: New York University Press.

NTC. (2005). Nutritional therapy council website. Accessed 20 January 2006. http://www.nutritionaltherapycouncil.org.uk/whatntis.htm.

O'Brien, M. (1995). Health and lifestyle: A critical mess? Notes on the dedifferentiation of health. In R. Bunton, S. Nettleton, and R. Burrows (Eds.), *The sociology of health promotion: Critical analyses of consumption, lifestyle, and risk* (pp. 191–205). London: Routledge.

Osgerby, B. (2003). A pedigree of the consuming male: Masculinity, consumption and the American 'leisure class'. In B. Benwell (Ed.), *Masculinity and men's lifestyle magazines* (pp. 57–85). Oxford: Blackwell.

O'Sullivan, T. (2005). From television lifestyle to lifestyle television. In D. Bell and J. Hollows (Eds.), *Ordinary lifestyles: Popular media, consumption and taste* (pp. 21–34). Maidenhead, England: Open University Press.

Ouellette, L. (2006). Honey, we're killing the kids, *Flow*. 4(8). Retrieved 1 August 2007 http://flowtv.org/?p=177.

PacificBrands. (2006). Jamie Durie signs up with KingGee. Retrieved 15 May 2006. http://www.pacificbrands.com.au/News/KingGee_Jamie_Durie.asp.

Palmer, G. (2003). *Discipline and liberty: Television and governance*. Manchester, UK: Manchester University Press.

Palmer, G. (2004). 'The new you': Class and transformation in lifestyle television. In S. Holmes and D. Jermyn (Eds.), *Understanding reality television* (pp. 173–190). London: Routledge.

Parker, B. J. (2003). Food for health: The use of nutrient content, health, and structure/function claims in food advertisements. *Journal of Advertising*, 32 (3): 47–55.

Pearson, K. and N. M. Reich. (2004). *Queer Eye* fairy tale: Changing the world one manicure at a time. *Feminist Media Studies*, 4 (2): 229–231.

Pendergast, T. (2000). *Creating the modern man: American magazines and consumer culture, 1900–1950*. Columbia: University of Missouri Press.

Petersen, A. (1997). Risk, governance and the new public health. In R. Bunton (Ed.), *Foucault, health and medicine* (pp. 189–206). London: Routledge.

Pew. (2006). Press release (Pew Internet and American Life Project). Retrieved 31 January 2007 from http://www.pewinternet.org/press_release.asp?r=132.

Popcorn, F. (2002). *Trends for 2003: The Popcorn Report.* 27 December. Retrieved 30 Jan 2006 from http://retailindustry.about.com/cs/ref_research_comp/l/bltrends2003.htm.

Probyn, E. (1997). New traditionalism and post-feminism: TV does the home. In C. Brunsdon, J. D'Acci, and L. Spigel (Eds.), *Feminist television criticism: A reader* (pp. 126–138). Oxford: Clarendon Press.

PTS. (2007). Taiwan public television service online—website for Taiwan fun cuisine. Accessed 18 April. http://www.pts.org.tw/php/_utility/ehomepage/detail.php?XHAENO=66.

RealAge.com. (2005). RealAge tip of the day: Heart-warming seasoning. Retrieved 19 December 2005 from http://www.realage.com.

Redden, G. (2007). Makeover morality and consumer culture. In D. Heller (Ed.), *Reading makeover television: Realties remodeled* (pp. 150–164). London: I. B. Tauris.

Reed, L. (2002). Governing (through) the internet: The discourse on pathological computer use as mobilized knowledge. *European Journal of Cultural Studies,* 5 (2): 131–153.

Ritzer, G. (1993). *The McDonaldization of society: An investigation into the changing character of contemporary social life.* Newbury Park, CA: Pine Forge Press.

Rogers, S. (2003). NBC rebroadcast of 'Queer Eye' draws 8 million viewers, wins timeslot in Adults 18–49. 25 August. Retrieved March 2005 from http://www.realitytvworld.com/index/articles/story.php?s=1628.

Rose, N. (1989). *Governing the soul: The shaping of the private self.* London: Routledge.

Rose, N. S. (1996). *Inventing our selves: Psychology, power, and personhood.* Cambridge: Cambridge University Press.

Rosenberg, B. C. (2005). Scandinavian dreams: DIY, democratisation and IKEA. *Transformations,* 11. Retrieved 12 August 2006 from http://transformations.cqu.edu.au/journal/issue_11/article_02.shtml.

Schiller, D. (2007). *How to think about information.* Urbana: University of Illinois.

Scrinis, G. (2002). Sorry, Marge. *Meanjin,* 61 (4): 108–116.

Seelye, K. Q. (2006). Stewart less visible in magazine offering. *New York Times,* 24 April: 7.

Sender, K. (2006). 'From cousin it to Brad Pitt': Audience responses to makeover media. Media Change and Social Theory Conference, CRESC. September 2006, Oxford, UK.

Sender, K. (2006). Queens for a day: *Queer Eye for the Straight Guy* and the neoliberal project. *Critical Studies in Media Communication,* 23 (2): 131–151.

Shrimsley, R. (2003). The new queens of makeover. *Financial Times,* London, 21 November: 17.

Shumway, D. R. (1997). The star system in literary studies. *PMLA,* 112: 85–100.

Skeggs, B. (2002). Techniques for telling the reflexive self. In T. May (Ed.), *Qualitative Research in Action* (pp. 349–375). London: Sage.

Smith, C. D. (2000). Discipline—it's a 'good thing': Rhetorical constitution and Martha Stewart living omnimedia. *Women's Studies in Communication,* 23 (3): 337.

Solier, I. de. (2005). TV dinners: Culinary television, education and distinction. *Continuum,* 19 (4): 465–481.

Stabile, C. A. (2004). Getting what she deserved: The news media, Martha Stewart, and masculine domination. *Feminist Media Studies,* 4 (3): 315–332.

Steemers, J. (2004). *Selling television: British television in the global marketplace.* London: British Film Institute.

Stevenson, N., P. Jackson, and K. Brooks (2003). Reading men's lifestyle magazines: Cultural power and the information society. In B. Benwell (Ed.), *Masculinity and men's lifestyle magazines* (pp. 112–131). Oxford: Blackwell.

Strange, N. (1998). Perform, educate, entertain: Ingredients of the cookery programme genre. In C. Geraghty and D. Lusted (Eds.), *The television studies book* (pp. 301–312). London: Arnold.

Summers, A. (2003). Message is still the same: Stay home, *Sydney Morning Herald Online*. 3 March. Retrieved 30 Jan 2007 from http://www.smh.com.au/articles/2003/03/02/10465400 68056.html.

Taylor, L. (2002). From ways of life to lifestyle: The 'Ordinari-ization' of British gardening lifestyle television. *European Journal of Communication,* 17 (4): 479–493.

Tomlinson, J. (2004). Globalisation and national identity. In J. G. Sinclair and G. Turner (Eds.), *Contemporary world television* (pp. 24–28). London: British Film Institute.

Tomlinson, M. (2003). Lifestyle and social class. *European Sociological Review,* 19 (1): 97–111.

Turner, G. (2004). *Understanding celebrity*. London: Sage.

Turner, G., F. J. Bonner, and P. D. Marshall. (2000). *Fame games: The production of celebrity in Australia*. Cambridge: Cambridge University Press.

Veblen, T. (1957). *The theory of the leisure class: An economic study of institutions*. London: Allen and Unwin.

Waisbord, S. (2004). McTV: Understanding the global popularity of television formats. *Television & New Media,* 5 (4): 359–383.

Warde, A. (1997). Consumption, food, and taste: Culinary antinomies and commodity culture. London: Sage.

Weaver, M. (2006). 'Supernannies' to tackle antisocial children, *Guardian*. 21 November. Retrieved 1 December from http://politics.guardian.co.uk/homeaffairs/story/0,,1953354,00.html.

White, C. L. (1970). *Women's magazines, 1693–1968*. London: Joseph.

Wilke, M. (2003). A Blackened Eye for Queer Guys, *Gully*. 1 October. Retrieved 14 February 2005 from http://www.thegully.com/essays/gay_mundo2/wilke/031001_bravo_queer_eye_ads.html.

Winship, J. (1987). *Inside Women's Magazines*. London: Pandora.

Wood, H. and B. Skeggs. (2004). Notes on ethical scenarios of self on British reality TV. *Feminist Media Studies,* 4 (2): 205–208.

Wood, H., B. Skeggs, and N. Thumim. (2008). It's just sad: Mediated intimacy and the emotional labour of reality television viewing. In S. Gillis and J. Hollows (Eds.), *Feminism, domesticity and popular culture*. New York: Routledge.

Xu, J. H. (2007). Brand-new lifestyle: Consumer-oriented programmes on Chinese television. *Media Culture & Society,* 29 (3): 363, 376.

Yue, A. (2003). Shopping. In F. Martin (Ed.), *Interpreting everyday culture* (pp. 124–139). London: Arnold.

Zdeb, C. (2004). How to eat your way to better grades. *Ottawa Citizen,* 9 November: A12.

Index

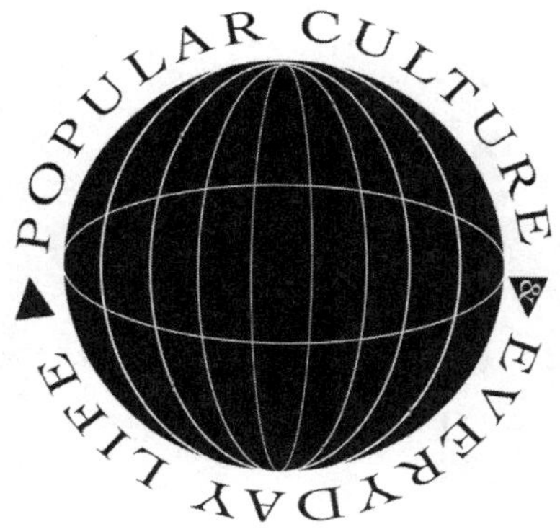

Toby Miller
General Editor

Popular Culture and Everyday Life is the new place for critical books in cultural studies. The series stresses multiple theoretical, political, and methodological approaches to commodity culture and lived experience by borrowing from sociological, anthropological, and textual disciplines. Each volume develops a critical understanding of a key topic in the area through a combination of thorough literature review, original research, and a student-reader orientation. The series consists of three types of books: single-authored monographs, readers of existing classic essays, and new companion volumes of papers on central topics. Fields to be covered include: fashion, sport, shopping, therapy, religion, food and drink, youth, music, cultural policy, popular literature, performance, education, queer theory, race, gender, and class.

For additional information about this series or for the submission of manuscripts, please contact:

Toby Miller
Department of Cinema Studies
New York University
721 Broadway, Room 600
New York, New York 10003

To order other books in this series, please contact our Customer Service Department:

(800) 770-LANG (within the U.S.)
(212) 647-7706 (outside the U.S.)
(212) 647-7707 FAX

Or browse online by series: www.peterlang.com